Sarbanes-Oxley and the
New Internal Auditing Rules

Sarbanes-Oxley and the
New Internal Auditing Rules

ROBERT R. MOELLER

WILEY

John Wiley & Sons, Inc.

This book is printed on acid-free paper. ∞

Copyright © 2004 by John Wiley & Sons, Inc. All rights reserved.

Published by John Wiley & Sons, Inc., Hoboken, New Jersey
Published simultaneously in Canada

No part of this publication may be reproduced, stored in a retrieval system, or
transmitted in any form or by any means, electronic, mechanical, photocopying,
recording, scanning, or otherwise, except as permitted under Section 107
or 108 of the 1976 United States Copyright Act, without either the prior written
permission of the Publisher, or authorization through payment of the appropriate
per-copy fee to the Copyright Clearance Center, Inc., 222 Rosewood Drive,
Danvers, MA 01923, 978-750-8400, fax 978-750-4470, or on the web at
www.copyright.com. Requests to the Publisher for permission should be
addressed to the Permissions Department, John Wiley & Sons, Inc.,
111 River Street, Hoboken, NJ 07030, 201-748-6011, fax 201-748-6008,
e-mail: *permcoordinator@wiley.com*.

Limit of Liability/Disclaimer of Warranty: While the publisher and author have
used their best efforts in preparing this book, they make no representations or
warranties with respect to the accuracy or completeness of the contents of this
book and specifically disclaim any implied warranties of merchantability or
fitness for a particular purpose. No warranty may be created or extended by
sales representatives or written sales materials. The advice and strategies
contained herein may not be suitable for your situation. You should consult
with a professional where appropriate. Neither the publisher nor author shall be
liable for any loss of profit or any other commercial damages, including but not
limited to special, incidental, consequential, or other damages.

For general information on our other products and services, or technical support,
please contact our Customer Care Department within the United States at
800-762-2974, outside the United States at 317-572-3993 or fax 317-572-4002.

Wiley also publishes its books in a variety of electronic formats. Some content
that appears in print may not be available in electronic books.

For more information about Wiley products, visit our web site at *www.wiley.com*.

Library of Congress Cataloging-in-Publication Data

Moeller, Robert R.
    Sarbanes-Oxley and the new internal auditing rules / Robert R. Moeller.
        p. cm.
    Includes bibliographical references and index.
        ISBN 0-471-48306-0 (CLOTH)
        1. Auditing, Internal—Law and legislation—United States.   2. United
    States. Sarbanes-Oxley Act of 2002.   I. Title.
    KF1357.M64 2004
    346.73'063—dc22   2003018290

Printed in the United States of America.

10 9 8 7 6 5 4 3 2

To my best friend and wife, Lois Moeller

contents

preface

After years of gradually changing, the profession of internal auditing in the late 1990s was very different from the internal auditing profession of an earlier decade. Perhaps one of the more significant changes was that the major public accounting firms were aggressively assuming responsibility for internal audit functions through what was called outsourcing. Many internal audit professionals suddenly found themselves working for their public accounting firms as outsourced internal auditors. Although there were many good things to say about this trend, new internal audit roles and responsibilities were evolving and the profession of internal auditing was changing. This was all happening during the dot-com bubble of the 1990s, during which time the stock market was going in only one direction—up—and some serious thinkers were predicting that there would never be another market downturn.

A series of events in the later 1990s and early 2000 changed all of this and the rules. Suddenly we were faced with a series of corporate failures and accounting scandals, many of which were caused by corporate executives who liberally bent the rules or blatantly reported false financial results for their organizations. Corporate scandals are nothing new in the United States; there has been a major failure about once every ten years over the last century. However, this was different. The traditional watchdogs—auditors and board members—appeared to be asleep at the switch. There was a clamor to do something! The end result was that, in 2002, the U.S. Congress passed the Sarbanes-Oxley Act, a major new rule that impacts both internal and external auditors, corporate senior management, their boards of directors, and more. Among other matters, the act prohibited the public accounting practice of outsourcing internal audit services. The Sarbanes-Oxley Act, often referenced as just SOA, is the major new rule discussed throughout this book. Internal auditors now have some new responsibilities with regard to their audit committees and external auditors and for overall corporate governance. This book explains these changes and how internal audit can help with other requirements, such as launching an ethics and whistle-blower program or performing effective internal controls reviews under the COSO (Committee of Sponsoring Organizations) framework.

Some of what we call new rules are not really rules at all but are best practices that have gained the attention of professionals worldwide. Business recovery and continuity procedures after the World Trade Center terrorist attack of September 11, 2001, are an example. Some organizations had processes in place that allowed easier recovery from that event, and we discuss those approaches. Even though internal auditors may not be initiating such practices, they need to have an understanding of such best practices as part of reviewing current approaches or recommending improvements.

This book also discusses other new trends or legislation that is creating new rules for internal auditors. One of these is the overall emphasis on privacy and security in many areas. We discuss several here, with Healthcare and Insurance Portability and Accountability Act (HIPAA) and its privacy rules as an example. Although that legislation is directed at healthcare, its requirements regarding such things as electronic signatures will cause changes in a wide range of organizations and systems. Fraud detection and prevention is another trend that is becoming a new rule. Auditors, both internal and external, often treated fraud matters in the past as "not my job"; however, the rules are changing here. The American Institute of Certified Public Accountants (AICPA) has issued new fraud-related auditing standards, with more changes to come. Risk management is yet another new rule area. As this book goes to press, a new COSO Enterprise Risk Management (ERM) framework has just been released in draft form. The book introduces this draft framework, which will soon become an important new rule for internal auditors.

This book attempts to describe the new rules impacting internal auditors and other professionals as they exist in mid-2003. We may have missed the point in some areas, or things may change in directions different from what we have anticipated. However, the Sarbanes-Oxley Act of 2003, as well as a series of other matters occurring at about the same time, have created a series of new rules for internal auditors and management professionals, both in the United States and worldwide. Although some final rules are yet to be issued and other matters may change, this book outlines some of the new rules as well as evolving trends that impact internal audit professionals.

ROBERT MOELLER

CHAPTER 1

Introduction

ACCOUNTING AND AUDITING SCANDALS
AND INTERNAL AUDIT

Despite all of the cataclysmic predictions of computer systems and other process-related disasters, the world survived the Y2K millennium change to the year 2000 with no major problems. However, the following year, 2001, became a real disaster for many U.S. accountants and auditors, as well as business in general. The long-running stock market boom, fueled by dot-com Internet businesses, was shutting down with many companies failing and growing ranks of unemployed professionals. Those same boom years spawned some businesses following new or very different models or approaches. One business that received considerable attention and investor interest at that time was Enron, an energy trading company. Starting as an oil and gas pipeline company, Enron developed a business model based on buying and selling excess capacity first over its competitors' pipelines and then moved to excess capacity trading in many other areas. For example, an electrical utility might have a power plant generating several millions of excess kilowatt-hours of power during a period. Enron would arrange to buy the rights to that power and then sell it to a different power company to get the latter out of a capacity crunch.

Enron applied its trading concept in many other areas, such as telephone message capacity, oil tankers, and water purification. Enron quickly became a very large corporation and got the attention of investors. Its business approach was aggressive but appeared to be profitable. Then, in late 2001, it was discovered that Enron was not telling investors the true story about its financial condition. It was found to be using off–balance sheet accounting to hide some major debt balances. It had been transferring significant financial transactions to the books of unaffiliated partnership organizations that did not have to be consolidated into its financial statements. Even worse, the off–balance sheet entities were paper-shuffling transactions orchestrated by Enron's chief financial officer (CFO), who made massive personal profits from these transactions. Such personal transactions were prohibited by Enron's Code of Conduct, but the CFO requested the board to formally exempt him from code violations. Blessed by the external auditors, the board then approved these dicey off–balance sheet transactions. Once its behavior was publicly discovered, Enron was forced to roll these side transactions back in to its consolidated financial statements, making the numbers look very bad and forcing a restatement of earnings. Certain key lines of credit and other banking transactions were based on Enron's pledge to maintain specific financial health ratios. The restated earnings put Enron in violation of these agreements. What once looked like a strong, healthy corporation was not, and Enron was forced to declare bankruptcy in 2002.

Because Enron was a prominent company, many "How could this have happened?" questions were raised in the press and by government authorities. Another major question was "Where were the auditors?" Commentators felt that someone should have seen this catastrophe coming if they had only looked harder. The press at the time was filled with articles about Enron's fraudulent accounting, the poor governance practices of Enron's board, and the failure of its auditors. The firm of Arthur Andersen had served as Enron's external auditors and also had assumed its internal audit function through outsourcing. With rumors that the Securities and Exchange Commission (SEC) would soon be on the way to investigate the evolving mess, Andersen directed its offices responsible for the Enron audit to clean-up all related records. The result was a massive paper-shredding exercise, giving the appearance of pure evidence destruction.

The federal government moved quickly to indict Andersen for obstruction of justice, effectively ending its 90-year run as an auditor under a cloud of scandal. In June 2002, Andersen was convicted by a Texas jury of a felony, fined $500,000, and sentenced to five years' probation. With the conviction, Andersen lost any level of public and professional trust. In the end, this formerly "Big 5" public accounting firm has essentially ceased to exist. In early 2003, Andersen was operating primarily as a used furniture dealer, selling the furniture and fixtures from its closed offices.

At about the same time, the telecommunications firm WorldCom disclosed that it had inflated its reported profits by at least $9 billion during the previous three years. WorldCom soon declared bankruptcy, and the telecommunications company, Global Crossing, failed at about the same time when its shaky accounting became public. The cable television company Adelphia failed in 2002 when it was revealed that top management, the founding family, was using company funds as a personal piggy bank, and the chief executive officer (CEO) of the major conglomerate Tyco was both indicted in 2002 and fired because of major questionable financial transactions. Only a few examples are mentioned here; in late 2001 and early 2002, many large corporations were accused of fraud, poor corporate governance policies, or sloppy accounting procedures. The press, the SEC, and members of Congress all declared that auditing and corporate governance practices needed to be fixed.

Public accountants and their professional organization, the American Institute of Certified Public Accountants (AICPA), received much of the initial criticism. The AICPA was responsible for financial auditing standards, and it governed public accounting quality standards through a peer review process. Because of Enron and the other failures, members of the U.S. Congress felt the existing process of establishing auditing standards and monitoring public accountants was not working. Although the AICPA initially resisted, the result was the Sarbanes-Oxley Act (SOA), passed in 2002. The most major and radical set of financial auditing changes in the United States since the 1930s, SOA has caused radical changes and strong new rules for public accounting, corporate governance, and others. Internal audit is one of those other groups. Although not specifically highlighted in the legislation, SOA has created some new rules and responsibilities for internal audit. In addition to SOA, a large number of other rules, improved standards, and technology developments are changing the environment for the internal audit professional.

WHAT ARE THE NEW RULES?

The Sarbanes-Oxley Act, with its public accounting firm regulatory authority, the Public Corporation Accounting Oversight Board (PCAOB), is a major component of new rules. SOA rules and other new standards and developments create a changed environment for the internal audit professional. A goal of this book is to introduce these new rules from the perspective of internal auditors and audit committee members with responsibility for their internal audit functions. We explain and interpret these processes and rules, giving some guidance on their effective implementation. The following paragraphs summarize this book on a chapter-by-chapter basis.

Chapter 2: Internal Audit and the Sarbanes-Oxley Act

An overview of the full SOA legislation is provided, with an emphasis on the requirements that will most impact internal audit, including relationships with external auditors and with the audit committee. The chapter also discusses the PCAOB (sometimes called "peek-a-boo" in the press) and its audit standards-setting responsibilities. With SOA, internal auditors will see major changes in their dealings with external auditors and the overall corporate governance processes. External audit firms are now barred from outsourcing the internal audit functions of their client companies and barred from accepting audit client consulting assignments. In addition, the audit committee, or at least a designate, is required to take a much more active role in understanding internal control processes. While the PCAOB is too new and its start-up process has been moving slower than anticipated, that process is described, as well as progress to date.

Chapter 3: Heightened Responsibilities for Audit Committees

Corporate boards of directors have had audit committees for some time, although in the past some did little more than appoint external auditors and approve annual audit plans. The Enron audit committee, for example, met for less than one hour only once each quarter. SOA has created a heightened responsibility for the corporate audit committee. This chapter describes these SOA responsibilities and suggests how internal auditors might work more effectively with their audit committee. An audit committee's new responsibilities include establishing a code of conduct for corporate executives, launching a whistleblower function for the corporation, and supervising a formal assessment of internal controls. As part of its service to management role, internal audit should be in an ideal position to help its audit committee to achieve these responsibilities.

Chapter 4: Launching an Ethics and Whistleblower Program

Ethics or compliance programs have been common in larger corporations since the mid-1990s and have existed at some other organizations for much longer. The key element for any ethics program is a strong code of conduct. Such codes originally applied primarily to workforce-related issues, such as the company's sexual harassment policy, and they received only passing blessings from executives. SOA now mandates that such codes be established at a higher level and tailored for corporate executives. Whistleblower programs started with U.S. federal contract laws in the late 1980s and usually became part of corporate ethics programs. Many corporations today still have never initiated these programs or certainly have not carried them up to senior management. This chapter discusses how to establish both ethics and whistleblower programs, per SOA guidelines. It also suggests how internal audit can help to launch ethics and whistleblower functions where they do not exist and explains how to help make them SOA-compliant and how to perform reviews of these functions.

Chapter 5: COSO, Section 404, and Control Self-Assessments

Although some of the rules discussed in this book are completely new, the COSO (Committee of Sponsoring Organizations) internal controls review framework has been with us since the mid-1990s and has been part of the AICPA's internal controls evaluation auditing standards. SOA reaffirms the importance of using the COSO approach to review and evaluate internal controls, and this chapter reintroduces COSO to internal auditors. The chapter provides an overview of the Organizational Sentencing Guidelines, a "carrot-and-stick" judicial approach to encourage effective compliance programs. Finally, the chapter discusses the Institute of Internal Auditor's Control Self-Assessment process, a methodology to review key business objectives, risks involved in achieving those objectives, and internal controls designed to manage those risks.

Chapter 6: Institute of Internal Auditors, CobiT, and Other Professional Internal Audit Standards

The Institute of Internal Auditors (IIA) recently has revised its Standards for the Professional Practice of Internal Auditing, the basic audit guidance for performing internal audits. All internal auditors should gain a basic understanding of these standards. This chapter provides an overview of these IIA Standards as well as the Information Systems Audit and Control Association (ISACA) CobIT control objectives framework. Not really a "standard," CobiT is a set of control objectives for understanding controls related to information systems. An uncomfortable acronym, CobiT stands for **C**ontrol **Ob**jectives for **I**nformation and related **T**echnology. Finally, IIA-oriented internal auditors involved in corporate-level audit activities often do not realize that a different professional group, the American Society for Quality (ASQ), has its own audit function and standards. ASQ internal auditors get involved in more quality assurance and process-oriented issues. The chapter introduces this group of auditing professionals and its standards.

Chapter 7: Disaster Recovery and Continuity Planning after 9/11

The World Trade Center terrorist acts of September 11, 2001, in New York became a major test for the effectiveness of information systems disaster recovery and continuity plans. Because of the extent of the destruction from this terrorist act, many established information systems disaster recovery plans did not work very effectively in the immediate aftermath. The result has been the introduction of new technologies and adjustments in emergency response approaches. What internal auditors once called disaster recovery now usually is called business continuity or business resumption planning, two separate but related concepts. This chapter introduces these topics as well as approaches for internal auditors to understand, review, and evaluate enterprise contingency planning in today's business environment.

Chapter 8: Internal Audit Fraud Detection and Prevention

Fraud can range from minor employee theft, to misappropriation of assets, to fraudulent financial reporting. The audit community, both external and internal, has perhaps for too long avoided procedures to prevent and detect financial fraud. Prior to SOA, for example, the AICPA mounted a major lobbying effort to declare that fraud detection was not its responsibility. As with so many things, SOA has changed these attitudes. This chapter provides guidance for internal auditors to help prevent and deter fraud at all levels. While there are few "new rules" here for fraud prevention and detection, auditor responsibilities are new. The chapter outlines how internal auditors can help to create a culture of honesty in their organizations, perform reviews to identify and mitigate fraud risks, and develop a fraud oversight process.

Chapter 9: Enterprise Risk Management, Privacy, and Other Legislative Initiatives

New rules for internal auditors have not just stopped with SOA and the IIA's new standards. This chapter discusses an important new ERM framework that has just been released in draft but soon will become important for management and auditors. We also introduce newer privacy-related rules and legislation that internal auditors should understand and consider in their reviews, when appropriate. Included here are the Healthcare and Insurance Portability and Accountability Act (HIPAA) and the Gramm–Leach–Bliley Financial Privacy Act (GLBA). Both of these outline some good practice minimum standards that internal auditors might consider in a variety of review areas.

Chapter 10: Rules and Procedures for Internal Auditors Worldwide

Although the IIA is an international organization, many of the new rules in this book focus primarily on current U.S. practices. SOA was passed by the U.S. Congress and is applicable only to companies whose securities are registered with the SEC. It is easy for non-U.S. auditors and professionals to say that this is just a U.S. problem and "We don't have those kinds of problems." There are movements in place to establish SOA-type procedures elsewhere in the world. This chapter reviews progress to date, with an emphasis on the United Kingdom's Turnbull Report and Canada's "CoCo" control objectives framework. The chapter also covers the importance of International Standards Organization (ISO) quality assurance guidance, the growing importance of the International Accounting Standards, and the SEC's efforts to extend SOA rules essentially worldwide. The chapter also discusses the best practices Information Technology Infrastructure Library (ITIL) process standards for service deliver and service support.

Chapter 11: Continuous Assurance Auditing Future Directions

Processes that allow a continuous audit-type review of operations have been the realm of academic researchers and a few information systems auditors in recent years. The idea was to establish a set of auditing controls similar to what are installed in nuclear power plants. When processes go beyond some critical boundary, the warning lights go on and corrective actions are taken. This concept is beginning to receive more serious attention. The AICPA is currently in the midst of a task force to explore this area, and these concepts soon will become much more common. This chapter explores continuous assurance auditing concepts and ways internal audit can implement this change-the-rules auditing concept.

Chapter 12: Summary: Internal Auditing Going Forward

This chapter summarizes the most important of these new rules for today's internal auditors and speculates on future directions. SOA and the PCAOB are new entities that will evolve over time. However, the rules have changed or are changing for internal auditors going forward in the twenty-first century. While much of the focus here is on the larger public corporations, these rules will translate to smaller public, privately owned organizations as well as not-for-profit entities. We also can expect to see sustainability reporting audit requirements where auditors may review or assess environmental and social responsibility matters. All internal auditors should have an understanding of these new rules and how they will apply to circumstances in individual organizations.

WHO WILL FIND THIS BOOK USEFUL?

This book is directed to all internal auditors, with an emphasis on the chief audit executive (CAE). That key internal audit officer needs to understand SOA as well as the PCAOB and how they will apply to the organization. The guidance on establishing whistleblower functions, establishing an ethics practice, and establishing a good internal controls review and evaluation processes should help internal auditors to better communicate with designated members of the audit committees responsible for establishing these practices.

Under SOA, at least one member of a corporate audit committee must be identified as a "financial expert." This person should be someone with certified public accounting or CFO experience who understands generally accepted accounting principles (GAAP) and accounting controls. The material in this book should help those designated financial experts to better understand the components of the COSO internal control model, to help initiate an effective whistleblower program in their organization, and to better appreciate the role of their internal audit function.

This book should be helpful to anyone interested in an overview of SOA and how it might apply to the organization. Although our interpretations of the act's text are just that, summaries and interpretations, the overview should provide the reader with a general overview of this important legislation. We also cover some technical areas, such as contingency planning today and setting up continuous auditing processes. These are described in such a way as to provide concepts to the technical auditor and a broad understanding to the audit manager and general reader.

Finally, this book should be of interest to anyone interested in good corporate and business governance. We are using "governance" here in broader terms than just the responsibilities of the board of directors in a public corporation. Since SOA's concepts will expand to a wide range of organizations, managers of public and private organizations of any size need to establish good governance practices. All should have in place ethical practices, effective internal controls, and some level of operations continuity planning.

CHAPTER 2

Internal Audit and the Sarbanes-Oxley Act

The beginning of the twenty-first century brought with it some major changes to what had been established financial auditing standards and practices. Corporate financial scandals, as discussed in Chapter 1, caused the investment community as well as the U.S. Congress to question and then reform the financial auditing standards setting process as well as a wide range of public accounting firm practices. The Institute of Internal Auditors (IIA) released a revised and very streamlined set of its Standards for the Professional Practice of Internal Auditing to replace what had become a too-large, too-detailed earlier set of standards. The Information Systems Audit and Control Association (ISACA) revised and fine-tuned its CobiT (**C**ontrol **Ob**jectives for **I**nformation and related **T**echnology) process framework to make them more acceptable to all auditors and management groups. The major change, however, has been the Sarbanes-Oxley Act (SOA) covering public accounting firms, financial auditing standards, and corporate governance. Through this legislative initiative, the public accounting profession has been transformed and the Auditing Standards Board of the American Institute of Certified Public Accountants (AICPA) has lost its responsibility for setting public accounting auditing standards. A new entity, the Public Corporation Accounting Overview Board (PCAOB), has been established, as part of SOA and under the Securities and Exchange Commission (SEC), to set public accounting auditing standards and to oversee individual public accounting firms.

This chapter discusses this very significant public accounting standards-setting and corporate governance legislation, the Sarbanes-Oxley Act, with an emphasis on the aspects that are most important to internal auditors. Chapter 6 discusses both the IIA and the ISACA standards. SOA and the PCAOB represent the largest change to public accounting, financial reporting, and corporate governance rules since the SEC was launched in the 1930s. SOA represents the most important set of new rules for auditing and internal auditing today. The effective internal auditor should have a good understanding of these new rules and how they apply to today's practice of internal auditing.

"WHERE WERE THE AUDITORS?" STANDARDS FAILURE

Chapter 1 highlighted some of the corporate accounting scandals and bankruptcies that surfaced in the early days of the twenty-first century, including Enron, WorldCom, and the demise of Arthur Andersen. These numerous examples of poor corporate governance, excessive corporate greed, and accounting fraud all occurred in the same general time frame, raising multiple questions along the theme of "Where were the auditors?" These questions generally were not directed at internal auditors, but toward the external auditor public accountants responsible for auditing the books of the failed companies and certifying that their financial statements were fairly stated. Initially it was easy to point out that the once highly regarded but now castigated Arthur Andersen represented what was wrong with major public accounting firms. Soon it became apparent that some audited financial statements were not at all fairly stated, per the traditional certified public accountant (CPA)/auditing terminology. The external auditors had missed some massive errors and frauds in their reviews of organization financial statements. Too often, the major public accounting firms were accused of selling their auditing services as a "loss leader" with the objective of using that audit work to gain assignments in more lucrative areas such as consulting. Many observers seriously questioned the whole concept of "independent outside auditors." How could a team of outside auditors be independent, the critics asked, if key members of the financial staff had recently been serving as external auditors and then had accepted positions on the other side? Too many close ties made independent, objective decisions difficult.

With a very few exceptions, there was also little evidence of internal auditors raising issues with these accounting scandal-implicated corporations. In addition, many of the internal audit departments at these corporations accused of accounting fraud had been "outsourced" to external audit firms. Prior to Enron's fall, published materials described the "great partnership" that existed between the Arthur Andersen–managed internal audit function at Enron and the Andersen external auditors. They shared offices, shared resources, and spoke essentially in one voice. This was in contrast to the somewhat uneasy alliances that independent internal audit functions had had with their external auditors in the past. Although these internal audit outsourcing arrangements had been in place for many corporations for some years, the Enron situation raised many questions about the independence and objectivity of outsourced internal auditors.

Outsourcing or contracting out some or all internal audit services had been a growing trend throughout the 1990s. An IIA-sponsored survey found that in 1996 in the United States and Canada, some 25 percent of the organizations surveyed had contracted out some if not all of their internal audit functions.[1] Public accounting firms were doing the bulk of this work. The reasons given for decisions to contract out internal audit services included saving costs, adding specialized audit skills, and "cleaning house of incompetent people or at least those with a perceived lack of value." That last comment received 10 percent of the IIA survey responses and certainly should have been disturbing to some internal audit professionals. This trend to outsource internal audit services continued, with the major public accounting firms becoming increasingly involved in internal auditing. Not much concern was expressed about independence and objectivity, except perhaps from internal audit managers who had lost their jobs because of outsourcing. Enron and the other accounting-scandal–related firms put these internal audit objectivity questions and concerns back on the table.

Beyond outsourced internal auditors, an even stronger criticism of the major public accounting firms at that time was aimed at their strong and lucrative practice of providing consulting services for the organizations they audited. The consulting arm of a firm might be hired to install a financial system at a client corporation, then auditors from that same firm would assess the internal controls for that just-implemented system. This arrangement pointed to objectivity issues and conflicts of interest, and Enron provided many examples here. This had been an ongoing concern of the SEC and other public accounting critics. In 2000, the SEC proposed rules that would limit the amount of consulting work that a public accounting firm could perform for the companies it also audited. That proposal was halted through a massive lobbying effort by the AICPA. With revenues from auditing always under pressure, the major public accounting firms did not want to give up their lucrative consulting practices.

As the professional organization for public accounting, the AICPA was responsible for establishing financial auditing standards as well as reviewing and initiating appropriate external auditor disciplinary measures through a peer review process. With the failure of Enron and Arthur Andersen, the AICPA found itself the target of considerable criticism. In addition to its fight to permit auditing and consulting at the same client, the AICPA was accused, in the late 1990s, of deferring to wishes of the "Big 5" accounting firms when it had backed off from proposed standards that would have made auditors more responsible for detecting financial fraud.[2] Questions also were raised about the AICPA quality review and disciplinary processes, which are based largely on a peer review process where member firms review each other. Peer reviews created an environment where almost everyone passed the test. Prior to Enron, Arthur Andersen had gone through peer review and passed with flying colors. The business world had changed after Enron and WorldCom, but the public accounting profession and the AICPA initially did not.

The end result of this was the Sarbanes-Oxley Act, passed in 2002 with its SEC-defined administrative rules ready early in 2003. A major component of SOA was the Public Accounting Oversight Board (PAOB), an independent entity to set auditing standards and to govern and regulate the public accounting industry. These are major changes that will impact auditing, corporate governance, and financial accounting.

SARBANES-OXLEY OVERVIEW: KEY INTERNAL AUDIT CONCERNS

The official name for this U.S. federal legislative act to regulate the accounting and auditing practices of publicly traded companies is the Public Accounting Reform and Investor Protection Act. Although it became law in August 2002, some detailed rules and regulations still were being released as this book went to press. As that official title is somewhat long, business professionals generally refer to it as the Sarbanes-Oxley Act, from the names of its principal congressional sponsors

SOA has introduced a totally changed process of issuing external auditing standards and of reviewing external auditor performance and has given new governance responsibilities to senior executives and board members. The PCAOB will issue financial auditing standards and also will monitor external auditor professional ethics and performance. As happens with all comprehensive federal laws, an extensive set of specific regulations and administrative rules is being developed by the SEC from the broad guidelines in SOA text.

The provisions of SOA have a major impact on internal auditors, particularly in U.S. publicly traded organizations. Internal audit now must act somewhat differently in its dealings with audit committees, senior—and in particular financial—management, and external auditors. Because of the breadth of U.S. business throughout the world, these SOA changes will have an impact on virtually all internal auditors. The effective modern internal auditor should develop a general understanding of SOA's provisions as well as its specific provisions impacting internal audit. This chapter contains an overview of SOA as well as the PCAOB auditing standards-setting activities to date with an emphasis on those elements of the act that will more directly impact internal auditors.

U.S. federal laws are organized and issued as separate sections of legislation called titles with numbered sections and subsections under each. Much of the actual SOA text only mandates rules to be issued by the responsible agency, the SEC, for the act. These specific SOA rules to be developed may or may not be significant to most internal auditors. For example, Section 602 (d) of Title I states that the SEC "shall establish" minimum professional conduct standards or rules for SEC practicing attorneys. Although perhaps good to know, an internal auditor typically will not be that concerned about these specific rules yet to be promulgated. Other rules can be of more interest to internal auditors. Section 407 of Title I says that the SEC will set rules requiring that at least one audit committee member must be a "financial expert." While the definition of a "financial expert" is going through ongoing interpretation, this is important information for a chief audit executive (CAE) who will be dealing with both members of the audit committee and senior management. That financial expert will or should have some understanding of an effective internal controls review process as well as audit committee and internal audit interactions. Since this financial expert may very well be new to the organization's audit committee, he or she may be a key liaison contact for internal audit.

SOA Title I: Public Company Accounting Oversight Board

The AICPA formerly had responsibility for public accounting firms through its administration of the Certified Public Accountant test and the restriction of AICPA membership to CPAs. State Boards of Accountancy actually licensed CPAs, but the AICPA had overall responsibility for the profession. Auditing standards for new issues or concerns were set by the AICPA's Auditing Standards Board (ASB) through a process that involved member task forces to develop the proposed standards changes, extensive individual member and firm review of draft standards, and the eventual issuance of those new or revised professional audit standards. Auditing standards were based on generally accepted auditing standards (GAAS) through a series of specific numbered auditing standards called Statements of Auditing Standards (SAS). Much of GAAS was just good auditing practices, such as the understanding that certain transactions must be backed by appropriate documentation. The SAS statements covered more specific areas requiring better definition. SAS No. 78, for example, defined internal control standards; the more recently issued SAS No. 99 was titled "Consideration of Fraud in a Financial Statement Audit." The AICPA's code of professional conduct stated that CPAs were required to follow and comply with those auditing standards when applicable.

The AICPA's GAAS and numbered SAS standards were accepted by the SEC in the past and set the foundation for what constituted the reviews and tests necessary for a certified audited financial statement. Much has changed since the adoption of SOA. Although previously there was not much noise about whether the process of establishing auditing standards was "broken," SOA has taken this audit standards-setting process out of the hands of the AICPA and the ASB, which are dominated by major public accounting firms.

The PCAOB is a totally new nonfederal, nonprofit corporation with the responsibility to oversee all audits of corporations subject to the SEC. It does not replace the AICPA but assumes responsibility for many functions that were formerly managed by AICPA members for themselves. The AICPA will continue to administer the CPA examination, with its certificates awarded on a state-by-state basis. The PCAOB is defined in Title I of SOA legislation along with nine separate legal sections as summarized below. The PCAOB is an entity regulating only external, not internal, auditors. However, because of the changes in the audit process and corporate governance, it will impact the manner in which internal auditors coordinate their work with external auditors as well as the overall process of corporate governance. If for no other reason, the new rules say that an internal audit function can no longer be run as an outsourced unit of a corporation's external auditors.

PCAOB Administration and Public Accounting Firm Registration

The PCAOB consists of five members to be appointed by the SEC; three of them are *required* to be public, non-CPA members. The legislation insists that the PCAOB is not dominated by CPA and public accounting firm interests. A board member can be considered as one of the two CPA representatives even if that member was only formerly a practicing CPA. In addition, the PCAOB chairperson must not have been a practicing CPA for at least five years. These strong rules aim to keep the board from being dominated by CPAs and public accounting firms. We can almost expect that PCAOB will be dominated by lawyers and public interest activists going forward. When this legislation was being drafted, the AICPA mounted a major lobbying effort to keep the PCAOB under CPA control. Ongoing accounting scandals, however, made its case worse, and the AICPA has lost much of its authority and responsibility for self-regulation. After a false start with a nominated PCAOB chair who was forced to resign due to past corporate governance questions, the first PCAOB chair is William J. McDonough, the former president of the Federal Reserve Bank of New York.

The PCAOB will be responsible for overseeing and regulating all public accounting firms that practice before the SEC. In essence, this means any corporation that has stock registered to trade on some U.S. exchange or has registered debt issuances. Private or small corporations are not included, nor are not-for-profits and governmental entities. PCAOB's responsibilities include:

- *Registration of the public accounting firms that perform audits of corporations.* This registration is much more detailed than just filling out an application form and beginning business. The registering firm must disclose the fees collected from the corporations it has audited, provide data on its audit and quality standards, provide detailed information regarding the CPAs who will be performing its audits, and disclose any pending criminal, civil, or administrative actions. A firm can be denied the right to register due to any PCAOB questions regarding its background.

- *Establish auditing standards.* These standards include auditing, quality control, ethics, independence, and other key audit areas. Although many of these initial standards probably will be essentially the same as the existing ASB standards, a new process for the overall setting of auditing standards has been established. As there are continuing demands for more continuous auditing and health and safety sustainability reporting audits, we probably can expect a whole different dimension of these standards in the future.

- *Conduct inspections of registered public accounting firms.* The PCAOB has responsibility for quality-related reviews of registered firms. In the past, the AICPA peer review process handled this, but the major firms often found little to criticize about their peers. This area will evolve as PCAOB establishes itself, but public accounting firms can almost certainly expect to receive more detailed, stringent reviews.

- *Conduct investigations and disciplinary procedures.* These procedures can apply to an entire registered firm or just to individuals within those firms. Wrongdoing discovered in formal investigations can result in sanctions that would prohibit a firm or an individual auditor from performing audits under PCAOB—a potential kiss of death.

- *Perform other standards and quality functions as the board determines.* The PCAOB may get into other areas to protect investors and the public interest. As the need for auditing services evolves, these standards will certainly change and evolve.

- *Enforce SOA compliance.* The following paragraphs outline many of the SOA rules. Although there is still much to be determined, PCAOB will be responsible for enforcing compliance to SEC rules beyond the overall SOA legislation. This responsibility may result in a variety of administrative law actions or other procedures as appropriate.

There is a required annual registration process for public accounting firms practicing before the board. This registration application data will become of public record, as will litigation matters and other traditionally somewhat confidential data about those firms.

This registration process and the available published data may be of particular value for an organization that is not using one of the Big Four accounting firms (formerly the Big Five, now sometimes called the Final Four). Many medium-size and smaller but very highly credible public accounting firms can provide an organization with excellent, high-quality service. However, if an organization is using one of these smaller public accounting firms, it would be very prudent for corporation financial management to check the firm's PCAOB registration records.

Auditing, Quality Control, and Independence Standards

SOA's Title I, Section 103 gives the PCAOB the authority to establish auditing and related attestation standards, quality control standards, and ethics standards for registered public accounting firms to use for their financial audits. The PCAOB has been given the authority to take over the standards-setting process that was built over many years by the AICPA's Auditing Standards Board. Using impartial language, SOA text recognizes that these new PCAOB auditing standards may be based on "proposals from one or more professional groups of accountants or advisory groups." This is an area still under development and subject to future change; at this time, the current set of auditing standards, known as Statements of Auditing Standards (SASs) will remain in effect. For example, the internal control review audit standard, SAS No. 78, was based on the Committee of Sponsoring Organizations (COSO) internal control framework and will almost certainly become one of the new PCAOB standards. Several new standards were released in late 2003, and we can expect new standards in other areas soon. Beyond SASs covering auditing, there have been other AICPA standards statements, such as the Statements on Standards for Attestation Engagements (SSAEs) and Statements on Standards for Accounting and Reviews (SSARs). The SSAEs cover situations where the CPA does not perform actual audit tests but examines or even observes some area or circumstance and then *attests* to what was observed or found. The SSARs are standards for the bookkeeping-type tasks that a CPA will perform. These are not formal audit procedures and are not included as part of PCAOB responsibilities.

The IIA's Standards for the Professional Practice of Internal Auditing fall into this latter category. They cover the work of internal auditors that may be used to support an external auditor's formal work in some area, such as internal controls. IIA Standards are designed to support all internal auditor review work but are not for an external auditor's audit and attest work. When an internal auditor had been working in support of the external audit counterparts on some review task, the work should have been done following external audit guidelines. Even with a new set of PCAOB standards, the reliance on traditional audit standards will continue. There would be a conflict only if some future PCAOB standard were widely divergent from some element of the IIA Standards. In that situation, the IIA Standards will have to be revised. SOA mandates that the PCAOB develop standards with the following minimum requirements:

- *Audit Workpapers Retention.* Standards will require that audit workpapers and other materials to support the auditor's report must be maintained for a period of not less than seven years. This requirement is certainly a response to the infamous Andersen document shredding, and every internal audit department should consider maintaining its materials for at least the same retention period. While an operational audit workpaper and report may not have the sane retention needs as the financial audit materials, members of the audit committee and others will expect the same level of retention from internal audit. In these days of electronic media, it is not enough to file workpapers as hard copy documents that are difficult to retrieve. Internal audit functions need to have documentation standards to define the necessary requirements for the set of workpapers necessary to support an audit. Too often, internal auditors have filed as a workpaper "permanent file" such trivia as the menu from a restaurant they visited on an extended audit to some remote location. Exhibit 2.1 outlines an action plan for establishing internal audit standards and maintaining internal audit workpapers and reports with a seven-year retention life.

EXHIBIT 2.1   Internal Audit Document Retention
Standards Checklist

Action Steps	
1.0 *Internal Audit Workpaper Retention Standards*	
1.1 Have documentation standards been established for internal audit workpapers?	_____
1.2 Is sufficient documentation included in the workpaper standards so that key internal audit findings are supported?	_____
1.3 Have the workpaper documentation standards been communicated to the audit committee and the internal audit staff?	_____
1.4 Do workpaper documentation standards cover both soft (electronic) and hard-copy versions?	_____
1.5 Are all workpapers retained for *at least 7 years?*	_____
2.0 *Workpaper Storage and Retrieval Procedures*	
2.1 Has a numbering or filing database been established for maintaining workpapers?	_____
2.2 Does the workpaper filing system contain linkages to easily retrieve workpapers by key attributes such as audit type or date?	_____
2.3 Is there a process for logging-in workpapers to identify dates and responsible parties?	
2.4 Are more-current workpapers stored in a secure location?	_____
2.5 Are there controls over workpaper storage to limit access only to authorized persons?	_____
2.6 Are there adequate fire, water damage, and other controls in place over hard-copy workpaper files?	_____

(continues)

EXHIBIT 2.1 Internal Audit Document Retention
Standards Checklist *(Continued)*

Action Steps	
2.7	Have arrangements been made with a secure off-site storage facility for older hard-copy workpapers? _____
2.8	Are retrieval procedures for that off-site facility tested periodically? _____
2.9	Are there adequate back-up and retention procedures in place for soft-copy or automated workpapers? _____
2.10	Are there adequate access and security controls over automated workpapers? _____
2.11	Have adequate allowances been given to storing automated workpapers in formats that will continue to be compatible? _____
2.12	When there are major file format or operating system upgrades, are older automated workpapers tested to ensure compatibility? _____
2.13	Is there a process in place to retrieve and destroy workpapers that have exceeded an often recommended 7-year retention limit? _____
3.0	***Workpaper Content Quality Standards***
3.1	Have minimum standards been established for workpaper documentation to support all audits? _____
3.2	Has a cross-reference process been established to allow cross referencing between all workpaper documentation? _____
3.3	Do all workpapers receive a quality review before the completion of the audit and being placed in storage? _____
3.4	Are all outstanding workpaper issues cleared before storage? _____
4.0	***Workpaper Sign-out and Access Controls***
4.1	Is there a process in place to control and monitor workpapers that have been signed out of storage to authorized persons? _____
4.2	Does the workpaper sign-out procedure cover both hard-copy and automated workpapers? _____
4.3	Is there a follow-up procedure in place to make certain that all signed-out workpapers are returned in a prompt manner? _____
4.4	Are returned workpaper packages monitored for quality and completeness? _____

- ***Concurring Partner Approval.*** Standards will be issued to require a concurring or second-party approval for each audit report issued. This concurrence or approval can be by another member of the same public accounting firm or an independent reviewer. All the major public accounting firms have had independent review processes for their issued reports and workpapers, but often these reviews were done more for an after-the-fact quality control review. Under the new SOA rules, a second external audit partner must "sign on the dotted line" and personally and professionally commit to the findings and conclusions in each audit. With the audit report requirements outlined in Section 204 of SOA, discussed below, the act says that both signing partners must agree to all of the potential alternative issues outlined there.

  There may be a message for internal auditors in this standard. Many internal audit departments are too small to allow having a second, concurring internal auditor assigned to the engagement. Even if a company has a larger internal audit department, this concept of a concurring auditor has generally not been used. In addition, the new IIA Standards outlined in Chapter 6 do not call for such a concept. The IIA Standards state only that the CAE—the audit director—is responsible for communicating the results of the audit to responsible parties. However, with an increasing emphasis on SOA rules, an effective internal audit function should perhaps consider installing ground rules for when a second audit report approval is appropriate.

  The concurring opinion here refers to the external auditor's formal opinion, at the conclusion of an audit, stating that the client's financial reports are "fairly stated" in accordance with generally accepted accounting principles (GAAP). Because of different interpretations of various GAAP rules in some audit situations, SOA has mandated those second, concurring opinions. The opinions expressed in internal audit reports typically do not require that same level of gravity. For example, an audit report on the internal auditor's observation of a physical inventory would not need a concurring opinion if the report covered primarily compliance observation findings, such as the failure to distribute documented inventory counting instructions. However, if, in the internal auditor's opinion, the inventory taking was so lacking in internal controls that the final results might be suspect, a second concurring or review auditor opinion might be helpful.

  SOA certainly does not cover standards for internal auditor report opinions or internal audit concurring opinions. However, it may be appropriate for an internal audit department to include a reviewing auditor or concurring auditor opinion on some reports. Exhibit 2.2 outlines guidelines for including a concurring internal auditor on the final report.

EXHIBIT 2.2   Guidelines for a Concurring Second Internal Auditor Opinion

Action Steps	
1. Does the CAE or a designate sign off on all audit reports issued?	_____
2. Does the senior auditor who performed the work and/or a responsible audit manager also sign the audit report?	_____
3. Prior to the CAE's sign-off, is there a process in place for the CAE's review of the detailed report findings and necessary supporting materials?	_____
4. When audit report findings are highly technical—such as for information systems or complex accounting issues—are all issues fully understood by persons signing the report?	_____
5. When consultants or other outside parties have been used to develop the audit conclusions, is this identified in the report and is their sign-off secured for documentation purposes?	_____
6. Are processes in place to ensure that all persons signing an internal audit report personally have acknowledged that they are personally and professionally responsible for the report content?	_____
7. If an internal auditor refuses to sign off on an audit report, are there procedures in place to document that refusal and secure a second opinion if necessary?	_____
8. For a smaller, limited resources audit department, have arrangements been made to secure a concurring signature from some other party, such as another knowledgeable person in the organization or an outside consultant?	_____

- ■ *Scope of Internal Control Testing.* SOA standards now require the external auditor to describe the scope of the external auditor's testing processes as well as the findings from that testing. The result will be more detailed descriptions of testing procedures in reports and report addendums as well as more extensive testing procedures. External auditors sometimes have used increasingly strained theories to justify the most minimal of test sizes. Often external auditors were faced with very large test populations and tested only a very small number of items. If no problems were found, they expressed an opinion for the entire population based on the results of this very limited sample. Although tests designed and administered by internal auditors typically have had a larger sample size, both internal and external auditors will need to pay greater attention to the scope and reasonableness of their testing procedures. As discussed in Chapter 1, prior to SOA, many external audit firms viewed their financial audits as loss leaders to allow them to better market other services. The situation now has changed, and we can certainly expect more comprehensive and detailed audit testing going forward.

- *Evaluation of Internal Control Structure and Procedures.* The PCAOB standards will include procedures for the review and evaluation of internal controls. Because it has become a recognized worldwide standard, the final PCAOB standards here will almost certainly follow the COSO model of internal control, as described in the AICPA's SAS No. 78. The AICPA currently has a major task force to evaluate internal controls in light of SOA. Chapter 5 discusses that COSO model and SOA reviews of internal controls. In addition, Chapter 9 introduces the new COSO Enterprise Risk Model (ERM). SOA further specifies, however, that the external auditor's evaluation contain a description of material weaknesses in such internal controls as well as any material noncompliance found on the basis of the auditor's testing. Again, we can expect to see more detailed and comprehensive reporting.

Internal auditors can assist the organization and senior management greatly through focused internal control reviews. If an internal audit function is emphasizing the COSO model as the basis for its current internal control review, the staff performing those reviews should take strong steps to get up to speed in developing a good understanding of the COSO model. For external auditors, responsibilities have changed but the bar really has been raised. External auditors will be required to attest to the effectiveness of internal controls as reviewed and documented by management, internal audit, or others. The absence of this documentation, per SOA, will be considered a weakness of internal controls. This new rule really puts a different spin on many internal auditor reviews that have been performed over the years. In the past, many times internal auditors reviewed systems, found them to have adequate internal controls, and only reported an audit finding that the documentation for the system reviewed was out of date or otherwise deficient. Such matters were reported, but often no one cared that much.

An interesting SOA internal control review comment, highlighted by the AICPA, is that for companies with many locations in the United States and/or internationally, all significant locations will have to be *evaluated annually* and not on a rotation basis for the purpose of determining the effectiveness of these internal control system.[3] Whether this work is performed by internal auditors or others, this comment greatly expands the scope of the overall audit. Preparations for internal control reviews at large, multilocation organizations will require detailed planning and coordination between internal and external audit under the overall supervision of the audit committee.

■ *Audit Quality Control Standards.* The PCAOB is mandated to release audit quality controls standards for the issuance of audited financial reports. In the past, the AICPA's quality standards were fairly high level and limited to its peer review processes for large firms. In October 2002, the AICPA became registered under the International Standards Organization (ISO) 9000 quality standards. Chapter 10 discusses the growing importance of these ISO standards. The ISO is a worldwide standards process, and internal auditors should gain a general understanding of the ISO process and how it fits into their organization.

The new IIA Standards, discussed in Chapter 6, require that internal audit departments have a quality improvement and assessment program. In the past, internal auditors had a single-sentence, general standard for internal audit quality assurance. The new IIA Standards have several distinct standards for quality assurance and improvement programs. This is much stronger guidance than in the past, and it should help the internal audit department better comply with this new era of ISO 9000 and SOA quality standards.

Although the PCAOB will not be expected to issue its own specific quality standards, SOA legislation states that every registered public accounting firm will be required to have standards related to:

□   Monitoring of professional ethics and independence

□   Procedures for resolving accounting and auditing issues within the firm

□   Supervision of audit work

□   Hiring, professional development, and advancement of personnel

□   Standards for acceptance and continuation of engagements

□   Internal quality inspections

□   Other quality standards to be prescribed by the PCAOB

These are general quality standards, and we can expect that over time the PCAOB or some other body will release a specific set of quality standards that can be applied to all registered public accounting firms, if not to all firms. In a similar sense, we can expect that the IIA or some other body will establish a set of quality standards that will be applicable to all internal audit departments.

■ *Internal Audit Implications of the PCAOB Standards.* An internal auditor might ask what all of the PCAOB standards stuff has to do with her. Some internal auditors may claim that, as internal auditors, there are the IIA Standards for the Professional Practice of Internal Auditing, and there is little need to be concerned here. However, although it cannot be predicted with absolute certainty, these newer PCAOB auditing standards to come will impact internal auditors as well as their external audit counterparts. The new SOA rules for corporate governance greatly increase the role and responsibility of the corporate audit committee and the internal audit function will become even more closely aligned with the audit committee. The audit committee "accounting expert" and other members will become exposed to the new SOA rules and will expect internal audit to follow similar processes and standards.

The effective internal audit function should closely monitor the evolving PCAOB standards and modify internal audit department processes to follow what eventually will be external and internal audit best practice standards. An example of this is the PCAOB rule for a recurring second auditor sign-off before the release of an audit report. Internal audit sometimes finds itself in a potentially contentious issue where a second audit opinion would be of help (see Example 2.1).

Example 2.1

Assume that an information systems internal auditor has been asked to review the security controls over a newly installed software application. The auditor reviews and tests this new application, finds some serious internal control weaknesses, and prepares an internal audit report that is signed by the CAE before release. As can be the case in a smaller audit department, the CAE does not have the technical knowledge to evaluate the results of the technical tests performed in the audit. The report is released based on the findings and documentation included in the audit workpapers as well as the internal auditor's professional reputation. Then assume that the business manager who approved the purchase of the software strongly objects to internal audit's internal control finding and recommendations, causing a major conflict in the organization. In this case, a second opinion on the internal audit report before its release might have helped. While securing a second opinion can be a problem for smaller organizations, consideration should be given to contracting with an outside consultant for that second opinion on an as-needed basis.

SOA standards will cause significant changes in the manner in which internal audits are planned, performed, and reported. An organization's external auditors will be working under SOA rules, and the audit committee will expect its external and internal auditors to operate in consistent manners. Whether it is quality standards, effective internal control testing, or the above-mentioned concurrent approvals, an internal audit department should begin to modify its procedures to comply with the evolving PCAOB standards. Exhibit 2.3 contains a checklist to help implement these new SOA rules. These standards should be consistent with the new IIA Standards discussed in Chapter 6. The end result will be a better, more effective internal audit department.

EXHIBIT 2.3   SOA Rules Checklist

Action Steps	
1.	The audit committee needs to have a procedure in place for recording and following up on accounting and auditing complaints or concerns. Internal audit should be able to provide support here. _____
2.	A hotline procedure needs to be implemented to allow anonymous, confidential complaints or tips from employees. There should be adequate follow-up procedures in place to investigate and take appropriate action based on those calls. _____
3.	Internal audit's CAE should take steps to establish an ongoing communications link with the designated independent audit committee "financial expert." The designated financial expert should be kept informed of ongoing audit and control issues. _____
4.	The CAE should establish a good communications link with the partner in charge of the external audit. If there are questions whether the registered external audit firm is following SOA rules for such matters as partner rotation, the CAE should discuss this first with the audit partner and bring it to the attention of the audit committee if there has been no corrective action. _____
5.	Documentation should be in place to ensure that published financial reports reflect all material correcting adjustments and off–balance sheet transactions. A member of internal audit should assist in this review. _____
6.	Using normal internal audit procedures to review audit evidence, the CAE should offer support for the organization's CEO if requested. _____
7.	Using internal audit confirmation letter type procedures, the CAE should offer help in establishing a confirmation procedure for the existence of executive loans. _____
8.	Internal audit should work with the treasurer to ensure that procedures are in place to disclose all insider stock transactions within SOA's required two-day limit. _____
9.	Internal audit should initiate reviews covering the effectiveness of internal controls supporting financial procedures. The findings and recommendations from those reviews should be reported to senior management. _____

EXHIBIT 2.3 SOA Rules Checklist *(Continued)*

Action Steps	
10. Working with the organization's existing code of conduct and SOA requirements, care should be taken to issue the existing or an SOA-specific code of conduct for all senior officers.	_____
11. Records should be established to confirm that the executive-level code of conduct has been acknowledged and signed.	_____
12. Internal audit should work with the organization's ethics function or others to launch a code of conduct for all organization employees.	_____

Inspections, Investigations, and Disciplinary Procedures

The PCAOB is empowered to conduct a continuing program of inspections of registered accounting firms to assess their compliance with SOA rules, SEC rules, and professional standards. Interestingly, here and throughout the legislation are references to public accounting professional standards but no specific reference to the AICPA. While groups such as the Canadian Institute of Chartered Accountants (CICA) play that role for companies headquartered there, the AICPA had set the auditing standards framework for all. The text of the SOA statute either ignores the AICPA or mentions it only in general terms. Still, the AICPA is a powerful professional organization and will continue to play a role in providing guidance to public accountants. The AICPA also is beginning to take a more active role in areas that are not covered in SOA. In the past, the AICPA's Peer Review standards and processes were limited to the major public accounting firms with many SEC-registered clients. With the PCAOB taking over this larger-firm quality review process, the AICPA announced in early 2003 that it would be administering and scheduling peer reviews for the many smaller firms that have no SEC-registered clients.

As part of the 2002 SOA legislation, the PCAOB quality inspections or reviews initially were scheduled to be performed annually at the larger registered public accounting firms and once every three years if a registered firm conducts less than 100 SEC financial statement audits per year. This was a very aggressive schedule, and the PCAOB got off to a slow start in 2003 in initiating these reviews. Due to a variety of review process start-up problems, only one of the Big Four firms was scheduled for review that year. That first review has been planned for up to 15,000 hours covering about 70 different offices.[4] Despite this slow start, the full PCAOB review process should be under way soon.

These PCAOB inspections focus on the public accounting firm's performance of the audits selected for review and on the issuance of associated audit reports. The reviews are empowered to identify any act or omission to act that is in violation of the rules established by SOA, the PCAOB, and the SEC as well as the AICPA–type professional standards and by that firm's own quality control policies. These reviews almost certainly will turn into lengthy and intense exercises as compared to the AICPA-administered peer reviews of the old days. Although not designated as reviews of an internal audit function, PCAOB peer reviews could greatly impact an internal audit department as well. Because internal auditors coordinate their work with their external audit counterparts, some internal audit work also could be subject to inspection as part of a PCAOB review. Because it is the external auditor's responsibility to review and monitor performance, problems could result in some nasty accusations.

These inspections will cover selected audits and reviews completed during the prior period and will cover selected offices and individual auditors. The reviews are to evaluate the quality control system of the firm reviewed as well as documentation and communication standards. Work performed by internal audit for a public accounting firm could be included here. The inspections will be documented in a formal inspection report that is to be reported to the SEC and state Boards of Accountancy. When appropriate, the PCAOB will begin disciplinary procedures.

The PCAOB reviews of public accounting firm audits probably will, and should, include activities performed by internal audit at the company reviewed. Following the COSO internal control model, internal audit is a key component of an organization's control foundation. Internal audit's plans, workpapers, and completed audit reports always should be ready and available for the possibility of such a PCAOB review.

Title I, Section 105 covers public accounting firm investigations and disciplinary procedures in some detail. The PCAOB is authorized to compel testimony, to require the examination of the audit work, and to conduct disciplinary proceedings. The latter may range from temporary suspension of an individual or firm, to substantial fines, or even to barring firms or individuals from the profession. The enforcement process follows the same general rules as for any federal administrative legal actions, whether violation of a SEC securities rule or a pollution complaint under the Environmental Protection Agency (EPA).

Section 106 consists of one brief paragraph on foreign public accounting firms that has resulted in much controversy. It says that if any foreign public accounting firm prepares an audit report for an SEC-registered corporation, that foreign public accounting firm is subject to the rules of SOA, the PCAOB, and related SEC rules. In addition, the board requires those foreign firms to register under SOA rules, with their audit workpapers and the like subject to inspection. The final procedures for this registration were in process as we went to press.

Our multinational world is filled with many non-U.S. non Big 4 but large public accounting firms. These foreign public accounting firms are governed by their own national public accounting standards, some of which are modeled on AICPA standards and others—so they claim—follow stronger than U.S. standards. Many firms follow the evolving set of International Accounting Standards discussed in Chapter 10. No matter what standards they have followed, SOA says that they now will be subject to SOA rules if one of their clients has its securities listed on a SEC-regulated stock exchange, such as the New York Stock Exchange or Nasdaq. This requirement has resulted in some firms no longer wanting to be listed on a U.S. stock exchange. They argue that the reach of U.S. law is too long or broad. The SEC and its PCAOB is standing firm on this issue at present, but we may see changes going forward.

Accounting Standards

Title I concludes with one section that affirms that the SEC has authority over the PCAOB, including final approval of rules, the ability to modify PCAOB actions, and the ability to remove board members. The PCAOB is an independent entity responsible for regulating the public accounting industry, but the SEC is really the final authority. The concluding section here recognizes the U.S. accounting standards-setting body, the Financial Accounting Standards Board (FASB), by saying that the SEC may recognize "generally accepted" accounting standards set by "a private entity" that meets certain criteria. The act then goes on to outline the general criteria that the FASB has used for setting accounting standards.

There is and always has been a major difference between accounting and auditing standards. The former define some very precise accounting rules, such as saying a certain type of asset can be written off or depreciated over no more than X years. These are the principles called GAAP. Auditing standards are much more conceptual, highlighting areas that an auditor *should consider* when evaluating controls in some areas. These auditing standards became increasingly loosely interpreted during the 1990s, as management was frequently under pressure to report short-term earnings growth and external auditors often refused to say no. The result was the financial scandals of Enron and others as well as the document destruction by Arthur Andersen auditors when they received news that the SEC was coming. SOA and the PCAOB now oversee all public accounting firms.

SOA Title II: Auditor Independence

Internal and external auditors historically have been separate and independent resources. External auditors were responsible for assessing the fairness of an organization's internal control systems and the resultant published financial reports while internal auditors served management in a wide variety of other areas. In the early 1990s, this separation began to change with external audit firms frequently taking responsibility for some internal audit functions. This change began when larger organizations began to "outsource" some of their noncore functions. For example, rather than having their own janitorial function, with company employees acting in those roles, an organization's janitorial function might be outsourced to a company that specialized in janitorial services for many organizations. The previous in-house janitors would be transferred to the janitorial services company, and, in theory, everyone would benefit. The organization that initiated the outsourcing would experience lower costs by giving a noncore function, janitorial services, to someone who better understood it. The outsourced janitor, in this example, also might have both better career possibilities and better supervision.

Internal audit outsourcing started in the late 1980s. External audit firms went to the management of their client firms and offered to take over existing internal audit functions. The idea made sense to senior management and audit committees on many levels. Senior management often did not really understand the distinctions between the two audit functions and sometimes were more comfortable with their external auditors. There were many reasons for this, and senior management and audit committee members were enticed by the promised lower costs of internal audit outsourcing. In addition, they looked at the external auditors as performing a more important role in the preparation of the annual financial statements while internal audit got involved in less important tasks such as compliance reviews.

Internal audit outsourcing became very much of an issue with the Enron scandal. Enron's internal auditor function had been almost totally outsourced to its external audit firm, Arthur Andersen. The two audit groups, both consisting of Andersen employees, worked side by side in Enron's offices. Many critics and commentators raised after-the-fact questions about how that outsourced internal audit department could have been independent of Andersen. In such an environment, it would have been very difficult for internal audit to raise concerns to the audit committee about the performance of their external auditors. This potential conflict became a major reform issue for SOA.

Limitations on External Auditor Services

Section 201 of SOA has made it illegal for a registered public accounting firm to contemporaneously perform both audit and nonaudit services at a client. The prohibitions include internal auditing, many areas of consulting, and senior officer financial planning. For the internal audit professional, the most significant element here is that it is illegal for a registered public accounting firm to provide internal audit outsourcing services if it is also doing the audit work. This rule means that the major public accounting firms are now essentially out of the internal audit outsourcing business. They can only do internal audit work for non-audit clients. Other firms, including independent spin-offs from public accounting firms, such as Protiviti, or other specialized "no conflict" financial or internal audit consulting firms such as Parson Consulting[5], can still provide internal audit services, but the era when an internal audit professional became a contractor or employee of his or her public accounting firm is over.

In addition to the ban on providing outsourced internal audit services, SOA prohibits public accounting firms from providing other services, including:

- *Financial Information Systems Design and Implementations.* Public accounting firms have been installing financial systems—often of their own design—at client firms for many years. This is no longer allowed. Internal auditors will need to have a greater understanding of installed financial systems and will no longer be pressured to look the other way because their external auditors were responsible for an installed financial system.

- *Bookkeeping and Financial Statement Services.* Public accounting firms previously offered accounting services to their clients in addition to doing the audits. Even for major corporations, it was not unusual for the team responsible for the overall financial statement audit to do much of the work necessary in building the final consolidated financial statements. Such actions are no longer allowed. In-house accounting groups will have the responsibility to analyze, document, and build their financial statements prior to audit.

- *Management and Human Resource Functions.* Prior to SOA, external audit firms took on many responsibilities in these areas. They often identified professionals from their own firms and helped to move them to client management positions. The result was an environment in which many times virtually all of the accounting managers in an organization were alumni of their external auditors. This situation sometimes was frustrating for internal auditors who were not from that same public accounting firm. Avenues for promotion above certain levels seemed limited because of "old-boy" network connections with the external audit firm.

- *Other Prohibited Services.* Although it does not have that much impact on internal audit, SOA also specifically prohibits external audit firms from offering actuarial services, investment advisor, and audit-related legal services.

Tax services are not prohibited under SOA. Although a prohibition was included in initial drafts of the act, there were massive protests from the public accounting firms. Tax services were allowed, but in early 2003 the chief executive officer (CEO) of the telecommunications company Sprint was forced to resign because of his personal involvement in a dodgy tax avoidance scheme that had been suggested by the firm's external auditors.[6] The tax scheme was based on stock options and the price of the stock, raising questions in the press about the external auditor's role and interests. There may be more to come in this area.

The overall SOA theme here is that external auditors are authorized to audit the financial statements of their client organizations and that is about all. SOA allows that beyond the prohibited activities just described, external auditors can engage in other nonaudit services only if those services are approved in advance by the audit committee. With the increased scrutiny of audit committees under the act, many will be wary of approving anything that appears to be at all out of the ordinary.

These SOA external audit service prohibitions will have major impacts on internal audit professionals for many organizations. Because external audit firms will now be *just the auditors,* internal audit professionals should find increased levels of respect and responsibility for their role in assessing internal controls and promoting good corporate governance practices. Internal audit's relationships with audit committees will be strengthened as the audit committee will seek increasing help for services that sometimes were assumed by their external audit firms. New groups of professional service firms will be organized to help with installing financial systems, providing bookkeeping services, or managing internal audit functions outsourced under the new SOA rules.

Organization management will find it necessary to use more scrutiny in their selection of outside service providers. With the changed environment under SOA, many new service providers already have appeared. Some are spin-offs from the traditional public accounting firms while others are new entities. Exhibit 2.4 is a checklist of things to consider when contracting for some of the types of services formerly supplied by external audit firms. Working with nonexternal audit consultants is discussed in more detail in a later section.

Audit Committee Preapproval of Services

Section 202 of SOA's Title I specifies that the audit committee must approve all audit and nonaudit services *in advance.* While audit committees have or should have been doing this all along, that approval often was little more than a formality prior to SOA. Audit committees in the old days sometimes received little more than a brief written and/or verbal proposal for added services from the external auditors that was approved in the same

EXHIBIT 2.4   Contracted Audit-Related Services Checklist

Action Steps
1. When the registered external audit firm proposes providing additional, nonaudit services, determine that the audit committee and other parties are aware of potential SOA prohibitions. _____
2. Working with corporate legal counsel, ascertain that any firm providing contracted services is properly SEC registered and licensed. _____
3. Through review and examination, determine that the firm providing contracting services has no direct connection with the current external auditor. _____
4. Also through review and examination, attempt to determine that the firm providing contracting services has no direct relationship with organization officers, board members, or their families. _____
5. If the services are to be supplied by the registered external audit firm and, if major in size, determine that the nature of these services has been presented to the audit committee and that approval has been received in advance. _____
6. For smaller nonaudit projects of less than 5 percent of the audit fee, establish a log to monitor the nature of the services and accumulated costs. _____
7. If nonaudit extra work proposed by the registered audit firm appears to violate SOA specific prohibitions, such as for financial systems consulting, consult with the responsible audit committee representative to resolve the matter. _____
8. Work with audit committee members responsible for approving additional work to establish appropriate project and accumulated cost documentation. _____
9. Develop a process to ensure that all additional services work approved by the audit committee is disclosed in the proxy. _____
10. Ascertain that all additional, nonaudit work is performed following good project management procedures, including a formal statement of work and documented completion procedures. _____
11. In cases where the outside provider work is performed by the external audit firm but could have been supplied by other consulting resources, provide potential alternative options to audit committee representative. _____

perfunctory manner that business meeting minutes are often approved. SOA changes all of this. Audit committee members can now expose themselves to criminal liabilities or stockholder litigation for allowing a prohibited action to take place.

Of course, many minor matters regarding external auditor activities should not have to go through this formal audit committee approval process in advance. These exceptions give the external audit firm and the audit committee some flexibility. However, the nature and accumulated dollar value of these additional nonaudit services must be monitored carefully throughout the course of a fiscal year to maintain a level of compliance. The CAE should become very involved in this process to help ascertain that all provided extra services continue in compliance with SOA rules. In addition, when an audit committee approves any material nonaudit services, they must be disclosed to investors through the annual proxy statement.

SOA does allow that the audit committee may delegate this nonaudit services preapproval authority to one or more of the outside directors on the audit committee. Doing this would relieve the strain of lengthy audit committee business matters, but will put even more responsibility on a few audit committee members over and above the many new legal responsibilities mandated by SOA. Chapter 3 discusses this heightened responsibility for corporate audit committees in much greater detail.

External Audit Partner Rotation

Another section of Title III makes it unlawful for a public accounting firm lead partner to head an engagement for over five years. This is a matter that the major public accounting firms had corrected well before SOA. Lead partners from the major firms had been rotated on a regular basis, although there may have been exceptions with smaller firms and smaller engagements. While lead partner rotation had been common, SOA makes the failure of a firm to not rotate a criminal act.

SOA does not really address the common practice in audit partner rotation where a given person will play the lead on an audit and then continue to serve in an advisory role after his or her term. That advisory role partner often can maintain the same level of responsibility as the designated lead partner. If the CAE sees this situation as a potential violation of SOA rules, the matter should be discussed with the chair of the audit committee for possible action.

Full audit partner rotation may bring a challenge to the internal audit function. Internal audit may have been working comfortably with the designated audit partner and the associated team over extended periods. Internal audit will need to become accustomed to working with a new audit team from time to time and playing a stronger role in introducing that new team to the organization.

External Auditor Reports to Audit Committee

External auditors always have communicated regularly with their audit committees in the course of the audit engagement as well as for any other matter of concern. In the aftermath of Enron and the other corporate scandals, it was discovered that this communication was often very limited. A member of management might negotiate a "pass" from the public accounting partner on a suggested accounting treatment change, but the matter was reported to the audit committee only in the most general of terms, if at all.

SOA has changed this. External auditors are required to report on a timely basis all accounting policies and practices used, alternative treatments of financial information discussed with management, the possible alternative treatments, and the approach preferred by the external auditor. The whole idea here is that external auditors must report to the audit committee any alternative accounting treatments, the approach preferred by the external auditors, and management's approach. The act really says that if there are disputed accounting treatments, the audit committee should be made well aware of the actions taken.

Conflicts of Interest and Mandatory Rotations of External Audit Firms

As discussed previously, it had been common for members of the external audit firm team to get promotions at client firms to become their chief financial officer (CFO) or other senior financial positions. SOA Title II, Section 206 now prohibits external auditors from providing any audit services to a firm where the CEO, CFO, or chief accounting officer participated as a member of that external audit firm on the same audit within the last year. In other words, an audit partner cannot leave an audit engagement to begin working as a senior executive of the same firm that was just audited. The news about Enron contained some outrageous examples of this switching of roles. As discussed earlier, Enron was the most notorious of corporate wrongdoers, and many of the questionable actions that Enron took moved almost directly to SOA regulations.

The CAE is not included in this prohibition of past external audit firm relationships. Also, staff members and managers still can move from the public accounting firm team to various positions in the audited organization. The prohibition is limited to public accounting partners. Persons beginning their careers in public accounting then can move to junior to midlevel management positions at organizations where they were assigned as external auditors.

In addition to required partner rotation, initial drafts of SOA proposed mandatory audit firm rotation. The initial proposal that a corporation was required to change its external auditors periodically was met with massive objections from the major public accounting and from many corporations. However, in the final versions of SOA, mandatory auditor rotation was put on hold. The General Accounting Office was mandated to perform a one-year review and study the potential effects of mandatory auditor rotation. Its results will go to a congressional committee, which may then take action in the future.

SOA Title III: Corporate Responsibility

While Title II of SOA set up new rules for external auditor independence, the next section, Title III, prescribes audit committee performance standards and a large set of new rules. The Title III regulations represent some major regulatory changes for audit committees that were not all that regulated until recently. Internal auditors should have a greater level of interest as well as a greater role in this area. While companies listed on the New York Stock Exchange as well as banks required that their audit committees be composed of independent directors, beyond that there were few governance rules covering corporate audit committees. Once again, SOA has changed all of that.

Public Company Audit Committee Governance Rules

Under SOA, all listed companies in the United States are required to have an audit committee composed of *only* independent directors. Each firm's external audit firm is to report directly to the audit committee, which is responsible for their compensation, oversight of the audit work, and the resolution of any disagreements between external audit and management. While major corporations in the United States have had audit committees for some years, audit committee rules have very much changed. Many companies with smaller boards of directors, often dominated by insiders, will have to make some major adjustments to become SOA compliant. Internal audit departments have had a reporting relationship to their audit committees for some years, but in the past that relationship often was a weak link. Many times the CAE had only a nominal direct-line reporting relationship to the audit commit with a very strong dotted line to the CFO. Internal audit reported to and met with the audit committee on a quarterly or monthly basis, but communications in the interim were limited. Now that reporting link will be much stronger and more active.

Each member of the board's audit committee must be a totally independent director. To be considered independent, an audit committee member must not accept any consulting or other advisory fees from the corporation and cannot be affiliated with any subsidiary or related organization unit. In addition, SEC regulations now require that at least one member of the audit committee must be a "financial expert." According to current SEC regulations, a "financial expert" is a person who, through education and experience:

- Understands GAAP and financial statements
- Is experienced in preparing or auditing financial statements of comparable companies and applying these principles in connection with accounting for estimates, accruals, and reserves
- Is experienced with the structure and nature of internal controls
- Has had experience with audit committee functions or operations

These are rather stiff rules for audit committee member qualifications. Many independent board member candidates who might otherwise be natural candidates to serve on an audit committee would have difficulty qualifying as such a financial expert. These qualification rules have since been softened through PCAOB rulings.

Audit committees are to establish procedures to receive, retain, and treat complaints and to handle whistleblower information regarding questionable accounting and auditing matters. In other words, an audit committee must become, in effect, an almost separate ongoing entity rather than a subset of the traditional board that flies to some location and meets quarterly for a day. While SOA allows the audit committee to hire independent counsel and other advisors, an organization's internal audit function should be a good resource to help establish these procedures. Internal audit is a truly independent resource within an organization and can be a major resource in helping the audit committee become SOA compliant.

An ethics department is another often quasi-independent function that exists in many larger corporations that can help an audit committee launch a whistleblower function. These corporate ethics functions are built around corporate codes of conduct and often have a hotline–type function to allow employees to point out a reported theft or to complain about some form of harassment. Both the U.S. Sentencing Commission's Organizational Sentencing Guidelines and the COSO internal control standards, discussed in Chapters 4 and 5, talk about the need for strong ethics standards in an organization. Chapter 4 also outlines some approaches to launching an effective ethics and compliance function in an organization, and Chapter 5 includes this in the COSO model. Internal audit can be a natural resource to help launch and facilitate these functions for the audit committee.

The whistleblower function described in SOA covers reported information regarding questionable accounting and auditing matters. The act is trying to address an issue reported during the Enron debacle where an accounting department employee tried to get the attention of the external auditors or an Enron financial officer to recognize some improper accounting transactions. The employee's concerns were rebuffed. An ethics whistleblower or hotline function could be a resource to respond to these types of issues.

Corporate Responsibility for Financial Reports

Prior to SOA, organizations filed their financial statements with the SEC and published the results for investors, but the responsible corporate officers who "signed" or authored those reports were not personally responsible. The bar has now been raised. The CEO, the principal financial officer, or other persons performing similar functions must certify each annual and quarterly report filed. The signing officer must certify that:

- The signing officer has reviewed the report.
- Based on that signing officer's knowledge, the financial statements do not contain any materially untrue or misleading information.
- Again based on the signing officer's knowledge, the financial statements fairly represent the financial conditions and results of operations of the organization.
- The signing officer is responsible for:
  1. Establishing and maintaining internal controls.
  2. Having designed these internal controls to ensure that material information about the organization and its subsidiaries was made known to the signing officer during the period when the reports are prepared.
  3. Evaluating the organization's internal controls within 90 days prior to the release of the report.
  4. Presenting his or her evaluation of the effect of the internal controls in the financial reports as of that report date.
- The signing officer has disclosed to the auditors, audit committee, and other directors:
  1. All significant deficiencies and material control weaknesses in the design and operation of internal controls that could affect the reliability of the reported financial data.
  2. Any fraud, whether or not material, that involves management or other employees who have a significant role in the organization's internal controls.
- He or she has indicated in the report whether there were internal controls or other changes that could significantly impact those controls, including corrective actions, subsequent to the date of the internal controls evaluation.

Given that SOA imposes the potential criminal penalties of fines or jail time on individual violators of the act, the above signer requirement places a heavy burden on responsible corporate officers. Corporate officers must take all reasonable steps to make certain that they are in compliance. There is a provision here that these requirements still apply even if the organization has moved its headquarters outside the United States (e.g., in 2000 and 2001, numerous U.S. corporations moved corporate registration to offshore locations, such as Bermuda, for income tax purposes).

This personal sign-off requirement has raised major concerns from corporation CEOs and CFOs. This requirement will cause a major amount of additional work for the accounting and finance staffs preparing these reports as well as signing officers. The organization needs to set up detailed paper-trail procedures such that the signing officers are comfortable that effective processes have been used and the calculations to build the reports are all well documented. An organization may want to consider using an extended sign-off process where staff members submitting the financial reports sign off on what they are internally submitting. Internal audit should be able to act as a consultant and help senior officers establish effective processes here. The audit workpaper model, with extensive cross-references, might be a good approach. Exhibit 2.5 provides an example of an Officer Disclosure Sign-off statement that officers will be requested to sign. This exhibit is not an official PCAOB form but is based on an SEC document, showing the types of things an officer will be asked to certify. We have highlighted a couple of phrases in the exhibit in *italics*. Under SOA, the CEO or CFO is asked to assert personally to these types of representations and could be held criminally liable if incorrect. Although the officer is at risk, the support staff—including internal audit—should take every step possible to make certain the package presented to the senior officer is correct.

In an interesting twist of the legal language used, this section makes references to the organization's "auditors" rather than using the term "registered public accounting firm" employed in Title II. Although there have been no legal rulings to date and although this author cannot hold himself out as a legal expert on such matters, Title III of the act would appear to refer to auditors in its broadest sense and certainly include both internal and external auditors. A CAE should recognize this fact and take appropriate steps to work with corporate officers to expand and improve internal controls and the like. An internal audit function must place a strong emphasis on performing reviews surrounding significant internal control areas. It can do this through a detailed risk assessment of the internal control environments, discussions of these assessments with corporate officers, and then a detailed audit plan documenting how these internal control systems will be reviewed.

Internal auditors should take particular care, given SOA rules, on the nature and description of any findings encountered during the course of audits, on follow-up reporting regarding the status of corrective actions taken and on the distributions of these audit reports. Internal audits may identify significant weaknesses in areas of the organization that are not material to overall operations. A breakdown in the invoicing process at one

EXHIBIT 2.5 Sample Officer Disclosure Signoff

Certificate of Employee Regarding Sarbanes-Oxley Compliance

Certification: Understanding that we intend to rely upon these statements, the undersigned hereby certifies, represents, and warrants to each of them and to the Company as follows:

1. I have read those portions of the accompanying draft of the covered filing that relate directly to the scope of my responsibilities as an employee of the Company (the "certified information").

2. Based on my knowledge, the certified information, as of the end of the period covered by such filing, did *not contain an untrue statement of a material fact* or omit to state a material fact necessary to make the statements therein, in light of the circumstances under which they were made, not misleading.

3. Based on my knowledge, to the extent of the scope of the certified information, the certified information fairly presents, in all material respects, the financial condition, results of operations, and cash flows of the Company as of the close of and for the period presented in the covered filing.

4. I am not aware of any deficiencies in the effectiveness of the Company's disclosure controls and procedures that could adversely affect the Company's ability to record, process, summarize, and report information required to be disclosed in the covered filing.

5. I *am not aware of any significant deficiencies or material weaknesses* in the design or operation of the Company's internal controls that could adversely affect the Company's ability to record, process, summarize, and report financial data.

6. I *am not aware of any fraud, whether or not material,* that involves the Company's management or other employees who have a significant role in the Company's internal controls.

Signature: _____

Dated this _____ day of _____, 200__

Print Name: _____

Title: _____

---

regional sales office may be significant to the performance of that sales region for the corporation. However, the weakness will not be a materially significant internal control weakness if the problem is local and does not reflect a wider, more pervasive problem and if the problem was corrected after being discovered by internal audit. The CAE should establish good communications links with key financial officers in the organization such that they are aware of audits performed, key findings, and corrective actions taken. Internal audit also should provide some guidance as to whether reported audit findings are material to the organization's overall system of internal control. Similar communication links should be established with members of the audit committee.

Materiality

The question of how much or what is "material" has been an open question among public accounting firms for years. Prior to SOA, public accounting firms used guidelines along the lines that only if an error or internal control failure altered reported earnings per share by some fraction of a cent would the matter be considered *material* for purposes of financial reporting. All other errors were considered nonmaterial. In other words, external auditors for a large corporation could discover an error in a transaction of a very large value—perhaps several million dollars—but sometimes would not investigate the reasons for that error or make some further adjustment because they considered it "nonmaterial" for an organization with accounts valued at hundreds of millions. This decision to define a transaction as material was an auditor's judgment call. Of course, an error that external auditors considered to be nonmaterial might be considered much more material or significant by internal auditors.

The SEC has indicated that *its* existing legal standards for materiality will now apply. That is, data or information now is generally considered to be material if:

- There is a substantial likelihood that a reasonable investor would consider it unimportant in making an investment decision, and

- There is a substantial likelihood that the information would be viewed by the reasonable investor as having significantly altered the total mix of available information.

The SEC has taken a further position that quantitatively small accounting errors still may be considered material under certain circumstances and that simple percentage thresholds for determining materiality are not appropriate.

In other words, all involved parties in the financial audit process need to develop a consistent understanding of what a material error is. An internal control error causing an accounting error that is reported in an internal audit report but ignored by the external auditors could cause trouble for the corporation's officers who sign the final financial reports if they are unaware or ignore the reported error. Given the era in which SOA was enacted, all parties probably would benefit from lowering standards for materiality such that more potential errors are viewed as material.

Internal audit needs to work closely with the external auditors as well as with the audit committee to ensure that both audit teams have a consistent definition of materiality when reporting errors or omissions. Both audit teams should try to coordinate findings here. There is no need for a situation in which external audit ignores some internal controls that a recently issued internal audit report has identified as "serious." Such a discrepancy places the senior officers signing off on the report in a potentially difficult situation.

Penalties for Reporting Failures

Section 906, located toward the end of the long, multiparagraph SOA legislation, schedules a series of criminal penalties for any corporate officer who signs or certifies a financial statement while knowing that the report is not in compliance with all of the requirements of the act. Maximum penalties are defined as fines of not more than $5 million and/or 20 years' imprisonment. Such fines will be imposed only if a wrongdoer is charged, tried, and convicted. The actual penalty would be based on the Organizational Sentencing Guidelines as discussed in Chapter 5. Thus, the senior manager who is found to be guilty of violating SOA financial statement rules is really at risk.

It is difficult to predict how this penalty process will play out over time. If good corporate governance practices become widespread and if no more Enron-type situations occur regularly, those penalty statutes will remain on the books with not much enforcement action. Some sort of major failure could turn things the other way with some corporate executives prosecuted because "they should have known." Strong internal control monitoring and reporting systems are needed. Internal audit can really help.

Improper Influence over the Conduct of Audits

SOA further states that it is unlawful for any officer, director, or related subordinate person to take any action, in contravention of a SEC rule, to "fraudulently influence, coerce, manipulate, or mislead" any external CPA auditor engaged in the audit for the purpose of rendering the financial statements materially misleading. These are strong words in an environment in which there often has been a high level of discussion and compromise between the auditors and senior management when a significant problem was found during the course of an audit.

In the past, management and the external auditors often had many "friendly" discussions regarding a financial interpretation dispute or proposed adjustment. Many times the result was some level of compromise. This is not unlike an internal audit team in the field that circulates a draft audit report with local management before departing. After much discussion and sometimes follow-up work, that draft internal audit report might have to be changed before its final issue. The same thing often happened in external auditor draft reports covering quarterly or annual preliminary results. SOA now has some very strong rules to prohibit such practices. The rules evolved during the congressional hearings leading up to the passage of SOA where testimony included tales of strong CEOs essentially demanding that external auditors "accept" certain questionable accounting entries or lose the audit business. These disputes and debates still can take place, but if an SEC ruling is explicit in some area and if the external auditors propose a financial statement adjustment because of that SEC rule, management *must* accept it without an additional fight.

There can be a fine line between management disagreeing with external auditors over some estimate or interpretation and management trying to improperly influence its auditors. External audit may have done limited testing in some area and then proposed an adjustment based on the results of that test. This type of scenario could result in management disagreeing with that adjustment and claiming the results of the test were "not representative." While the external auditors, particularly under SOA, have the last word in such a dispute, internal audit often can play a facilitating role here. Internal audit resources, for example, can be used to expand the population of some audit sampling test or to perform other extended observations or testing regarding the disputed area. Doing this, internal audit is not helping to improperly influence the conduct of an audit but helping to resolve the matter.

Forfeitures, Bars, and Penalties

Title III concludes with a series of other detailed rules and penalties covering corporate governance. Their purpose is to tighten existing rules that were in place before SOA or to add new rules for what often seemed to be outrageous or at least very improper behavior prior to the act. These new rules, outlined below, will not impact the audit committee or internal or external auditors directly, as they are directed at other areas of what was believed to be corporate governance excess.

Forfeiture of Improper Bonuses

Section 304 requires that if an organization is required to restate its earnings due to some material violation of securities laws, the CEO and CFO *must reimburse* the company for any bonuses or incentives received on the basis of the original, incorrect statements issued during the past 12 months. During SOA hearings, multiple instances were cited where a company had issued an aggressive but unsupportable earnings statement, its key officers had benefited from bonuses or the sale of stock from that good news, and then the company soon had to restate its earnings due to some material noncompliance matter. SOA places a personal penalty on senior corporate officers who benefit from materially noncompliant financial statements.

Bars to Officer or Director Service

Section 305 is another example of how SOA has tightened up the rules. Prior to SOA, federal courts were empowered to bar any person from serving as a corporate officer or director if that person's conduct demonstrates "substantial unfitness to serve as an officer or director." SOA changed the standard here by eliminating the word "substantial"; now the courts can bar someone from serving as a director or officer for *any* conduct violation.

Pension Fund Blackout Periods

A standard rule for 401-K and similar retirement plans is that a fund administrator can establish a blackout period over a limited time period that prohibits plan participants from making investment adjustments to their personal plans. A plan participant with a substantial amount of retirement funds in company stock could, because of bad company news, transfer funds from that stock to a cash-based money market fund or some other investment option. These blackout periods usually are instituted for purely legitimate reasons, such as a change in plan administrators. An Enron-related complaint during SOA hearings was that there was a blackout in place during those final weeks before bankruptcy, preventing employees but not corporate officers from making changes to their plan. SOA rules now state that the same blackout periods must apply to everyone.

Attorney Professional Responsibility

Section 307 covers revised rules for attorney professional conduct and is very controversial. An attorney is required to report evidence of a material violation of securities law or a similar company violation to the chief legal counsel or the CEO. If those parties do not respond, the attorney is required to report the evidence "up the ladder" to the audit committee of the board of directors. SOA's initial rules also allowed that if an attorney discovered such a securities law violation, the attorney should withdraw from the engagement reporting the violation particulars; this is called a "noisy withdrawal" approach.

The controversy here is that SOA is effectively requiring an attorney to violate the rules of attorney-client privilege. Under traditional rules, if a subsidiary executive met with an attorney to discuss some matter that constituted a potential violation of SOA, the attorney and the subsidiary manager client would work out the issues. Now that attorney is supposed to blow the whistle on this discussion and bring the matter potentially all the way to the audit committee.

Fair Funds for Investors

The final section of Title III states that if an individual or group is fined for a violation through administrative or legal action, the funds collected will go to a "disgorgement" fund for distribution to the investors who suffered because of the fraud or improper accounting actions. The same rule applies to funds collected through a settlement in advance of court proceedings. Properties and other assets seized will be sold and also go into that disgorgement fund. The whole idea here is that investors who lost because of individual corporate wrongdoing may be subject to some financial settlement from such a fund.

SOA Title IV: Enhanced Financial Disclosures

This title of SOA is designed to correct some financial reporting disclosure problems, to tighten up conflict of interest rules for corporate officers and directors, to mandate a management assessment of internal controls, to require senior officer codes of conduct, and other matters. There is a lot of material here, and internal auditors might give particular attention to the Section 404 internal controls review rules outlined in the paragraphs following.

Disclosures in Periodic Reports

Many of the unexpected bankruptcies and sudden earnings failures of companies around the time of the Enron failure were attributed to extremely aggressive, if not questionable, financial reporting. With the approval of their external auditors, companies pushed to the limits and often used such tactics as issuing questionable—dicey—pro forma earnings to report their results. While these tactics were in accordance with GAAP and existing laws, the public outcry caused SOA to tighten up some rules and make some of these tactics difficult or illegal.

SOA mandated that the SEC develop rules that pro forma published financial statements must not contain any material untrue statements or omit any fact that makes the reports misleading. Further, the pro forma results also must reconcile to the financial conditions and results of operations under GAAP. However, there has been no standard definition and no consistent format in the financial world for reporting pro forma earnings. Depending on the assumptions used, it was possible for an operating loss to become a profit under pro forma earnings reporting. For example, for its 2001 fiscal year, Cisco Systems Inc., a San Jose, California–based maker of computer networking systems, reported net income of $3.09 billion on a pro forma basis but simultaneously reported a net loss of $1.01 billion on a GAAP basis. Cisco's pro forma profit specifically excluded acquisition charges, payroll tax on the exercise of stock options, restructuring costs and other special charges, an excess inventory charge, and net gains on minority investments. Cisco certainly was not alone here; many companies reported pro forma earnings showing ever increasing growth while their true, GAAP results were not so favorable. The problem with these two sets of numbers is that investors and the press frequently ignored the GAAP numbers, focusing on the more favorable pro forma results.

Perhaps the major issue that brought Enron down was a large number of off–balance sheet transactions that, if consolidated with regular financial reports, would have shown major financial problems. SOA now requires that quarterly and annual financial reports must disclose all such off–balance sheet transactions that may have a material effect on the current or future financial reports, including contingent obligations, financial relationships with unconsolidated entities, or other items. Although many of SOA financial disclosure rules are really the responsibility of external auditors, this is an area where internal auditors might be of help through their visits to distant units of the company, where they may encounter these types of off–balance sheet arrangements.

There may be more to come regarding the rules for off–balance sheet transactions. The SEC is directed to complete a study on off–balance sheet disclosures within 18 months after the mid-2002 passage of SOA and to submit a report to Congress and the president six months later. This would push any potential new rules out further into the future.

Expanded Conflict of Interest Provisions and Disclosures

The hearings that led to the passage of SOA often pictured corporate officers and directors as a rather greedy lot. Large relocation allowances or corporate executive personal loans were granted and subsequently forgiven by corporate boards. It is difficult to see these arrangements as anything other than potential conflict of interest situations. A CEO, for example, who convinces the board to grant his CFO a large personal "loan" with vague repayment terms and the right to either demand payment or forgive certainly creates a conflict of interest situation. Although a series of exceptions are allowed, SOA makes it unlawful for any corporation to directly or indirectly extend credit, in the form of a personal loan, to any executive officer or director.

Another section of Title IV requires that all disclosures under SOA, as discussed previously, must be filed electronically and posted "near real time" on the SEC's Internet site. Doing this would make the filing of such information much more current. Internal audit should consider evaluating the control systems in place to handle such SEC online reporting. In the past, reporting was often hard-copy based, and without proper internal control procedures, the company could be at risk for improperly transmitted data or security leaks. Chapter 11 discusses these trends in terms of continuous assurance auditing.

Management's Assessment of Internal Controls: Section 404

SOA requires that each annual report filing must contain an internal control report that states management's responsibility for establishing and maintaining an adequate system of internal controls as well as management's assessment, as of the fiscal year ending date, of the effectiveness of those installed internal control procedures. This information is what has popularly been known as the Section 404 rules. Internal audit, outside consultants, or even the management team—but not the external auditors—have the responsibility to review and assess the effectiveness of their internal controls. The external auditors are to attest to the sufficiency and rely on the sufficiency of these internal control reviews made by management. This is a major change in the auditor's review of internal controls. Under Section 404, external auditors will attest to the results and sufficiency of these internal control reviews but will be dependent on management, other consultants, or internal audit who actually performed the reviews. This major change in the internal control review process is discussed in greater detail in Chapter 5.

Financial Officer Codes of Ethics

SOA requires that corporations must adopt a code of ethics for their senior financial officers, including the CEO and principal financial officers, and disclose to the SEC their compliance to this code as part of the annual financial reporting. Employee codes of ethics or conduct have been in place in some organizations for many years. They evolved to more formal ethics functions in larger corporations in the early 1990s, but often were established with the main body of employees in mind rather than the officers. These codes defined a set of rules for all employees covering such matters as the protection of company records, acceptance of gifts from vendors, and many other issues. Exhibit 2.6 shows the types of topics that might be included in an organization's code of conduct. These codes were designed for all employees rather than just corporate officers. Chapter 4 contains a more detailed discussion on launching a whistleblower function and ethics program, including a code of conduct, under SOA rules.

Although this area has become very important for many companies since the 1990s, SOA brings organization codes of conduct to new levels. With a growing public concern about the needs for strong ethical practices, many organizations have appointed an ethics officer and launched a code of conduct as a first step. However, although those codes of conduct received senior officer endorsement, they were typically directed at the overall population

EXHIBIT 2.6   Sample Code of Business Conduct Topics

I.   **Introduction**
     A. Purpose of this Code of Conduct
     B. Our Commitment to Strong Ethical Standards
     C. Where to Seek Guidance
     D. Reporting Noncompliance
     E. Your Responsibility to Acknowledge the Code

II. **Fair Dealing**
     A. Our Selling Practices
     B. Our Buying Practices

III. **Conduct in the Workplace**
     A. Equal Employment Opportunity Standards
     B. Workplace and Sexual Harassment
     C. Alcohol and Substance Abuse

IV. **Conflicts of Interest**
     A. Outside Employment
     B. Personal Investments
     C. Gifts and Other Benefits
     D. Former Employees
     E. Family Members

V.   **Company Property and Records**
     A. Company Assets
     B. Computer Systems Resources
     C. Use of the Company's Name
     D. Company Records
     E. Confidential Information
     F. Employee Privacy
     G. Company Benefits

VI. **Complying with the Law**
     A. Inside Information and Insider Trading
     B. Political Contributions and Activities
     C. Bribery and Kickbacks
     D. Foreign Business Dealings
     E. Workplace Safety
     F. Product Safety
     G. Environmental Protection

Source: Adapted from Robert Moeller and Herbert Witt, *Brink's Modern Internal Auditing,* 5th ed. (New York: John Wiley & Sons, 1999).

of employees, not the senior officers. This author recalls leading an effort to launch an ethics function for a large organization where he secured the endorsement of all senior officers for the policy rules outlined in the code of conduct. However, when certain of those code rules later ran contrary to the business practices of some of those senior officers—a vendor offered senior managers paid trips to the Super Bowl for what was called a sales planning meeting—the managers requested exceptions, stating that rules prohibiting employees from accepting and taking vendor-paid promotional trips were "different" for certain senior officers and thus permissible. Although this example is from a different time frame and only one company, it is an example of how corporate senior managers often felt, prior to SOA, that the company code of conduct rules were good in general but did not always apply to them.

SOA does not address the content of these organization-wide codes of ethics but focuses on the need for the same standards for senior officers as for all other employees in the organization. SOA specifically requires that an organization's code of ethics or conduct for senior officers must reasonably promote:

1. Honest and ethical conduct, including the ethical handling of actual or apparent conflicts of interest between personal and professional relationships.

2. Full, fair, accurate, timely, and understandable disclosure in the organization financial reports.

3. Compliance with applicable governmental rules and regulations.

Many larger organizations today have established ethics-type functions, but smaller ones have not. Internal audit can play an important role in helping an organization achieve compliance with SOA ethical rules for officers. If an ethics function is not in place, internal audit can help to launch such a function for all members of the organization, board members, officers, and employees.

If an organization has a code of conduct, the CAE can play a key role in assuring that this code applies to all members of the organization and is consistent with SOA. With the approval of the audit committee, the CAE should launch a project to assure that the existing code of conduct procedures are consistent with SOA rules and are communicated to all members of the organization, including the officers. Exhibit 2.7 is an action plan to assure an existing code of conduct is consistent with SOA rules. The key issue here is that the existing code of conduct covers the above SOA rules, that it has been communicated to senior management, and that these officers have agreed to comply with it. While others in the organization can make certain that the existing code of conduct is consistent with SOA, the CAE is a key person to communicate that information to the audit committee.

EXHIBIT 2.7   Action Plan to Ensure Code of Conduct
Is Consistent with SOA

Action Steps
1. Does the organization have a formal code of business conduct? _____
2. Is the code of conduct updated regularly to reflect current business activities? _____
3. Has the code been modified to reflect any recent changes that are mandated by SOA? _____
4. Is the code distributed to all employees, key other stakeholders, and officers? _____
5. Are all employees and officers required to acknowledge their acceptance of the code? _____
6. Are permanent records maintained of employee and officer code acknowledgments? _____
7. Are there formal programs in place to educate employees on the ethical issues covered in the code as well as on other compliance issues? _____
8. Do employees have an effective mechanism to confidentially report violations of the code or other questionable acts? _____
9. Is there a process in place to investigate reported compliance violations? _____
10. Are reported compliance violations subject to disciplinary action and programs of corrective action? _____
11. Does the organization have a formal ethics office or ombudsman program? _____
12. Is there a program in place to formally report issues related to the code of conduct, including any disciplinary violations, to the audit committee? _____

An organization faces a greater challenge here if it has no formal ethics function, no code of conduct, or a code that has not been effectively communicated throughout the organization. Here again the CAE can play a key role in establishing SOA code of conduct compliance for the officer group as well as throughout the organization. Although SOA code of conduct compliance processes can be established just for the senior officers enumerated in SOA, this is the ideal time to launch an ethics function throughout the organization that applies to senior management and to all employees.

The ethical requirements of SOA can help any organization to better set itself up for ongoing ethical business conduct practices. With an overall understanding of how to establish such ethics programs, internal audit can work with both management and the audit committee to establish a program that will be SOA compliant and will enhance overall organization ethical standards. See Chapter 4 for more detailed guidance.

Other Required Disclosures

Title IV concludes with three other sections that will not directly impact internal audit but do have ongoing impacts on organizational governance. SOA legislation authorizes the SEC to develop the detailed rules necessary to implement these new rules. Although these rules, discussed below, have been largely established, they may continue to change over time. Internal auditors and all members of management always should consult counsel or other advisors for detailed current interpretations of SOA rules when implementing compliance programs. These final three sections cover the following topics.

Audit Committee Financial Expert Disclosures—Section 407

As discussed earlier, at least one member of every corporate audit committee must be identified as a "financial expert." Some CPA-qualified internal auditors who have worked on financial audits and who have trouble managing their personal household budgets may wonder about the requirements of such a financial expert. Some current audit committee members have expressed the same concerns.

The SEC has released guidance for these specific SOA financial expert rules. To qualify, the audit committee financial expert should have had experience as a public accountant, internal auditor, or principal financial officer. With that experience, the financial expert should have:

1. An understanding of generally accepted accounting principles and financial statements

2. Experience in the preparation or auditing of financial statements of comparable organizations with an emphasis on accounting for estimates, accruals, and reserves

3. Experience with internal accounting controls

4. An understanding of audit committee functions

These are strong requirements for any audit committee member. Many board and audit committee members today do not come from an audit or accounting background but from such areas as finance or overall corporate management. They had relied on their financial "experts" to supply the necessary support. This financial expert requirement has resulted in new board of director searches for persons who can claim such qualifications. It probably also will result in one or another audit committee member being designated as that financial expert, whether the candidate's background meets SOA requirements to the letter of the law or not. The downside is that the person designated as the financial expert may become liable if there is a corporate SOA rules violation problem.

Often the CAE is more qualified to be a financial expert than the designated audit committee member. Internal audit might consider taking a role of advising the audit committee "expert" on the ongoing internal control and financial issues impacting the organization. This advisory role could be limited to as little as sending press clippings to that audit committee member on current financial issues in the specific company or industry, or it could be expanded to more detailed consultations. This would be a further expansion of internal audit's service to management.

SEC Enhanced Disclosure Reviews—Section 408S

All listed U.S. corporations are required to file Form 10-K and other financial reports with the SEC. Although the issuing companies filing those reports could anticipate an SEC review, the hearings leading to SOA revealed that SEC reviews were not always that timely or comprehensive. Just as an individual hopes that his or her federal income tax return will not be subject to a detailed audit, corporations and their external auditors certainly have had the same hopes. Some of the massive corporate accounting and financial problems leading up to the passage of SOA might have been detected earlier had there been a more diligent SEC review.

SOA mandates that the SEC perform an "enhanced review" of the disclosures included in *all* company filings on a regular and systematic basis and no less often than once every three years. As part of that disclosure review, the SEC is mandated to do a detailed review of the reports' supporting financial audit materials. The SEC can decide to perform an enhanced review of disclosures triggered by any one of these six situations:

1. If the corporation has issued a material restatement of its financial results
2. If there has been a significant volatility in stock prices compared to others
3. If the corporation has a large market capitalization
4. If this is an emerging company with significant disparities in its stock price to earnings ratio
5. If corporation operations significantly affect material sectors of the national economy
6. Any other factors the SEC may consider relevant

In other words, the SEC may schedule more regularly such extended disclosure reviews for large Fortune 500–size companies, leaders in some sectors of the economy, or where stock prices are out of average ranges. Of course, with the "other factors" consideration, virtually any corporation might move to the head of the list for such an extended review.

SOA text and the SEC rules published to date do not provide much detail on the nature of these planned enhanced reviews. Financial statement disclosures that are part of published financial reports are included in the section called Management's Discussion & Analysis (MD&A) in the SEC's 10-K report. It covers a wide range of issues, including transactions with unaffiliated subsidiaries or derivative trading activities. Unusual or hard-to-classify transactions are disclosed and discussed here. Exhibit 2.8 lists a few, but certainly not all, of the types of financial statement disclosures that could be subject to an SEC enhanced review. The exhibit also contains some extracts from actual reports.

Financial disclosures are documented as footnotes on published financial reports. They are stated in terms of complex financial gibberish that few people understand. A recent article in *Business Week* magazine summarized the problem: "[N]o amount of reform will matter if people don't bother to read the information companies give them. And the sad fact is, few investors and shockingly few professional analysts ever bother combing through financial documents."[7]

EXHIBIT 2.8   SEC-Mandated Financial Statement Disclosure Examples

Financial reporting disclosures are mandated by the SEC and appear on an organization's 10-K annual and 10-Q quarterly reports in the Management's Discussion & Analysis sections. Matters are discussed in the form of detailed legal-sounding text and often are not easily understandable by investors. Examples of the types of matters discussed include:

- ***Restatements of Previously Issued Financial Statements.*** If necessary, this discussion explains why an organization had to restate its earnings. Often, it is described in fairly lengthy text discussions along the lines of:

    an oversight in collecting data for the calculation for certain postretirement benefit liabilities at the fiscal years . . .

- ***Changes in Accounting Principle.*** Again, this will be a detailed description but can be difficult to understand and interpret. It is stated along the lines of:

    the Company implemented a change in accounting principle to reflect more appropriately investment returns and actuarial assumptions . . .

- ***Critical Accounting Policies.*** This may be a general discussion covering such matters as policies for revenue recognition, certain government contracts, or environmental costs.

- ***Liquidity and Capital Resources.*** This would be a series of broad and very general statements asserting to the company's health.

The CAE as well as many others in the organization can argue that a proposed disclosure is unreadable, but the lawyers preparing the disclosure may argue otherwise. Good corporate governance practices would argue that these documents need to be better understood by investors, but legal and accounting specialists will insist on the precise but convoluted language of many financial disclosures.

The SEC plans to require simplified language and to perform these enhanced reviews the financial statement disclosures for the corporations selected. It has allowed that this disclosure review may lead to a full audit of the financial statements for the period reviewed. This type of review really puts the SEC in an almost financial audit role. If it finds inconsistencies between the disclosures and reported financial statements, this could lead to financial statement restatements. Detailed rules have not been released at the time of publication, but the rules for Section 408 enhanced reviews could have some interesting implications going forward.

With the large number of SEC-registered companies, the not-unlimited number of SEC staff members to do such reviews, and the probable time requirements for any such enhanced review, completing its once-every-three-years enhanced reviews probably will present a challenge for the SEC. The many smaller SEC-registered corporations with no unusual accounting statement disclosures and low total capitalization values may very well miss the review window mandated by SOA legislation.

Real-Time Financial Statement Disclosures—Section 409R

The last section under Title IV mandates that the reporting corporation must disclose to the public "on a rapid and current basis" any additional information containing material financial statement issues. Formal SEC rules have not yet been established here, but corporations are allowed to include trend and quantitative approaches as well as graphics for those disclosures. This is a change from traditional SEC report formats that allowed only a pure text format with the exception of corporate logos. Internal audit can help to ensure that the organization has such a real-time financial disclosure facility. The Internet might be an ideal facility for transmitting such data to an investor's web site, and Chapter 11 discusses some standards and approaches here. The application needs to be reviewed for controls and security. Only company-authorized data should be reported to investors, and the site should have appropriate security controls.

Internal audit should consider offering to perform a controls-related review for any application that is scheduled for this disclosures reporting. The results of the audit should be well documented, and there should be a follow-up process to ensure that corrective actions have been taken to repair any control problems encountered during that audit.

SOA Title V: Analyst Conflicts of Interest

SOA Title V and other subsequent sections do not directly cover financial reporting, corporate governance, audit committees, and both external and internal audit issues. They are designed to correct some of the other perceived abuses that were encountered during SOA congressional hearings. The internal audit professional should be interested in them only from a general knowledge basis. Title V is designed to rectify some securities analyst abuses. Investors have relied on the recommendations of securities analysts for years. These analysts often were tied to large brokerage houses and investment banks, and were analyzing and recommending securities to outsiders. Strong separations of responsibility between the people recommending a stock for investment and those selling it to investors were supposed to exist. In the frenzy of the late 1990s investment bubble, these traditional analyst controls and ethical practices broke down. In the aftermath of the market downturns, analysts sometimes recommended stocks seemingly only because their investment bank employer was managing the initial public offering. Also, investigators found analysts publicly recommending a stock to investors as "great growth opportunity" while simultaneously telling their investment banking peers that the stock was a very poor investment or worse.

Abuses of this manner existed in many circumstances. While investment analysts once relied on their own strong self-governing professional standards, SOA hearings revealed that strong and prominent securities analysts ignored many of these standards. Title V attempts to correct these securities analyst abuses. Rules of conduct have been established with legal punishments for violations. SOA has reformed and regulated the practices of securities analysts. The result should be better-informed investors.

SOA Titles VI and VII: Commission Authority, Studies, and Reports

These final two SOA legislative titles cover a series of issues ranging from the funding authorization SEC appropriations to plans for future studies. These sections of the legislation include new rules to tighten up what had been viewed as past regulatory loopholes. The SEC can now ban persons from promoting or trading penny stocks because of past SEC misconduct or can bar someone from practicing before the SEC because of improper professional conduct. The latter rule gives the SEC the authority to effectively ban a public accounting firm from acting as an external auditor for corporations.

The professional misconduct ban could represent a major penalty to any public accounting firm or individual CPA who was found, through SEC hearings, to have violated professional or ethical public accounting standards. Although SOA discusses a necessary process of hearings before any action is taken, individual CPAs or entire firms can be banned temporarily or permanently. This title takes the monitoring and policing process away from the AICPA's key peer review process of the past and gives the regulatory authority to the SEC. While an individual negligent CPA still can work in non-SEC practice areas such as small business accounting or internal audit, even a temporary ban can be a death knell for a public accounting firm. All individuals concerned must be aware of and follow SEC rules and procedures, particularly this new set authorized by SOA.

Title VII authorizes the SEC to engage in a series of studies and reports with specified due dates for the delivery of those reports to appropriate congressional committees or federal agencies. An untold number of such legislatively authorized reports are filed with the Congress or with government agencies, and some just disappear in some bureaucratic swamp. SOA authorizes five of these studies and reports:

1. ***Consolidation of Public Accounting Firms.*** This study is charged with looking at the factors that have led to consolidations among public accounting firms; the problems, if any, that business organizations face because of those consolidations; and whether and to what extent state and federal agencies impede competition among public accounting firms.

2. ***Credit Rating Agencies.*** The role these agencies play and their importance to investors will be studied.

3. ***Securities Professionals Violations and Violators.*** Securities professionals here include investment bankers and advisors, public accountants and their firms, attorneys, and others practicing before the SEC. The study looked at violations and disciplinary practices over the four-year period ending in 2001.

4. ***Analysis of SEC Enforcement Actions.*** Violations of security law reporting requirements will be studied over a five-year period.

5. ***Study of Investment Banks.*** Here the study will focus on whether investment banks and their advisors have assisted corporations in manipulating reported earnings. There is a specific emphasis here on Enron and Global Crossing.

The ongoing impact, if any, of these studies is yet to be determined. The analysis of enforcement actions is designed to help the SEC formulate the detailed rules that are still being released at this writing.

SOA Titles VIII, IX, and X: Fraud Accountability and White-Collar Crime

Sections VIII and IX of SOA seem to be a reaction to the failure of Enron and the subsequent demise of Arthur Andersen. Earlier this chapter discussed some of the events surrounding the failure of Enron, including the conviction of the then major public accounting firm Arthur Andersen for its destruction of Enron's accounting records. At that time, even though Andersen seemed to outside observers very culpable for its massive efforts to shred company accounting records, Andersen initially argued that it was just following its established procedures and had done no wrong. The courts eventually found this to be a criminal conspiracy, and Arthur Andersen is essentially no more. Now Title VIII of SOA has established specific rules and penalties for the destruction of corporate audit records.

The words in the statute are much broader than just the Andersen matter and apply to all auditors and accountants, including internal auditors. The words here are particularly strong regarding the destruction, alteration, or falsification of records involved in federal investigations or bankruptcies: "Whoever knowingly alters, destroys, mutilates, conceals, covers up, falsifies or makes false entry in any record, document, or tangible object with the intent to impede, obstruct, or influence the investigation . . . shall be fined . . . [or] imprisoned not more than 20 years, or both." Taken directly from the statute, these are strong words indeed. In view of this statute, any organization should have a strong records retention policy. While records can be destroyed in the course of normal business cycles, any hint of a federal investigation or the filing of bankruptcy papers for some affiliated unit should trigger activation of that records retention policy.

A separate portion of this section establishes rules for corporate audit records. Although we tend to think of SOA primarily in terms of rules for external auditors, it very much applies to internal auditors as well. Workpapers and supporting review papers must be maintained for a period of five years from the end of the fiscal year of the audit. SOA clearly states that these rules apply to "any accountant who conducts an audit" of an SEC-registered corporation. While internal auditors sometimes have argued that they only do operational audits that do not apply to the formal financial audit process, the prudent internal audit group should closely align their workpaper record retention rules to comply with this SOA five-year mandate.

Several of the sections of the legislation are designed to tighten up things and to correct what were viewed by others as excesses. One of the reported excesses leading up to SOA was instances where corporate officers got large loans from their board of directors based on corporate stock manipulation or performance that was later found to be improper. Boards of directors regularly forgave those loans after some period of time. Now SOA states that these debts cannot be forgiven or discharged if they were incurred in violation of securities fraud laws. The executive—now probably ex-executive—who received the forgiven loan is now obligated to repay the corporation. Another section extends the statute of limitations for securities law violations. Now legal action may be brought no later than two years after discovery or five years after the actual violation. Since securities fraud can take some time to discover, this change gives prosecutors a bit more time.

The Organizational Sentencing Guidelines is a published list of corporate penalties for violations of certain federal laws. If an organization is found to be guilty, the punishment or sentencing could be reduced if there had been an ethics program in place that normally should reduce the possibility of such a violation. While the basic concepts of the sentencing guidelines are still in place, SOA modifies them to include the destruction or alteration of documents as offenses. Chapter 5 discusses the sentencing guidelines in greater detail.

Section 806 adds whistleblower protection for employees of publicly traded organizations who observe and detect some fraudulent action and then independently report it to the SEC or some other outside parties. By "employee," the section means officers, contractors, or agents. Any person who observes an illegal act can "blow the whistle" and report the action with legal protection from retaliation. SOA adds whistleblower language for securities law violations but does not include the provision that whistleblowers will be rewarded with some percentage of the savings reported. Securities law violations and whistleblowing raises an issue for internal auditors. More than almost anyone in the organization, internal audit has access to virtually all organization records. Following the code of ethics, as defined by the IIA, any violations discovered here should be handled not by a report to the SEC but through a report to proper levels of senior management. If the internal auditor discovers a security law violation by a senior financial officer, the matter normally would be first reported to the CEO. However, if the CEO is involved in the action, internal audit should report the matter to the audit committee for resolution. While an employee at a different level in the organization may not feel comfortable reporting something to an audit committee member, internal audit certainly has that established level of communication. Internal audit standards, as they exist today, are covered in Chapter 6. Where a standard appears to be in conflict with a law, such as SOA, the law will take precedence over professional standards.

Title VIII concludes with a very brief Section 807 defining the criminal penalties for shareholders of publicly traded companies. Summarized here, it simply states that whoever executes or attempts to execute a scheme to defraud any persons in connection with a corporation's securities or fraudulently receives money or property from that sale shall be fined or imprisoned not more than 25 years or both. A strong potential penalty for securities fraud. The regulations, rules, and penalties outlined in SOA have made following the rule extremely important.

Title IX then contains a series of white-collar crime penalty enhancements. It goes through existing criminal law penalties and raises maximum punishments. For example, the maximum imprisonment for mail fraud has now grown from 5 years to 20, and the maximum fine for ERISA retirement violations has gone from $100,000 to $500,000. These increased penalties coupled with the provisions of the Organizational Sentencing Guidelines create an environment where many persons found guilty of white-collar crimes may have to spend time in prison.

Finally, Section 906 of SOA Title IX introduces a strong new requirement on corporate CEOs and CFOs. Both must sign a supplemental statement with their annual financial report that certifies that the information contained in the report "fairly represents, in all material respects, the financial condition and results of operations." These effectively personal certifications are coupled with penalties of fines up to $5 million and 10 years in prison for anyone who certifies such a statement while knowing it is false. Since these are personal penalties, the prudent CEO and CFO must take *extreme care* to make certain that all issues are resolved and that the annual financial statements are correct and fully representative of operations.

Title X then is a "Sense of the Senate" comment that corporate income tax returns should be signed by the CEO. Again, responsibility is placed on the individual officer, not the anonymous corporate entity.

SOA Title XI: Corporate Fraud Accountability

Prior sections focused on the individual responsibilities of the CEO, CFO, and others; the last SOA title defines overall corporate responsibility for fraudulent financial reporting. Various sections here focus on other existing statutes, such as the Organization Sentencing Guidelines, and reaffirm the rules for corporations and increase penalties. The SEC also is given authority to impose a temporary freeze on the transfer of corporate funds to officers and others in a corporation subject to an SEC investigation. This was done to correct some reported abuses where corporations were being investigated for financial fraud while they simultaneously dispensed huge cash payments to individuals. A corporation in trouble should retain some funds until the matter is resolved.

Section 1105 also gives the SEC the authority to prohibit persons from serving as corporate officers and directors. This prohibition applies to persons who have violated certain of the SOA rules outlined above. While not automatic, the SEC has the authority to impose this ban where it feels appropriate. The idea is to punish the corporate wrongdoer who has been found culpable of securities law violations at one corporation, only to leave that troubled corporation to serve at another.

IMPACT OF THE SARBANES-OXLEY ACT ON THE MODERN INTERNAL AUDITOR

The previous sections provided a general overview of the Sarbanes-Oxley Act. While this discussion did not cover all sections or details, the intent was to give internal auditors an overall understanding of key sections that will impact the annual audit of an organization and its audit committee. Whether a large, Fortune 100–size corporation, a smaller company not even traded on Nasdaq, or a private company with a bond issue registered through the SEC, all will come under SOA and its public accounting regulatory body, the PCAOB. Internal auditors will see these changes first in their dealings with their external auditors. Relationships have changed, and the internal audit professional will no longer see consultants from the public accounting firm installing a new accounting system or perhaps fear that the internal audit department will be outsourced.

New rules and responsibilities have been established for audit committees, and the CAE with a good general knowledge of the provisions of SOA can become a valuable advisor to both that audit committee and corporate management. Both will be exposed to many other sources of information, such as specialized consultants, but an internal auditor should be able to provide very valuable insights.

NOTES

1. Jamie Kusel, Ralph Schull, and Thomas H. Oxner, "What Audit Directors Disclose about Outsourcing," Institute of Internal Auditors, Altamonte Springs, FL, 1996.
2. "CPAs: Bloodied and Bowed," *Business Week,* January 20, 2003.
3. *AICPA Business & Industry News,* issue 30, February 18, 2003.
4. "Accountancy Watchdog Admits It Will Fall behind on Targets," *Financial Times,* February 12, 2003.
5. In the interest of full disclosure, the author is a consultant for Parson Consulting. Parson Consulting is a no-conflict financial management consulting firm specializing in helping clients realize greater accuracy, speed, and efficiency in finance and business support functions but not compromised by other interests.
6. "Sprint Case Shows New Risk to CEOs When Things Go Bad," *Wall Street Journal,* February 11, 2003.
7. "What Good Are Disclosures That Go Unread?" *Business Week,* March 26, 2002.

CHAPTER 3

Heightened Responsibilities for Audit Committees

Internal audit has had a long-term reporting relationship to the audit committee of the board of directors, although much has changed since enactment of the Sarbanes-Oxley Act (SOA). In the past, many audit committees met only quarterly in conjunction with regular board meetings; those meetings often were limited to little more than approving the external auditor's annual plan, approving quarterly and year-end reports, and reviewing internal audit activities on what often appeared to be little more than a perfunctory basis. While New York Stock Exchange (NYSE) rules, prior to SOA, required that audit committees consist of only outside directors, many audit committees directors often appeared to be "buddies" of the chief executive officer (CEO) with apparently little independent action. While the chief audit executive (CAE) always has had a direct reporting relationship to the audit committee, often the relationship was little more than theoretical, with the CAE having limited contact with the audit committee beyond scheduled board meetings. SOA has changed all of that.

A major issue that evolved from the collapse of Enron and other firms was the publicity and testimony that boards and their audit committees were not exercising a sufficient level of independent corporate governance. Frequently, the Enron audit committee was highlighted as an example of what was wrong. It was reported to have met less than 60 minutes a quarter prior to the company's fall. Given the size of the corporation at that time and the many directions it was pursuing, the audit committee's attention appeared to be very limited at best. Even before Enron, the Securities and Exchange Commission (SEC) was becoming interested in seeing audit committees acting as more independent, effective managers of a company's external and internal auditors.

In 1999, the Blue Ribbon Committee on Improving the Effectiveness of Corporate Audit Committees, formed by the NYSE, the SEC, the American Institute of Certified Public Accountants (AICPA), and others, issued recommendations for improving the independence, operations, and effectiveness of audit committees. The stock exchanges adopted new audit committee standards as listing requirements to be phased in over the next 18 months, and the then Auditing Standards Board (ASB) of the AICPA raised standards for external auditors with respect to their expectations of audit committees. The legislative work that led to SOA showed these earlier initiatives were not enough. This chapter emphasizes those heightened audit committee responsibilities and how internal audit can better work with audit committees under SOA rules.

AUDIT COMMITTEE CHARTERS AND OTHER REQUIREMENTS

Internal audit organizations regularly operate through an audit charter, a formal document approved by the audit committee and senior management that outlines internal audit's roles and responsibilities. Although the Institute of Internal Auditors (IIA) provided some guidance, these internal audit charters did not follow any specific standards or format but formally stated, among other matters, that internal audit had full access to all records and facilities within the organization. Those charters covered internal audit but not the corporate audit committees. The NYSE had proposed formal audit committee charters in December 1999 with suggested audit committee improvements, but SOA has now mandated that each audit committee develop a formal audit charter to be published as part of the annual proxy statement.

The purpose of this audit committee charter is to define the audit committee's responsibilities regarding:

- The identification, assessment, and management of financial risks and uncertainties
- The continuous improvement of financial systems
- The integrity of financial statements and financial disclosures
- Compliance with legal and regulatory requirements
- The qualifications, independence, and performance of independent outside auditors
- The capabilities, resources, and performance of the internal audit department
- The full and open communication with and among the independent accountants, management, internal auditors, counsel, employees, the audit committee, and the board

The audit committee is required to go before the overall board of directors and obtain authorization through this charter document for board audit committee activities, just as the CAE regularly has gone before the audit committee. This audit committee charter is to be published annually as part of the organization's annual meeting proxy statement.

Although some may look on this audit charter requirement as just some additional pages to add bulk to the proxy statement, it is a formal commitment by the board audit committee to ensure the integrity of financial statements and to supervise the internal and external audit functions. There is no single required format for this charter document, but the NYSE has published a model charter that has been adopted by many public corporations. Formats vary from one corporation to another, but audit committee charters generally include:

1. Purpose and Power of Audit Committee
2. Audit Committee Composition
3. Meetings Schedule
4. Audit Committee Procedures
5. Audit Committee Primary Activities
   a. Corporate Governance
   b. Public Reporting
   c. Independent Accountants
   d. Audits and Accounting
   e. Other Activities
6. Discretionary Activities
   a. Independent Accountants
   b. Internal Audits
   c. Accounting
   d. Controls and Systems
   e. Public Reporting
   f. Compliance Oversight Responsibilities
   g. Risk Assessments
   h. Financial Oversight Responsibilities
   i. Employee Benefit Plans Investment Fiduciary Responsibilities
7. Audit Committee Limitations

Although audit committee charters vary, many contain descriptions of the above items. Some appear to have been developed by corporate legal counsels with language to cover every possible contingency; others are clearer and more succinct. An excellent example of an easy-to-follow charter is Microsoft Corporation's 2002 audit committee charter, part of their web site and shown in Exhibit 3.1. Although not included in this exhibit, the charter also outlines some 30 specific activities for the audit committee. For example, number 29 in that list states: "Meet with the General Auditor in executive sessions to discuss any matters that the Committee or

EXHIBIT 3.1   Microsoft Corporation 2002 Audit Committee Charter

Role

The Audit Committee of the Board of Directors assists the Board of Directors in fulfilling its responsibility for oversight of the quality and integrity of the accounting, auditing, and reporting practices of the company and such other duties as directed by the Board. The Committee's role includes a particular focus on the qualitative aspects of financial reporting to shareholders, and on the company's processes to manage business and financial risk, and for compliance with significant applicable legal, ethical, and regulatory requirements. The Committee is directly responsible for the appointment, compensation, and oversight of the public accounting firm engaged to prepare or issue an audit report on the financial statements of the company.

Membership

The membership of the Committee shall consist of at least three directors who are generally knowledgeable in financial and auditing matters, including at least one member with accounting or related financial management expertise. Each member shall be free of any relationship that, in the opinion of the Board, would interfere with his or her individual exercise of independent judgment. Applicable laws and regulations shall be followed in evaluating a member's independence. The chairperson shall be appointed by the full Board.

Communications/Reporting

The public accounting firm shall report directly to the Committee. The Committee is expected to maintain free and open communication with the public accounting firm, the internal auditors, and the company's management. This communication shall include private executive sessions, at least annually, with each of these parties. The Committee chairperson shall report on Audit Committee activities to the full Board.

Education

The company is responsible for providing the Committee with educational resources related to accounting principles and procedures, current accounting topics pertinent to the company, and other material as may be requested by the Committee. The company shall assist the Committee in maintaining appropriate financial literacy.

Authority

In discharging its oversight role, the Committee is empowered to investigate any matter brought to its attention, with full power to retain outside counsel or other experts for this purpose.

Responsibilities

The Committee's specific responsibilities in carrying out its oversight role are delineated in the Audit Committee Responsibilities Checklist. The responsibilities checklist will be updated annually to reflect changes in regulatory requirements, authoritative guidance, and evolving oversight practices. As the compendium of Committee responsibilities, the most recently updated responsibilities checklist will be considered to be an addendum to this charter.

EXHIBIT 3.1   Microsoft Corporation 2002 Audit Committee Charter
(Continued)

The Committee relies on the expertise and knowledge of management, the internal auditors, and the public accounting firm in carrying out its oversight responsibilities. Management of the company is responsible for determining the company's financial statements are complete, accurate, and in accordance with generally accepted accounting principles. The public accounting firm is responsible for auditing the company's financial statements. It is not the duty of the Committee to plan or conduct audits, to determine that the financial statements are complete and accurate and are in accordance with generally accepted accounting principles, to conduct investigations, or to assure compliance with laws and regulations or the company's internal policies, procedures, and controls.

Microsoft Corporation Audit Committee Responsibilities Checklist

A detailed list of responsibilities follows along with a schedule of the quarterly meeting when the activity will be covered.

---

the General Auditor believes should be discussed privately with the Audit Committee" and highlights that this activity will occur two times per year.

Audit committee charters are often very specific regarding relationships with internal audit and typically require the audit committee to:

1. Review the resources, plans, activities, staffing, and organizational structure of internal audit.

2. Review the appointment, performance, and replacement of the chief audit executive.

3. Review all audits and reports prepared by the internal audit department together with management's response.

4. Review the adequacy of financial reporting and internal control systems with management, the CAE, and the independent accountants. This review should include the scope and results of the internal audit program, and the cooperation afforded or limitations, if any, imposed by management on the conduct of the internal audit program.

These items have been part of the relationship between internal audit and its audit committee over time, but a charter published in the proxy formalizes this arrangement. The CAE should work closely with the audit committee to ensure that the effective communication links are in place. The third point in the list above, about audit reports, is an example. Some internal audit departments have developed the habit, over time, of supplying their audit committees with only summaries of internal audit report findings or just submitting what internal audit has decided are significant audit report findings. SOA put this in a new perspective. Internal audit should not just send the audit committee what it *thinks* committee members need to see. Rather, the act mandates that internal audit should provide the audit committee with all audit reports and the management responses. Even when internal audit generates a large number of audit reports, such as for a retail organization with audits of many smaller store units that often have few significant findings, the audit committee should receive detailed information on *all audits* performed. Even though summary reports are provided, complete reports for all audits should be provided as well.

Not every corporation is a Microsoft Corporation in terms of its size and resources, but all corporations with SEC registration must conform to SOA rules. Smaller entities will not have the resources or need to release a Microsoft-like web-based audit committee charter. But smaller corporations still must have an audit committee composed of independent directors, as mandated by SOA, as well as an audit committee charter. Exhibit 3.2 is an example of a smaller corporation audit committee charter for the hypothetical XYZ Corp. This type of board of directors' resolution document would be part of corporate records.

Whether larger or small, an organization still needs to have effective internal controls as well as an internal audit function. This is even more important in these post-SOA days when a limited internal audit resource can no longer rely on its external auditors to perform required tasks it had expected in the past. The CAE for that smaller corporation should review materials published by the IIA, the Information Systems Audit and Control Association (ISACA), or the AICPA and work with internal auditors from other smaller firms to develop ideas and approaches. Interestingly, the AICPA, having been stripped of its responsibilities for large-corporation audit standards by the Public Accounting Oversight Board (PCAOB), has announced that it will be emphasizing services to smaller businesses in the future. Local IIA chapters typically have as members CAEs from other nearby similar-size companies who should be willing to share thoughts and ideas.

BOARD'S "FINANCIAL EXPERT" AND INTERNAL AUDIT

A major audit committee criticism after the fall of Enron was that many boards did not appear to understand financial and internal control issues. SOA now requires that at least one of the audit committee independent directors must be what the act calls a "financial expert"; and as outlined in Chapter 2, there are some fairly specific requirements for that role. This financial expert board member could very well be internal audit's best or closest audit committee ally and may very well be the starting point for the CAE to introduce or reintroduce internal audit to the board's audit committee. Today's typical audit committee member and certainly that financial expert are in a new and challenging position with legal mandates and a lot of pressure.

EXHIBIT 3.2   Smaller Corporation Audit Committee Charter

Whereas, the XYZ Corp. Board has designated an Audit Committee and such committee has two initial members, and the Bylaws of XYZ specify that the Board may determine the power and authority of such committee,

Resolved, that the power and authority of the XYZ Audit Committee shall generally be to review the internal accounting controls of XYZ, to review its financial statements, and to appoint an independent auditor. This Audit Committee shall have general authority and responsibility to act on behalf of XYZ in dealing with such external auditor with respect to the financial statements of the Company, and the Audit Committee shall have the following specific duties and shall report to the Board on its activities at least annually and at other meetings as may be appropriate:

1. Review and approve XYZ's annual financial statements and any significant disputes between management, the external auditor and internal audit that arose in connection with the preparation of those financial statements.

2. Review and approve the procedures employed by XYZ in preparing published financial statements and related management commentaries.

3. Consider major changes and other questions of choice regarding the appropriate auditing and accounting principles and practices to be followed when preparing XYZ's financial statements.

4. Consider, in consultation with the external auditor and the chief audit executive, the adequacy of XYZ's internal financial controls to provide reasonable assurance that XYZ's financial statements are presented fairly and in conformity with generally accepted accounting principles.

5. Serve as a channel of communication between the external auditor and the board as well as between the chief audit executive and the board. Among other matters, meet with each in periodic private sessions to discuss any matter of concern and to take action where appropriate.

6. Recommend which firm to engage as XYZ's external auditor and review that external auditor's compensation, terms of engagement, its independence, and whether to terminate that relationship.

7. Review the annual internal audit plan as well as the appointment and replacement of the chief audit executive.

8. Review the results of each external audit including any qualifications in the external auditor's opinion. any related management letter and management responses to external auditor recommendations.

9. Review the results of each internal audit including management's responses and plans for corrective actions based on internal audit recommendations.

10. Meet periodically with management to review XYZ's major financial risk exposures and review appropriate insurance coverage.

11. Contract for other outside services as appropriate.

12. Perform such other functions as delegated by the board.

EXHIBIT 3.3   Internal Audit Health Check Assessment

Internal Audit (I/A) Processes
1.   Does I/A have a formal set of standards, and are those standards consistent with IIA Standards? _____
2.   Are new I/A members educated on the use of I/A standards, and is overall compliance to standards monitored regularly? _____
3.   Does I/A prepare an annual audit plan, and is performance against the plan monitored regularly? _____
4.   Are audit plans developed through a formal risk assessment process? _____
5.   Are individual audits planned and supervised with sufficient attention given to adequate planning and staffing? _____
6.   Is all I/A work documented through a formal set of workpapers, and are those workpapers reviewed by appropriate levels of management? _____
7.   Are audit findings reviewed, as appropriate, with management before release of final audit reports? _____
8.   Are recipients of audit reports required to respond to recommendations with plans for corrective action, and are those responses monitored? _____
9.   Are there special I/A procedures in place in the event of fraud or suspected fraud encountered during reviews? _____
10.   Does I/A report the results of its activities regularly to the Audit Committee? _____
11.   Are overall budgets developed for all I/A work and is performance monitored against those budgets? _____
12.   Do all members of I/A receive adequate training on accounting, internal controls, and technology issues? _____

SOA has caused many changes to corporate governance, the board of directors, and certainly the audit committee. The role of external auditors has changed very much, and since the demise of Arthur Andersen, an organization also may be using a new external audit firm. In many situations, the CAE and internal audit may be a unique thread of corporate governance continuity, and internal audit can help the audit committee in this new era through a three-step approach:

1. Provide, through a report and presentation, a detailed summary of current internal audit processes for risk assessments, planning and performing audits, and reporting results through audit reports.

2. Work with human resources and other resources to present plans to the audit committee to assist in launching the SOA-required ethics and whistleblower program. This function is discussed in Chapter 4.

3. Develop detailed plans for reviewing and assessing internal controls in the organization. A key component of SOA's Section 404, internal control assessment requirements, is discussed in Chapter 5.

The first step here is that internal audit should make a concentrated effort to explain its processes and procedures to the audit committee, the board, and senior management with an emphasis on internal audit changes since SOA. Once this board presentation is launched, it should become part of the annual internal audit planning process with ongoing changes reported. However, even before launching any such presentation, internal audit should go through its own processes and perform what might be called a health check to assess current internal audit practices. This review might point to areas where there is ongoing room for internal audit improvement. Exhibit 3.3 shows an internal audit health check assessment that can be expanded or modified, depending on current conditions. The idea here is that internal audit should go through a formal self-assessment, asking itself how it is doing at present and what it should do to improve, and then make changes as required.

Once internal audit has gone through such a self-correction process, internal audit processes and ongoing activities should be presented to the audit committee as well as the overall board and management. The idea is make certain that all parties are aware of internal audit's processes and ongoing issues. Exhibit 3.4 outlines such a presentation, showing how internal audit is contributing to overall corporate governance in light of SOA. This type of presentation should be given to key members of management first before the audit committee presentation to ensure that internal audit's message is well understood and consistent with other management initiatives. Depending on the organization and its past history, internal audit may receive too little or even too much credit for its role in the corporate governance process.

HELPING TO ESTABLISH DOCUMENTATION PROCEDURES

Rules of the SEC state the audit committee must establish procedures for the receipt, retention, and treatment of complaints regarding accounting, internal accounting controls, or auditing matters, including procedures for the confidential, anonymous submission by employees of concerns regarding questionable accounting or auditing matters. These procedures can be a documentation challenge since much of this material must be held in a secure, confidential manner. Often the CAE is the only non-CEO and non–chief financial officer (CFO) link between the audit committee and the

EXHIBIT 3.4   Internal Audit Activities Presentation Outline

Note: This outline represents the types of topics that the chief audit executive might present to the Audit Committee, the overall board, and members of senior management to introduce internal audit and to describe its activities.

- Internal audit organization including its staff size and location of operations
    - Audit member backgrounds including education and professional credentials
    - Internal audit department budget for current period
    - Internal audit's understanding and use of technology
- Discussion of the internal control environment in the organization and internal audit's role in assessing controls
- Overall description of the internal audit process including planning, risk assessments, and execution of internal audits
- Summary of audits planned and performed over the most recent period including an overview of significant findings
- Discussion of internal audit's relationship with outside auditors in light of Sarbanes-Oxley changes
- Internal audit plans for the upcoming period
- Internal audit identified problems, concerns, or issues that may be of interest

corporation. Internal audit should offer its services to the head of the audit committee—probably the designated financial expert—to establish documentation and communication procedures in three areas:

1. ***Documentation Logging Whistleblower Calls.*** SOA mandates that the audit committee establish a formal whistleblower program where employees can raise their concerns regarding improper audit and internal controls matters with no fear of retribution. A larger organization may already have an ethics function, as discussed in Chapter 4, where these matters can be handled in a secure manner. When a smaller organization does not have such a resource, internal audit should offer its facilities to log in such whistleblower communications, recording the date, time, and name of the caller to facilitate investigation and disposition. With a heritage of handling secure internal audit reports, internal audit is often the best resource, particularly in a smaller organization, to handle such matters.

2. ***Disposition of Whistleblower Matters.*** Even more important than logging in initial whistleblower calls, documentation must be maintained

to record the nature of any follow-up investigations and related dispositions. Although SOA mandated whistleblower program does not have any cash reward program, complete documentation covering actions taken as well as any net savings should be maintained. Again, with its tradition of handling confidential matters, internal audit should offer to take responsibilities here in a secure confidential manner. This activity can be very important. If an employee calls in a whistleblower report and it is later proven that this call information was leaked causing some level of retaliation, the reporting employee can bring legal action against the corporation.

3. *Other Accounting and Auditing Matters.* Particularly in the post-SOA era, the audit committee frequently may receive questions and queries regarding various accounting and auditing matters. Internal audit can offer to act as a secretary to the audit committee in documenting and handling these matters.

The points discussed in this section outline areas where internal audit can help the audit committee in handling some of its new SOA-mandated administrative chores. Even in very large corporations, audit committees may consist of no more than perhaps six persons, and such committees in smaller corporations typically have only two members. In addition, the typical independent director audit committee member is a busy person serving on multiple boards and with little direct administrative support. While the administrative support staff of the CEO or CFO usually handles many administrative duties for board members, the new SOA rules require that the audit committee must act independently. Internal audit is a natural resource to provide help.

CONTROLLING OTHER AUDIT SERVICES

SOA requires that the audit committee approve all external audit services, including comfort letters, as well as any nonaudit services provided by the external auditors. At the time of this publication, external auditors still are allowed to provide tax services as well as certain *de minimus* service exceptions. External auditors are prohibited from providing other nonaudit services contemporaneously with their financial statement audits:

- Bookkeeping and other services related to the accounting records or financial statements of the audit client
- Financial information systems design and implementation
- Appraisal or valuation services, fairness opinions, or contribution-in-kind reports
- Internal audit outsourcing services

- Management function or human resource support activities
- Broker or dealer, investment advisor, or investment banking services
- Legal services and other expert services unrelated to the audit
- Any other services that the PCAOB determines to be not permitted

Even though prohibited by external auditors, corporations still will need to contract for and acquire many of these types of services. These arrangements must be treated as special contracting arrangements, reported as part of the annual financial reports. While it is in the best interests of the external audit firm not to get involved with such nonaudit services, internal audit should consider offering its services where appropriate and consistent with internal audit's charter.

ESTABLISHING OPEN COMMUNICATIONS

Under SOA, the audit committee takes on a new and important role, and internal audit is in perhaps one of the best positions to help facilitate that new role. The CAE has an opportunity for open access to the audit committee through presentations at periodic meetings and confidential one-on-one meetings. However, for many organizations in the past, that was often little more than a formality with limited true communications. As discussed throughout this book, SOA has changed these rules.

The audit committee and certainly its designated financial expert have been tossed a whole series of new responsibilities. Internal audit is an excellent source to help audit committee members to fulfill their SOA new responsibilities through close communications and by offering to take on certain audit committee documentation tasks.

CHAPTER 4

Launching an Ethics and Whistleblower Program

The Sarbanes-Oxley Act (SOA) financial disclosures Section 406 requires companies to adopt a "code of ethics" applicable for their chief financial officer (CFO) or principal accounting officer. In addition, that code of ethics must include standards reasonably necessary to promote honest and ethical conduct, including the handling of actual and apparent conflicts of interest between personal and professional relationships. The standards also should promote full, fair, accurate, timely, and understandable disclosures in SEC periodic reports and compliance with applicable governmental rules. Changes in or waivers of this SOA-mandated code of ethics must be disclosed immediately via the Form 8-K report, the Internet, or other electronic methods. However, the board and its audit committee are required to implement this code of ethics *only* for the CFO.

Section 806 of SOA also mandates that organizations establish a "whistleblower" program to allow employees and others to anonymously report potential fraudulent activities. Whistleblower programs have been a requirement in many federal laws such as health and safety, environmental standards, and federal contracts. Some of those programs have provisions for the employee reporting the matter to receive a share of damages recovered. The SOA whistleblower requirement covers accounting, internal control, and auditing issues, a broad new expansion of whistleblower protection.

While the SOA-mandated ethics program focuses on just CFO-level persons, any ethics or code of conduct initiative should be broadened to cover the entire organization. Similarly, the mandated whistleblower program can be broadened to a help or "hotline" type of concept where all interested parties can report anonymously any of a wide range of concerns or questions. This chapter describes how to establish ethics and whistleblower functions that are consistent with SOA requirements but also add value to all stakeholders: employees, officers, vendors, and contractors. Going beyond SOA objectives primarily to prevent fraudulent financial reporting, an effective ethics program can be an important governance and compliance tool for the entire organization. The chapter concludes with guidelines for performing operational and compliance audits over these functions.

LAUNCHING AN ORGANIZATION ETHICS PROGRAM

Although SOA mandates that corporate boards must have their CFO sign an ethics statement, this is not a guarantee that the CFO always will follow ethical business practices. The risks to the CFO of a major fine or even prison are stronger inducements! A strong set of CFO personal values and an ongoing commitment to always to "do the right thing" are even more important. An effective ethics program requires a formal commitment between the organization and its employees and all stakeholders to "do the right thing." Some organizations today assume they have good ethics practices because there have been no recent problems. All too often those established "ethics programs" amount to little more than an employee code of conduct given to new hires on their first day on the job plus a few employee posters or brochures. That new employee is asked to read and sign the organization's code of conduct along with completing such new-hire materials as W-2 tax withholding forms, medical plan selections, and other employee benefit options. Many times, that code of conduct is signed, filed away, and forgotten. Such a program does not constitute an effective ethics program for an organization.

The next sections outline the elements of an effective organization ethics program, starting with understanding the risk environment and launching an effective code of conduct. While SOA requires such a program for senior financial managers, effective organizations should launch an ethics program that applies to all involved stakeholders. Often, the ethics program will be headed by someone with the title of chief ethics officer, an important component of corporate governance. Adapted from materials published by the Ethics Officer Association, Exhibit 4.1 outlines the responsibilities for a chief ethics officer.[1] Although the emphasis may be a bit different at various levels, an ethics officer should be aware of the organization's values and overall mission. As another party interested in good, ethical business practices, internal audit should be in a key position to help launch an organization-wide ethics function if one really does not exist or to help to improve any current programs. This is an improvement of corporate governance—clearly more than just SOA compliance.

Understanding the Risk Environment

Virtually every organization faces a mix of risks that might hamper its business operations, growth, or profitability. In the aftermath of the dot-com bubble of the 1990s, many organizations failed or experienced severe business

EXHIBIT 4.1   Chief Ethics Officer Responsibilities

The responsibilities of a Chief Ethics Officer might include:

- Responsibility and accountability for developing and directing the ethics, compliance, and business conduct function for the total organization including compliance with the Sarbanes-Oxley Act

- Leadership, oversight, and expert advice to ensure appropriate development, interpretation, and implementation of ethics and compliance strategies, policies, and programs impacting the organization

- Accountability for all ethics program activities relating to the organization's code of conduct, including ethical relationships with employees, customers, contractors, suppliers, shareholders, and other stakeholders

- Providing leadership in the development of a compliance risk management program to assess, prioritize, and effectively manage legal and regulatory compliance

- Accountability for the organization-wide confidential whistleblower reporting program allowing employees, customers, suppliers, and other stakeholders to report violations of the organization's ethical standards, violations of law or corporate policy, without fear of retaliation

- Setting the strategy for and administering the organization's annual or periodic ethics and compliance training and regular communications on ethics, compliance, and business conduct issues

- Conducting investigations into alleged violations of ethics, compliance, or business conduct practices and making recommendations for resolution of misconduct, including disciplinary action

- Measuring and assessing organization performance in compliance and ethics arenas

- Providing comprehensive reports to the top executive and various committees of the board of directors

Source: Ethics Officers Association.

downturns. In order to keep showing growth as the dot-com era was beginning to slow down, too many companies ignored risks and bent accounting and good internal control rules to show improved financial performance. Understanding an organization's risk environment and what risks to accept is a first step to launching an effective ethics program. Chapter 9 also discusses risks in the context of the new COSO (Committee of Sponsoring Organizations) Enterprise Risk Model.

Although an effective ethics program certainly cannot shield an organization from the risk of a major earthquake or some other cataclysmic event, an ethics program can help to shield it from a variety of other operational and business risks by discouraging bend-the-rules kinds of attitudes.

The office worker who copies company software for personal use on his or her home computer, the factory worker who skips product final inspection procedures to save time, or the vendor that ships fewer items than ordered because "they will never check" are all examples of bending rules and increasing risks to the organization. These kinds of practices often develop because of a perception that no one really cares or that senior management is doing things just as bad, if not worse.

Do we have a problem? An ethics survey is a very good way to understand organization attitudes and is an aid to support corporate governance processes. Ethics attitudes and risks can be assessed through a review of findings from past audits or special, targeted reviews; employee and stakeholder ethics attitude surveys; or detailed employee interviews. Formal ethics functions, internal audit, or human resources can perform these types of surveys to assess the opinions of employees and sometimes all stakeholders. If there is no basis for understanding the ethical attitudes in the organization or if there is no formal ethics function, internal audit should launch a survey of organizational ethics using some mix of these three approaches:

1. Ethics-related findings from past audits or special audits
2. Employee and stakeholder ethics attitude surveys
3. Detailed employee ethics interviews

Ethics-Related Findings from Past Audits or Special Audits

If internal audit has completed a large number of compliance-related operational and financial audits over recent periods, a reexamination of workpapers, audit report findings, and responses to them may provide some insights into overall ethical attitudes. Consistent workpaper findings covering the same "minor" infractions may document and point to overall trends in ethical attitudes. An example here would be an ongoing failure of employees to follow some relatively minor processes or procedures, such as securing a second approval signature on certain smaller-value transactions, despite a policy calling for this second approval signature. Another would be the ongoing failure to document new information systems, despite systems development documentation requirements. The responsible audit team may have decided the matter was too minor to include in the summarized final audit report, but these workpaper–documented findings point to potential ethical attitude problems. Even worse, sometimes these types of findings may have been reported in audit reports, only to be brushed off in management responses.

Some of these ongoing "minor" findings may not point to ongoing ethical violations, but only to areas where rules are not practicable and need to be changed. Some organizations, for example, have travel expense rules calling for "every" travel expense to be supported by a receipt, even minor highway tollbooth fares of 50 cents each. The driver incurring the expense can get this minor toll receipt only by waiting in the cashier's line rather than driving through a faster highway toll line that accepts coins without providing receipts. Employees then submit their expense reports without these receipts because they feel the rule is "stupid." The submitted reports then are approved with receipts for items of less than $1.00 missing. A violation here may be noted in audit workpapers but almost certainly will not be formally reported in audit reports. Does this situation represent an ethical violation for the organization? On one level, the answer may be yes, because a rule is a rule. However, an internal auditor reviewing past audit reports and workpapers for ethical problems might do best to work with the employee expense accounting area to get such unreasonable rule procedures changed.

Internal audit might consider initiating a special audit to assess organization ethical attitudes. This audit could cover compliance practices in some key areas across the organization or could be a highly focused review within

EXHIBIT 4.2 Compliance Practices Audit Sample Report Finding

> Internal audit completed a detailed review of total compliance with established procedures for travel expense reporting for the ABC and DEF divisions for a two-year period ending on June 30, 20XX. The purpose of this review was to assess overall compliance with established travel policy rules for all reports filed for all levels of employees. The exceptions noted here were documented in internal audit workpapers but may not have been included in formal internal audit reports. However, in all instances, internal audit records indicate that these matters were discussed at the conclusion of each audit.
>
> - ***Approved Travel Reports Lacking Item Documentation.*** Travel policy requires that all submitted expense reports must include original receipts. We found that XX percent of all reports did not have receipts for highway tolls and XX percent were lacking receipts for taxi fares.
>
> - ***Failure to Use Authorized Vendors.*** Company policy requires all employees to use the authorized travel agent. We found that XX percent of all approved expense reports did not use the authorized agency. In addition, we found XX instances where the field marketing group did not comply with this policy.
>
> - ***Expense Limitations for Meals.*** Company policy requires that all employees are limited to no more than XX dollars per day for meal expenses. We found XX percent of reports submitted exceeded this daily limit with all approved by the direct supervisor. In a further investigation of approving managers, we found only XX instances where report violation notes were issued.

one department or group. Exhibit 4.2 provides a sample audit report finding from such a review. These findings would have been based on a detailed review of past audit workpapers and point out a pattern of small exception items that might have been documented in past reviews but otherwise ignored.

Employee and Stakeholder Ethics Attitude Surveys

Employee, officer, and stakeholder surveys can be an excellent way to assess ethical attitudes throughout the organization. Although the ethics attitude survey would include some common questions, each stakeholder group also would receive very specific questions that apply to that stakeholder group. The senior officer group, for example, would receive the same set of organizational attitude questions given to all but also might receive questions related to specific SOA items and internal controls. Drafting a fact-gathering survey that seeks a high response level is never easy, and using specialized help should be considered. Rather than a series of questions requiring just yes-or-no responses, the survey should consist of many "Have you ever . . . ?" types of questions where persons completing the survey can provide as long or as short an answer as they wish. Such open-ended responses make compiling results more difficult, but provide interesting and valuable information to be retained. Exhibit 4.3 is an example of an ethics attitude survey that might be directed to a senior officer.

A key requirement is that the survey must be as anonymous as possible. The surveys should be sent directly to employee homes along with a cover letter from the CEO explaining the survey's objectives and purpose. Return envelopes, prestamped, to a special post office box, should be included. The primary objective of the survey would be to understand ethics attitudes; however, if the organization has an established a whistleblower hotline function, as discussed later in this chapter, the survey also could allow people to report violations. Summarizing survey results can be a major challenge with this type of survey, particularly if respondents have provided free-form responses. Internal audit or the ethics officer could be responsible for preparing such a report with an objective of reviewing results with the audit committee and senior management. Due to confidentiality reasons, this type of report would not be distributed back to the employee/respondent group. Respondents should receive only a general thank-you type of letter.

Detailed Employee Ethics Interviews

Individual one-on-one interviews are perhaps the best way to understand stakeholder ethical attitudes. A broad sample of stakeholders should be selected with arrangements made to meet with these people individually. The sample group should be drawn from all stakeholders, including contractors

EXHIBIT 4.3   Ethics Environment Survey Questions

1. Do you have access to current company policies and procedures?

2. If you have questions or need clarifications, do you have a mechanism to ask questions or seek advice?

3. When an established procedure does not appear applicable, given current conditions, is there a process for submitting it for review?

4. Do you feel the rules and procedures apply just to other groups, such as regular employees if you are part-time or the headquarters operation if you are at a remote subsidiary?

5. Has your supervisor ever told you to ignore some rule or procedure?

6. Do you feel some of the published rules and procedures are trivial or out of date?

7. Are you familiar with the organization's mission statement?

8. What does the mission statement mean to you?

9. Are you familiar with code of business conduct?

10. Do you feel this code of conduct is updated regularly to reflect current business activities and issues?

11. Do you feel the code of conduct is applicable to other stakeholders, such as officers, contractors, or vendors?

12. Have you participated in any company-sponsored ethics training?

13. Do you understand how to report accounting, internal control, or auditing concerns under the company's whistleblower program?

14. Do you feel there is an effective mechanism to confidentially report violations of the code of conduct or other questionable acts?

15. Do you feel there is an effective process in place to investigate reported code of conduct compliance violations?

16. Have you observed any evidence that reported compliance violations are subject to disciplinary action?

17. Would you be reluctant to report a violation for fear of employer retaliatory actions?

and vendors. However, this broader selection requires careful planning, preparation, and stakeholder briefings. The interviews should be conducted by a nonthreatening person who should operate from a prepared script to assure consistency in the questions. The persons interviewed should be told that they were selected randomly because of management's overall desire to improve the ethical environment in the organization. The employees interviewed should be strongly advised that their responses will be kept strictly confidential. The ethics individual interview questions should cover such matters as the employee perceptions of the organization's ethics or any pressure on the employee to bend the rules. Since some people get concerned about talking in the presence of a tape recorder, a third party might be used to take notes. This approach requires a larger organization.

With a skilled interviewer, individual ethics surveys often can gather the best information about ethics attitudes from a representative but detailed sample. However, this method of gathering information is often the most expensive and can be risk-prone. Transportation costs can be high unless most employees are located in the same geographic area. The survey will fail miserably if too many employees fear a lack of confidentiality or just have a general mistrust, wondering why they are being asked such questions.

Any of the three methods described here, or a combination of them, will allow an ethics office team to gain a general understanding about the ethics environment in the organization. This is a first step to launching a formal ethics function or upgrading and enhancing an existing function. These surveys will provide general management some insights into the organization's overall ethics atmosphere. Although not required under SOA, this information will bolster corporate governance practices by highlighting areas where improvements are needed.

Summarizing Ethics Survey Results: Do We Have a Problem?

The summarized results of these ethics attitude surveys or assessments may provide some assurances that things are pretty good throughout the organization. More often, however, they may point to some troubling signs, ranging from small but ongoing compliance deviations that had been reported in earlier audit reports, to surveyed vendors claiming heavy-handed negotiation tactics, or to employees stating they have been asked to bend rules. The hard question now is whether the responses represent troubling exceptions or the tip of a much larger ethics problem iceberg. At this point, internal audit, the ethics officer, or whoever else compiled these survey results should meet with management and develop some next steps.

Based on any potential disturbing red flags from the surveys, it may be best to expand the mail surveys or interview process. The preliminary information gathered may point to a need to expand the assessments to such groups as customers, agents, or vendors. Concerns that came out of those initial surveys can be reiterated here. If the survey results ended with inconclusive or mixed messages, another appropriate step would be to set up a series of focus group sessions. Small groups of employees and stakeholders could be selected randomly and asked to meet together at an off-site location to discuss their perceptions of organizational ethical values. With a strong emphasis that any responses from such sessions are anonymous, a skilled often non-employee facilitator could lead the group through a discussion. With a poor or weak facilitator, some of these focus sessions can become little more than bitch sessions directed at management or others. A strong facilitator is necessary to ask general questions and to gain accurate information; all data gathered here, along with other inputs, should form the basis for evaluating current practices.

ESTABLISHING A MISSION OR VALUES STATEMENT

Every organization, no matter how big or small, needs a mission statement to describe its overall objectives and values. It should be a source of direction or a compass to let employees, stakeholders, customers, and even stockholders know what the organization is about and what it is not. Once often little more than a nice but tired-sounding slogan, the mission statement has become very important for strong organizational ethics and good corporate governance. Effective mission statements can be a great asset to an organization, allowing it to better achieve organizational goals and purposes.

The Johnson & Johnson Tylenol crisis of the late 1980s provides a good example of the importance of strong corporate mission statements. Johnson & Johnson, a major medical products provider, manufactures a popular over-the-counter pain reliever medication called Tylenol. In those days, such nonprescription medications were sold in stores in unsealed, screw-top bottles. Someone in the Chicago area opened a series of these Tylenol bottles, added cyanide poison to the contents, and replaced the cyanide-laced bottles on the store shelves. Several people who purchased this tainted Tylenol subsequently died. An investigation quickly pointed to Johnson & Johnson and the poison-tainted Tylenol.

This whole matter put Johnson & Johnson under massive pressure. The corporation knew that it had extremely strong quality control processes that would prevent such poison contamination from occurring within its own manufacturing facilities. It also knew that the contaminated products had appeared only in the Chicago area, although Tylenol was found on store shelves worldwide. Any total product recall would be both extremely expensive and damaging to its image. However, Johnson & Johnson quickly did the right thing. It recalled the entire product from all store shelves worldwide and subsequently rereleased Tylenol in a newly designed sealed package. When asked why it was able to make such a very expensive recall decision so quickly, the corporation stated that there was no need for a delayed decision. The Johnson & Johnson Credo, the company's mission statement, dictated that decision. That Tylenol-era mission statement stated that Johnson & Johnson's first responsibility was to supply high-quality products, contributing to the health of its customers. Everyone at Johnson & Johnson knew this, the credo had been posted widely in organization facilities, and there was no need for a protracted decision. Although the strategy and procedures for such a recall, if any, could have consumed hours of legal wrangling, the company made its right decision very quickly. The whole unfortunate matter highlighted the importance of a strong mission statement for an organization.

A strong corporate mission statement is an important element in any ethics and corporate governance initiative. Although most organizations will never face a crisis on the level of Johnson & Johnson with its tainted Tylenol, a stronger ethics approach of this sort might have helped some organizations to better avoid the recent accounting scandals that led to SOA. It is certainly impressive when an organization can make a difficult decision based on the words in its mission statement. Today's organizations should look at their existing mission statements to see if they might be of help in making difficult decisions. Too often, however, mission statements sound good but do not really say very much. Working with ethics office function and senior management, internal audit can help to evaluate and potentially rewrite an existing mission statement or help launch a new one if needed. The stakeholder ethics surveys discussed previously should have pointed out any potential problems in an existing mission statement. If employees or other stakeholders are not really aware of any existing corporate mission statement or if they view it with little more than cynicism, there is a need to revisit and revise that document. A poorly crafted mission statement often can do more harm than good, potentially creating cynical and unhappy organizational members. If the organization has no mission statement, or an ineffective one, a team should be formed to develop and review a statement and, if necessary, make changes that better reflect the organization's overall values and purposes. If the existing statement was met with cynicism during the ethics survey, it is time to rework and revise it. However, any revised statement should be crafted and delivered carefully. If it just is rolled out with minimal thought or preparation, it may be viewed with even more cynicism.

A good mission statement should make a positive difference, inspiring organizational stakeholders to harness their energy, passion, and commitment. The goal is to create a sense of purpose and direction that will be shared throughout the organization. Perhaps one of the best examples of a mission statement was expressed by President John F. Kennedy in the early 1960s:

> *This nation should dedicate itself to achieving the goal, before this decade is out, of landing a man on the moon and returning him safely to Earth.*

Those simple words describe a mission and vision much better than an extensive document of many pages. Sometimes called values statements or credo, examples of these statements can be found in the annual report of many organizations. Some are lengthy while others seem to be little more than fluff. The best are closer in style to Kennedy's statement or to Johnson & Johnson's credo.

Once an organization has developed a new mission statement or has revised an existing one, it should be rolled out to all organization stakeholders with a good level of internal publicity. Using webcasts or other tools, senior managers should explain the reasons for the new mission statement and why it is important. The mission statement should be posted on facility billboards, in the annual report, and in other places to encourage all stakeholders to understand and accept it.

CODES OF CONDUCT

While a mission statement represents a keystone holding together the overall structure of corporate governance, the code of conduct represents a series of supporting rules that define good practices, what is allowed or prohibited. SOA requires that corporations *must develop* a code of ethics for their senior financial officers to promote the honest and ethical handling of any conflicts of interest and compliance with applicable governmental rules and regulations. This code of ethics or conduct is to be disclosed in the organization's periodic financial reports, and a financial officer's willful violation of the code could result in personal criminal penalties. While the SOA code of ethics is mandated, all organizations should benefit from a code covering all stakeholders. SOA uses the expression "code of ethics," but we refer to it here by its more common name, the organization code of conduct.

Today's effective organization should develop and enforce a code of conduct that covers a set of appropriate ethical, business, and legal rules for all organization stakeholders including the financial officers highlighted in SOA as well as all employees and other parties, such as contractors or vendors. Although internal audit typically is not the catalyst group to draft or launch such a code of conduct, internal audit can be a key participant in helping to determine that the organization has an effective code of conduct that promotes ethical business practices throughout the organization. Internal audit also can then help to formally launch this code of conduct.

The Contents: What Should the Code's Message Be?

A code of conduct should be a clear, unambiguous set of rules or guidance that outlines what is expected of the members of the organization, whether officers, employees, contractors, vendors, or any other stakeholders. The code should be based on both the historic values and any legal issues surrounding an organization. If the business is a traditional one that has been around for many years, the code should reflect on that heritage when applicable. While the codes for organizations should have strong prohibitions against sexual and racial discrimination, a defense contractor with many issues related to military rules will have a code that sounds somewhat different from that of a fast food store operation. Whatever the industry or type of business, the code should apply to all members of that organization, from the most senior level to a part-time clerical employee. A code of conduct rule prohibiting erroneous financial reporting should have the same meaning whether directed at the CFO for incorrect financial reporting or the part-timer for an incorrect or fraudulent weekly time card. While one has more serious consequences, both represent erroneous financial reporting.

If the organization already has a code of conduct, the enactment of SOA should provide a rationale to revisit it. Older codes often were drafted as rules for the lower-level employees, with little attention to the more senior members of the organization. The Ethics Officer Association has reported that, prior to SOA, only a minority of senior officers in the large organizations sampled even formally signed and acknowledged their organizations' codes of conduct. The thinking then was that the code of conduct was meant for the troops, but the officers did not need such rules. Of course, SOA has changed this. SOA code of conduct requirements and overall corporate governance rules are directed specifically at senior financial officers. A general theme of this book is that although SOA guidance was meant for senior members of the organization, corporate governance processes should apply to everyone in the organization. Working with senior members of management and the audit committee, internal audit can examine any existing code of conduct to determine if its rules still fit today's post-SOA era.

Whether a revision to an existing code of conduct or a new code, a team from a cross-section of management, including legal and human resources, should be assembled to develop it. Team members should examine the business issues facing them and then draft a set of code rules applicable to the organization. The code rules must be written in a clear manner such that they can be easily understood by all. Exhibit 4.4 lists sample code of conduct topics. Although this list does not apply to all organizations, these topics are appropriate for many modern organizations. The key is that the message delivered in the code must be clear and unambiguous. This author was involved in drafting a code of conduct for a large U.S. corporation several years ago. An extract from that code on a section covering company assets provides an example:

> We all have a responsibility to care for all of the company's assets including inventory, cash, supplies, facilities, and the services of other employees and computer systems resources. If you see or suspect that another employee is stealing, engaging in fraudulent activities, or otherwise not properly protecting company assets, you should report these activities to your manager or to the ethics office.

EXHIBIT 4.4   Example Code of Conduct Topics

The following topics are found in a typical organization code of conduct.

I. **Introduction**
   A. Purpose of this Code of Conduct: A general statement about the background of this Code of Conduct.
   B. Our Commitment to Strong Ethical Standards: A restatement of the Mission Statement and printed letter from the CEO.
   C. Where to Seek Guidance: A description of the ethics hotline process.
   D. Reporting Noncompliance: Guidance for whistleblowers—How to report.
   E. Your Responsibility to Acknowledge the Code: A description of the code acknowledgment process.

II. **Fair Dealing**
   A. Our Selling Practice: Guidance for dealing with customers.
   B. Our Buying Practices: Guidance and policies for dealing with vendors.

III. **Conduct in the Workplace**
   A. Equal Employment Opportunity Standards: A strong commitment statement.
   B. Workplace and Sexual Harassment: An equally strong commitment statement.
   C. Alcohol and Substance Abuse: A policy statement in this area.

IV. **Conflicts of Interest**
   A. Outside Employment: Limitations on accepting employment from competitors,
   B. Personal Investments: Rules regarding using company data to make personal investment decisions.
   C. Gifts and Other Benefits: Rules regarding receiving bribes and improper gifts.
   D. Former Employees: Rules prohibiting giving favors to ex-employees in business.
   E. Family Members: Rules about giving business to family members, creating potential conflicts of interest.

V. **Company Property and Records**
   A. Company Assets: A strong statement on employees' responsibility to protect assets.
   B. Computer Systems Resources: An expansion of the company assets statement to reflect all aspects of computer systems resources.
   C. Use of the Company's Name: A rule that the company name should be used only for normal business dealings.

(continues)

EXHIBIT 4.4   Example Code of Conduct Topics *(Continued)*

     D. Company Records: A rule regarding employee responsibility for records integrity.

     E. Confidential Information: Rules on the importance of keeping all company information confidential and not disclosing it to outsiders.

     F. Employee Privacy: A strong statement on the importance of keeping employee personal information confidential to outsiders and even other employees.

     G. Company Benefits: Employees must not take company benefits where they are not entitled.

VI. Complying with the Law

     A. Inside Information and Insider Trading: A strong rule prohibiting insider trading or otherwise benefiting from inside information.

     B. Political Contributions and Activities: A strong statement on political activity rules.

     C. Bribery and Kickbacks: A firm rule of using bribes or accepting kickbacks.

     D. Foreign Business Dealings: Rules regarding dealing with foreign agents in line with the Foreign Corrupt Practices Act.

     E. Workplace Safety: A statement on the company policy to comply with OSHA rules.

     F. Product Safety: A statement on the company commitment to product safety.

     G. Environmental Protection: A rule regarding the company's commitment to comply with applicable environmental laws.

These words are a good example to the tone and style of a good code of conduct. Such a code places the responsibility on the recipient of the code, tries to explain the issues in an unambiguous manner, and suggests expected responses and actions.

In addition to the code topics and rules, many organizations have found value in adding a set of questions and answers to accompany the points in the code. Doing this allows the reader to better understand the issues as well as the types of questions that more unsophisticated employees might ask regarding a code rule. The format of the supporting questions and answers for the code of conduct might be:

Q: May I release the addresses of the employees in my department to an outside organization that wishes to offer them very attractive discounts at a local store?

A: No. Regardless of the well-intentioned purpose, you may not release this confidential information to outsiders without the specific permission of each employee.

These Q & A materials should apply to specific organization issues and can be very helpful in rooting the code of conduct in workplace reality. This book does not provide any full sample codes of conduct; almost every organization's code of conduct looks different in terms of its style, format, and size. Some organizations publish elaborate documents while others are very bare bones. Corporate codes of conduct, by their natures, are not company trade secrets. A call to a corporate information or public relations office or to the corporate ethics department or the CAE typically will result in their sending sample copies of their code of conduct. The reader should start with organizations in an industry of interest to see how they have built their codes.

Global corporations have another issue when developing a code of conduct. Although a corporation may be headquartered in the United States, it may have significant operations worldwide where key managers, employees, and other stakeholders do not use English as their prime language. Despite the added costs of translation, consideration should be given to producing code versions in at least several of the major languages used in corporate operations. If there exist many locations and just small numbers of various foreign-language stakeholders, a summary of the main code of conduct in each of the local languages might be appropriate. However, those summary versions should emphasize the same SOA financial fraud and whistleblower guidance that is contained in the prime code of conduct.

Communications to Stakeholders and Ensuring Compliance

An organization's code of conduct must be a *living document*. It has little value if it has been developed, delivered to all stakeholders with much hullabaloo, and then essentially filed and forgotten after that initial launch. The organization should undertake a major effort to deliver a copy of the new code of conduct, or even a major revision of the existing code, to all employees and stakeholders. Given today's SOA era, a good first step would be to present that new code of conduct formally to the organization's top managers, particularly the financial officers. The reported financial scandals leading up to SOA highlighted this discrepancy. Both Enron and WorldCom had adequate corporate codes of conduct; however, corporate officers evidently did not feel the rules applied to them.

A disturbing example of high-level corporate officer code of conduct acceptance can be found with the Enron ex-CFO, Andrew Fastow. Aware of the Enron code of conduct and because he knew that he would be violating it with his off–balance sheet schemes, Fastow went to the Enron audit committee and asked to be formally voted an exemption from code of conduct rules. The audit committee did grant this exemption as one more step leading to the ultimate failure of Enron.

Members of the senior management group should acknowledge formally that they have read, understand, and will abide by the code of conduct.

With the management team standing behind it, the code of conduct should then be delivered to all other stakeholders. Distribution can take place in multiple phases with delivery to local or major facilities first followed by smaller units, foreign locations, and other stakeholders. Rather than just including a copy of the code with employee payroll documents, an organization should present their code in a manner that will gain stakeholder attention. It should not be the "program of the month," an unfortunate happening in some organizations.

The code can be communicated through a video by the CEO, training sessions, or other means to stress its importance and meaning. Special communication methods might be used for other groups, such as vendors or contractors, but an organizational objective should be to get all stakeholders to formally acknowledge the code. Confirmation can be accomplished by an Internet or telephone response–type of system where every organization stakeholder is asked to respond to these three questions:

1. Have you received and read the Code of Conduct? Answer Yes or No.

2. Do you understand the contents of the Code of Conduct? Answer Yes if you understand this Code of Conduct or No if you have questions.

3. If you understand the contents of the Code, do you agree to abide by the policies and guidelines in this Code of Conduct? Answer Yes if you agree to abide by the Code and No if you do not.

The whole idea is to require *every* employee and other stakeholder to acknowledge their understanding and acceptance of the organization's code of conduct. Responses should be recorded on some form of computer database listing the stakeholder name and the date of review and acceptance or nonacceptance. Any questions from question 2 can be handled through the whistleblower program described later in this chapter. The idea is to have all of the stakeholders receiving it to buy in to the issued code of conduct and agree to abide by its terms. If someone refuses to accept the code because of questions, supervisors or others should discuss the matter with that person to gain eventual resolution. Following that code of conduct can be characterized as just another required work rule. Consistent failure to abide by these rules should be grounds for termination. Acceptance of the code of conduct should be made a condition of employment as well as any stakeholder relationship arrangement. Procedures should be modified to emphasize this requirement. Doing this would create grounds for termination for any employee who subsequently refuses to acknowledge the code of conduct.

The whole concept behind this code acknowledgment requirement is to avoid any "I didn't know that was the rule" excuses in the future if any code violations are encountered. It is a good idea to go through the code acceptance process on an annual basis or at least after any revision to the code document. Also, review and acceptance of the code should be required for new employees within their first days of employment.

Code Violations and Corrective Actions

A code of conduct lays out a set of rules for expected individual behavior in the organization. SOA requires that financial officers must subscribe to a code containing rules prohibiting fraudulent financial reporting, among other matters. Any financial officer who violates these rules is subject to strong penalties under the act. However, the organization should release one code of conduct with guidance for *all* stakeholders—SOA-impacted financial officers as well as all other persons. In addition to publishing its code of conduct and obtaining stakeholder acceptance, a mechanism to report code violations and for the investigation and disposition of those violations is required.

If the organization issues a strong code of conduct along with a message from the CEO about the importance of good ethical practices, all stakeholders will be expected to follow those rules. However, people are people, and there will always be some who violate the rules or run on the edge. An organization needs to establish a mechanism to allow employees or even outsiders to report potential violations of the code in a secure and confidential manner. Much of that reporting mechanism can be handled through a whistleblower facility, which is discussed later. Other potential violations must be handled on a different level. Consider the female staff employee who has a male supervisor who "hints" that sexual favors with him present a good way for the female employee to advance in the organization. A sexual harassment prohibition in the code of conduct will not necessarily stop that supervisor, and often the employee cannot easily report this situation to a manager one level above the supervisor. Recriminations and denials could be the result. A process should be established for anonymously reporting this and all types of ethics violations.

In addition to the whistleblower or ethics hotline function, the organization should establish other mechanisms for reporting potential code of conduct violations. Since some people do not want to call an ethics hotline, a well-publicized post office box address is sometimes very effective. Stakeholders could be encouraged to write to such a P.O. box, anonymously or not, to report ethics violations. Based on these responses, the ethics function, human resources, or some other appropriate function in the organization should investigate matters and take action as necessary.

A code of conduct describes a series of rules for expected actions. When violations are found, the matter should be investigated and actions taken on a consistent basis, no matter what rank the organization stakeholders. If the code of conduct prohibits making copies of corporate software—and it should—the penalties for a staff analyst in a remote sales office or a senior manager in corporate headquarters should be the same. Assuming they both have read the prohibition in the code and acknowledged understanding and acceptance, penalties for violations should be consistent. Otherwise, an atmosphere in which the rules appear to apply only to some will exist.

Code of conduct violations can be handled through the organization's normal human resources procedures. These functions typically have some processes where there may be verbal counseling or probation for a first offense and termination if there are multiple recurrences. Some matters must be reported to outside authorities. A violation of SOA rules, such as a recently discovered undocumented off–balance sheet arrangement, would be reported to the SEC; the theft of goods from a warehouse would be reported to a county prosecutor. When these matters are discovered and reported to outside authorities, the matter moves outside of the organization's hands. The overall goal is for the organization to have some process in place to encourage all stakeholders to follow good ethical practices, as defined in its code of conduct, and to provide a consistent mechanism for both reporting violations and taking disciplinary action when necessary.

Keeping the Code Current

Many of the basic rules of good ethical behavior and basic organization rules will not change from year to year. The example rule about the protection of company assets, cited previously, will not change over time. Other code of conduct rules may change due to business or other conditions. The author was involved with a retail organization, company A, which originally had a code rule prohibiting employees working for competitors. That rule was appropriate when a shopping mall salesperson worked for company A full time. However, in a changing era of a lot of part-time work, it was not appropriate to tell a half-time shopping mall salesperson that she could not work part time for another retailer, company B, located in the same shopping mall. The code of conduct rule here was changed to state that while on the job for company A, the employee's loyalty *had to be* just with A and not for B.

Organizations should review their published codes of conduct on a periodic basis and at least once every two years to make certain the guidance material there is still applicable and current. All organizations today should review any current published code of conduct to determine if it reflects changes introduced by SOA. This might include a code statement regarding the need for accurate and timely financial reporting at all levels or the organization's commitment to avoid any type of financial fraud. Changes to the code of conduct should not be treated lightly. Any revision should go through the same announcement and rollout process described for code introductions. The revised code should be issued to all stakeholders along with an explanation of the changes and a requirement to reacknowledge acceptance as discussed previously.

A new code of conduct revision and requests for stakeholder reaffirmation can be an expensive task requiring dedicated organization resources from the ethics function, human resources, or others. It is generally not a good idea to roll out a new version of the code annually, as it should stand with the mission statement as a set of foundation stones for the organization. Rather, an organization should keep its code of conduct and supporting principles in front of all stakeholders at all times. Doing this can be accomplished through constant references to the code of conduct, such as in bulletin board posters in all facilities, instructive questions and answers in company publications, or segments in employee training classes. Internal audit should play a key role in promoting the code and monitoring compliance through audit reviews and ongoing contacts through the organization.

WHISTLEBLOWER AND HOTLINE FUNCTIONS

Section 301 of SOA mandates that the audit committee establish procedures to "handle whistleblower information regarding questionable accounting or auditing matters." This whistleblower provision is an important part of the act. Many of the questionable accounting practices that originally gave rise to SOA came to light, at least in part, because of employees who blew the whistle. Even before the scandals at Enron, WorldCom, and others broke, whistleblower protections have been part of many federal laws as a means to help regulators ferret out violations and wrongdoing. The whistleblower provisions of SOA are patterned after similar statutory schemes for protecting workers in the airline and nuclear power industries.

Whistleblower laws allow an employee or stakeholder who sees some form of wrongdoing to report independently and anonymously that action with no fear of recrimination against the whistleblower. Recriminations can take many forms, ranging from a supevisor's "tut-tut" comments to job downgrades or worse. The matter can be reported to the organization or to regulatory authorities. Per SOA whistleblower rules, there can be no recrimination against the employee, or the whistleblower can initiate legal action for damages. These whistleblower cases can inflict serious damage on an organization's reputation as well as on the careers of accused managers. While whistleblower programs have been around for some years to support federal contracting laws, health and safety regulations, and others, SOA moves these rules into the business offices of *all* publicly traded U.S. organizations. The audit committee is required to establish these whistleblower procedures, but other functions, such as the ethics department, human resources, or internal audit, will need to actually set things up.

Organizations that have established ethics functions usually also have hotline or similar ethics questions telephone lines. While these ethics hotlines can provide a starting point for the SOA whistleblower function, they usually need adjustments or fine tuning. Too often, reported incidents are not investigated in a proper manner and whistleblower confidentiality is not as strong as necessary. A slip-up here can cause major problems for an organization if the whistleblowing stakeholder feels matters have not been resolved or individual confidentiality has been compromised. Internal audit often can be a major aid to management and the audit committee in this process through its reviews of the existing ethics hotline process, recommendations of appropriate controls, and provision of guidance to the audit committee.

Whistleblower functions have been part of federal laws for stakeholders in any organization involved in a wide range of activities, from federal contracts to employee health and safety. Any employee or stakeholder who observes some type of improper or illegal activity can "blow the whistle" and report the incident. The matter then should be investigated and corrected if the allegations prove true. The original whistleblower sometimes may receive a proportionate reward from the savings. An employee whistleblower, for example, may know that a contract calls for some machine part, under a federal contract, to be of certain gauge steel but may discover that the organization is using a cheaper gauge of steel, violating contract terms and potentially endangering the safety of the component. The employee has a right and, really, an obligation to blow the whistle on this practice by contacting the organization's contract compliance office, human resources, or some procurement or internal audit function. If no action is taken by the company, the employee can blow the whistle again to federal contract administration authorities. Once the matter has been reported, either internally or externally, the whistleblower is legally protected from any form of workplace recrimination.

The SOA-mandated whistleblower program adds accounting and auditing issues to topics for whistleblower complaints, although it does not promise cash rewards beyond out-of-pocket expenses. This SOA whistleblower provision provides a new challenge to the responsible audit committee member. The typical audit committee member *may* be aware of existing whistleblower processes within the organization, but almost certainly will not be aware of the necessary processes to establish an effective whistleblower program. Internal audit often can help the audit committee representative to establish an effective whistleblower program that will comply with SOA.

Federal SOA Whistleblower Rules

The U.S. Department of Labor (DOL) administers and enforces more than 180 federal laws covering workplace activities for about 10 million employers and 125 million workers. Most labor and public safety laws and many environmental laws mandate whistleblower protections for employees who complain about violations of the law by their employers. SOA now adds federal whistleblower protection to all employees of SEC-registered organizations, and public companies will need to pay special attention to these new protections for corporate whistleblowers. SOA Section 806 establishes a system for whistleblower protection for stakeholders in publicly traded companies. That provision provides that no public company or any officer, employee, contractor, or agent of such company "may discharge, demote, suspend, threaten, harass, or in any other manner discriminate against an employee in the terms and conditions of employment because of any lawful act done by the employee." Those lawful acts are when the employee provides information or otherwise assists in an investigation conducted by a federal regulatory or law enforcement agency, the Congress, or company personnel regarding any conduct that the employee "reasonably believes" constitutes a violation of SEC rules and regulations or fraud statutes; or files, testifies, participates in, or otherwise assists in a proceeding—pending or about to be filed—relating to an alleged violation. In other words, the employee or stakeholder who perceives some financial wrongdoing and then reports the matter is legally protected during its investigation and resolution.

In many respects, these whistleblower provisions are designed primarily to protect employees who think they have discovered some wrongdoing rather than to increase the organization's internal controls. Virtually any personnel action taken against a whistleblower employee, including a demotion or suspension, can potentially be subject to legal action under this provision. Although minimal SOA-related whistleblower experience is available at this time, if the experiences from other whistleblower statutes are applied to SOA, the SEC and the DOL will broadly protect accounting and auditing whistleblower employees. In other words, an employee or stakeholder who registers a whistleblower complaint will be protected until the matter is resolved. SOA does seek to avoid frivolous complaints here by requiring that the whistleblower must have a "reasonable" belief that the practice reported constitutes a violation.

SOA Section 1107 makes it a crime for anyone "knowingly, with the intent to retaliate," to interfere with the employment or livelihood of any person—a whistleblower—who provides a law enforcement officer any truthful information relating to the possible commission of a SOA violation offense. Any whistleblower employee who then faces adverse employment action could potentially become a "protected informant" witness. Several legal sources have emphasized that this employee protection legislation is extraordinary and underscores the seriousness with which the Congress viewed this subject.

Stakeholders who believe they have been unlawfully discharged or discriminated against, due to their whistleblower action, may seek relief by filing a complaint, within 90 days after the date of the violation, with the DOL or initiating federal district court action. The aggrieved typically will need to secure legal help to seek relief, but numerous law firms will be waiting to get involved. The process can be time-consuming and expensive for the accused corporation. The procedural rules governing whistleblower incidents, including the burdens of proof for the employer and employee, will follow the Air 21 statute for airline employees.[2] For example, to prevail on a complaint before the DOL, the employee must demonstrate that discriminatory reasons were a "contributing factor" in the unfavorable personnel action. Relief will be denied, however, if the employer demonstrates by "clear and convincing evidence" that it would have taken the same personnel action in the absence of protected activity.

An employee prevailing in such an action is entitled to full compensatory damages including reinstatement, back pay with interest, and compensation for the litigation costs and attorney fees. However, if DOL does not issue a final decision within 180 days of the whistleblower's complaint filing, the matter may be moved to the federal district court. Complicating matters further, the harmed whistleblower can take action on several fronts, seeking protection under federal and state laws as well as any applicable collective bargaining agreement. Employers are exposed to potential "double jeopardy" for whistleblower actions with liability under both SOA provisions as well as state or federal laws on wrongful discharge and similar causes of action. In addition, the aggrieved whistleblower can seek punitive damages through separate court actions.

Based on administrative and judicial experiences in the nuclear energy and the airlines industries, whistleblower protection laws can become a potential minefield for corporations. If an employee raises any sort of SOA accounting or auditing matter regarding an improper or illegal act, that whistleblower is totally protected until the matter is investigated and resolved. There will be many trial lawyers in the wings eager to help the whistleblower and to file actions, particularly against major corporations with deep pockets. A substantial body of DOL and court precedent exists in this area. Because SOA reforms are substantially similar to Section 211 of the Energy Reorganization Act and Air 21, it can be expected that they will share common legal standards, such as the definition of "protected activity" and legally sufficient proof of causation (between the protected activity and the adverse personnel action) to support regulatory sanctions and personal remedies.

Based on over 20 years of experience with whistleblower protection laws, an impacted organization should attempt to strike a balance between the rights of employees to raise whistleblower concerns and the ability to manage the workforce. A positive work environment is needed in which employees feel free to raise concerns to management coupled with effective mechanisms to deal with any concerns raised. The strong ethics-related programs discussed in the first sections of this chapter—including mission statements and codes of conduct—will support this strategy.

SOA Whistleblower Rules and Internal Audit

Under SOA, any employee or other stakeholder can become a whistleblower by reporting an illegal or improper activity covering accounting, internal control, and auditing. This should be an effective process when the potential whistleblower is a member of the corporate accounting staff who hears of plans for some fraudulent transactions or an employee at a remote unit that is not visited frequently by corporate staff, such as internal audit. Whistleblower rules are designed to encourage stakeholders to report these fraudulent or illegal acts and to protect the person who reported the matter. This raises a series of issues regarding internal auditors and internal audit reviews.

An objective of internal auditing is to review and discover the types of accounting, internal control, and auditing issues specified in SOA. Internal audit findings are reviewed with management and presented in a formal audit report where management can outline its plan for corrective action. However, what if the internal audit team discovers an accounting, internal control, or auditing matter that is not formally reported to management in the audit report? Can one of the audit team members independently report the matter under SOA whistleblower procedures? Can an internal auditor who encounters a SOA accounting and internal control matter that is not part of a scheduled audit go through the whistleblower protection route to report the matter? What if the internal audit team member has not been performing well and fears termination? Can that shaky-status auditor dig up some potential findings, perhaps from past workpapers, and report them outside of the audit department to obtain whistleblower protection and job security until the matter is resolved?

The internal audit team is clearly part of management, and internal auditors have a responsibility to report any improper or illegal matters encountered during an audit visit first to internal audit management for disposition. Internal audit team members should not attempt to work as independent whistleblowers as part of their internal audit work. Internal audit should develop a clear policy stating that any SOA accounting, internal control, or auditing matters encountered during the course of a scheduled audit review should be documented in the audit workpapers and communicated to internal audit management for resolution. Exhibit 4.5 outlines a potential internal auditor whistleblower policy. Both the internal audit team and general management should understand that the purpose of internal audit is not to let loose a team of potential whistleblowers in a department's books and records. Any illegal or improper items should be investigated and reported through the normal internal audit process.

A situation could exist where an internal auditor does find an SOA accounting or internal controls matter that is somehow dropped from the audit process, perhaps in a senior auditor's workpaper review. The internal

EXHIBIT 4.5   Internal Audit Whistleblower Policy

To: Internal Auditors

Federal law, under the Sarbanes-Oxley Act, allows any employee of our company to "blow the whistle" and independently and confidentially report any improper or illegal matters involving accounting, internal control, or auditing issues. These matters can be reported to our "800-HELP" facility for investigation and resolution. However, as a member of our internal audit team, your reporting responsibilities are different.

As a member of the internal audit team responsible for assessing our overall operations, you may regularly encounter major or minor improper or illegal matters involving accounting, internal control, or auditing issues. It is your responsibility to investigate, document, and report such matters as part of your normal internal audit work. The matters will be handled though our normal Internal audit reporting processes. If you feel your supervisor on an audit assignment is not giving sufficient attention to some matter, your first responsibility is to report and discuss the matter through internal audit channels, up through the audit committee.

You may encounter situations where it is necessary to report incidents such as material wrongdoing in our internal audit department. In those instances, you have a right and indeed an obligation to report them through our "800-HELP" facility.

John Doe
Chief Audit Executive

auditor has a first responsibility to get resolution on the matter through the internal audit department up through the CAE or even the audit committee. If the internal auditor documents and reports the issue, but audit management elects to drop or ignore the matter, the internal auditor certainly then has the right and responsibility to report the matter through the organization's hotline functions or even through the SEC. Audit management and other processes should be in place to prevent such a frustrated internal auditor/potential whistleblower situation.

Launching the Organization Help or Hotline Function

Many organizations already have established help or hotline functions. Most include confidential telephone line facilities administered through the ethics department, human resources, or an independent provider. These toll-free telephone operations, which often operate on 24 hours, 7 days a week, allow any stakeholder to call anonymously and ask a question, report a concern, or "blow the whistle" on some matter. The idea is to provide an independent facility where all stakeholders can ask questions or report possible wrong-doings at any level. These hotlines are not legally required functions, but where established, the items reported may range from allegations of theft of company property, human resource complaints, or just troubling questions. In most cases, the telephone operator will take all of the necessary information, asking questions when needed, and then pass the reported incident to an appropriate authority for investigation and resolution. The hotline operator typically assigns the reported incident a case number so the caller can later check on resolution.

Employee hotlines were established in many larger organizations beginning in mid-1990. Often staffed with knowledgeable human resources veterans, many of the operators often are particularly skilled at answering human resource issues, such as treatment in the workplace. With allegations of wrongdoing, the recorded case is shifted to others for investigation, such as to the legal department. In some instances, these lines have turned into little more than corporate "snitch" lines where many minor gripes or infractions are reported. However, organizations such as the Ethics Officer Association, mentioned previously, have reported that these facilities have been generally very successful.

Many established ethics hotlines were set up to be "friendly" in answering employee questions and giving some advice in addition to investigating reported incidents. Using this same, already established facility for the SOA whistleblower program places some new controls and responsibilities on the function. While the more friendly help aspects of an ethics hotline still can apply, federal whistleblower rules require that the function have much more formalized processes, particularly in areas such as confidentiality, documentation requirements for all records, and efficient processing of any investigations. In addition, the employee calling in an SOA whistleblower allegation is legally protected from any future recrimination. In some respects, a bubble has to be encapsulated around the whistleblower employee such that no actions of any sort can be directed at that whistleblower by the employer until the whistleblower action is resolved. While they have not yet occurred under SOA, under other federal whistleblower laws an employee who called in a matter and then had his desk moved was able to bring legal action for whistleblower discrimination. There is no reason to establish separate ethics help lines and SOA whistleblower lines. Doing so would confuse callers about which one to call. However, with the SOA whistleblower requirement, control procedures need to be enhanced in any established ethics hotline facility. Exhibit 4.6 contains some guidelines for setting up an ethics hotline program that will also serve as a SOA whistleblower facility.

The existence of an ethics hotline and whistleblower facility will be of little value unless it is communicated and "sold" to all members of the organization. A good way to launch these processes initially is through the employee code of conduct, discussed previously. Even if such a hotline has

EXHIBIT 4.6   Guidelines for Setting Up a Whistleblower Call Center

- Establish independent—preferably toll-free—telephone lines for facility. The lines must not go through other company switchboards.

- Train all operators in the facility with the basic provisions of federal whistleblower rules. Also, establish scripts such that operators can ask the same general questions.

- Advertise and promote the facility throughout the organization with an emphasis that all items will be reported, the caller will be able to check status, all callers will be treated anonymously, and there will be no recrimination for caller actions.

- Implement a logging form to record all calls. Maintain the date and time of the call, the caller name or identification, and the details reported.

- Establish a routing and disposition process such that the status of who has the call information and the status of any investigation can be determined.

- Establish a secure database for all whistleblower data with appropriate password protection,

- Working with human resources, develop procedures to fully but anonymously protect any whistleblower from recrimination of any sort.

- Develop a process for closing out all whistleblower calls, documenting all actions, if any.

been launched already, the fact that the line can be used for any potential SOA whistleblowers needs to be communicated. The goal should be to investigate and promptly resolve all calls—and especially whistleblower calls—internally to avoid outside investigators and lawyers.

Hotline and Whistleblower Functions in the Smaller Organization

The provisions of SOA apply to all SEC-registered corporations, whether large or small. While organizations that are Fortune 500 in size probably have such resources as an established ethics department and a larger internal audit function, many smaller corporations do not. Nevertheless, SOA applies to all, and smaller organizations need to take steps to demonstrate compliance with the act. While there will be numerous consulting firms circling around to offer SOA-compliance help, smaller organizations often can establish effective SOA compliance through a dedicated team effort led by the CFO, internal audit, human resources, and legal counsel resources.

While many SOA areas are fairly easy to implement, such as having an audit committee "financial expert" or complying with COSO internal controls, regardless of organization size, the ethics and whistleblower requirements discussed in this chapter may present a challenge for smaller organizations. Often internal audit can play a lead role here. We have used the term "internal audit" rather than the chief audit executive referenced in other chapters because the head of internal audit in a smaller organization may be a very hands-on manager responsible for a relatively small staff of perhaps ten or fewer internal auditors.

Many specialized resources are available to help a smaller organization achieve SOA compliance. In some respects, it depends on how much time and cost the organization wants to devote to this area, ranging from minimal compliance to a well-designed program. The smaller corporation director of internal audit coupled, perhaps, with the head of human resources might be the key resources to launch SOA ethics and whistleblower compliance programs.

Smaller Organizations: Corporate Mission Statement and Code of Conduct

Many smaller corporations are closely held and led by a founding CEO or family members. Things such as mission statements and codes of conduct often are not published in this type of environment because everyone is considered "family." While the smaller corporation often has this one-big-happy-family approach, SOA provides an appropriate reason to formally develop and release a corporate mission statement and code of conduct. That mission statement will become a statement of purpose for the organization, stating where it is and where it hopes to be going in a very high level sense. Once drafted and communicated, this smaller organization's mission statement can be the driver for other SOA compliance efforts.

As discussed, SOA requires that all organizations have a code of conduct or code for their senior financial officers. No matter the organization size, such a code should be developed, communicated, and accepted by all its members. Beyond SOA accounting and internal control financial fraud issues, a general code of conduct will outline the rules to all stakeholders. Consultants are available to help draft such materials, but the key managers for most organizations should be able to develop their own code based on their business and what they feel should be right or wrong. Although the topics do not apply to all organizations, the sample code of conduct topics outlined in Exhibit 4.4 can serve as a starting point here. The idea is to lay out the rules of right or wrong.

No matter how small the organization, once the code has been released, all employees should be asked to acknowledge formally their understanding and acceptance of the code. Doing so affirms to them the rules of right or wrong in business dealings. The smaller organization should request that all of its stakeholders, such as contractors and vendors, also sign and acknowledge the code of conduct. Requiring this sometimes is difficult for a relatively small corporation that may be dealing with much larger vendors or suppliers. A $10 billion corporation that supplies or is a vendor for a $10 million corporation will almost certainly refuse to formally acknowledge the small company's code of conduct. Often the best way to handle such an issue is to send a copy of the code to appropriate units in the larger company along with a note that unless those units object, they are expected to follow the code's general precepts.

Ethics and Whistleblower Training

The whistleblower provisions of SOA have the potential to cause major problems for the smaller organization. The goal should be to promote good ethical behavior such that whistleblower issues are reported only for true accounting issues and internal control issues and that they are reported to the corporation's whistleblower help facility rather than to regulators or outside lawyers. A series of formal training programs should be launched to introduce the program. Key things to consider for this ethics and whistleblower training include:

- The training should be more than a speech about the "new rules" and the need to follow them.
- There should be a strong statement that senior management has endorsed this program and expects all employees to follow the ethics program.
- Specific whistleblower rules should be outlined, including how to report matters and how they will be resolved. In addition, it must be emphasized that there will be no retribution to whistleblowers.
- The training should focus on ethical dilemma types of issues where there is no easy right or wrong answer, but the employee is expected to do the right thing.
- Although larger organizations often launch multiple levels of training sessions for various groups of employees, the smaller organization might be most successful in one session that covers the entire organization, from executive to the shop floor.

Ethics and whistleblower training is an effective way to launch these initiatives. The training should not be a one-time endeavor; the material should be presented periodically, perhaps once a year, to keep all members of the organization familiar with the ethics program.

Implementing the Whistleblower Program in Smaller Organizations

The training program just discussed also would launch an ethics and whistleblower program in a smaller organization. However, a key additional element is to establish a resource for the receipt and disposition of any whistleblower calls. The often internally staffed hotline function discussed previously is just too expensive for the smaller organization. Whistleblowers need a facility to report any such concerns anonymously. We have not made any specific recommendations here, but an Internet search for a topic such as "Sarbanes-Oxley whistleblower" will yield a variety of service organizations that provide telephone banks for reporting such matters. These providers will assign the company a toll-free hotline number supported by trained agents round-the-clock to answer whistleblower calls. Daily reports then are distributed to a designated contact person in the subscribing company for investigation and resolution.

These commercial hotline services provide essential services to the smaller organization seeking SOA compliance. However, investigation, resolution, and whistleblower confidentiality are key factors that the outside hotline provider cannot supply easily. The designated hotline contact person just mentioned must be someone who can totally preserve the whistleblower's confidentiality with no hint of retribution. Implementing this role can be very challenging in smaller organizations.

Keeping SOA Programs Current and Active

Once ethics and whistleblower programs are launched, organizations of any size need to keep their programs current and active. Doing this can be an even greater problem for smaller organizations that do not have sufficient resources to assign even one individual to the program. The team that originally launched this program should review the program on probably an annual basis by revisiting and updating the code of conduct and assessing the progress or problems with the hotline whistleblower program.

We have suggested some action steps smaller corporations can take to launch an ethics and SOA whistleblower program. Internal audit can be a key resource to making these things happen, as internal audit typically has exposure to all levels of the organization through its financial and operational audits. Also, internal audit will have regular contact with the audit committee, through frequent reports and meetings, as well as with key financial management. This role becomes another of the "new rules" for internal audit—an overall theme of this book.

AUDITING THE ORGANIZATION'S ETHICS FUNCTIONS

The ethics and hotline function should not be exempt from the same types of operational or financial reviews that internal audit performs in all other segments of the organization. Different from asset management, marketing, or design engineering, which are subject to periodic internal audit reviews based on potential audit risks, the ethics function should be included in the same type of risk-analysis model used by internal audit for audit planning. Although the ethics code of conduct function may introduce minimal risks, the whistleblower function—particularly if it is administered internally— may present some major security and confidentiality risks. In addition, the CFO and other key officers are very much at risk if there are problems here.

The purpose of an internal audit review of the ethics and whistleblower function is to assess whether that ethics group is following good internal control procedures, making effective use of its resources, complying with good confidentiality procedures, and following its department charter author- izing the ethics function. Although all ethics and whistleblower functions may be a little different, internal audit should gain a detailed understand- ing of how the function operates and the procedures normally performed. As the organization's *ethics function,* internal audit should expect to find the ethics department procedures at least as good as internal audit regard- ing compliance with document confidentiality and with organization poli- cies, such as travel expenses. Other ethics functions responsibilities may point to areas where internal audit can suggest improvements. For exam- ple, the ethics department's code of conduct normally should have an acknowledgment form or process where employees indicate that they have read and understand the code. An ethics function may not have established appropriate procedures here to ensure that all newly hired employees go through this code acknowledgment process. Internal audit can assess this process and recommend improvements where appropriate.

Exhibit 4.7 describes some audit procedures for an internal audit review of an organizational ethics and whistleblower function. Because of the close, ongoing relationship that should exist between the ethics function and inter- nal audit, if an operational review of ethics does come up as part of audit's risk analysis, the CAE should discuss in some detail the planned review with the ethics director to explain the reasons for it and its objectives. Privacy and confidentiality may become an issue in this type of review. A call to the hotline may have pointed to some form of potential employee malfeasance or an SOA whistleblower revelation, which ethics will want to keep highly confidential until the matter is resolved. Despite internal audit's ongoing exposure to other sensitive areas and issues in the organization, the direc- tor of the ethics function may be reluctant to have internal auditors review certain materials. The CAE should point out internal audit's ongoing expo- sure to other sensitive information and the requirements that it follow appropriate professional standards. Assuming that these matters can be resolved appropriately, an operational review of an ethics function will give management additional assurances as to the integrity of controls in the ethics function, a component of operations where most managers have had little exposure or experience.

EXHIBIT 4.7   Auditing the Ethics Function: Sample Audit Program

1. *Ethics Function Administration*

   1.1. Develop an understanding and document the organization structure of the ethics function including organization structure and reporting relationships.

   1.2. Review ethics function's charter and other key process documentation.

   1.3. Assess ethics function office security procedures for the adequacy of such matters as records, file, and workstation security.

   1.4. If outside contractors are used to provide ethics or hotline services, review and document contractual arrangements.

2. *Code of Conduct Processes*

   2.1. Obtain copy of current Code of Conduct.

      2.1.1. Determine whether code is current and updated regularly.

      2.1.2. Discuss code with a sample of organization staff to determine that they understand the code document.

      2.1.3. Discuss code with sample of managers to determine if there are concerns about the code's issues or content.

   2.2. Assess the adequacy of processes for obtaining code acknowledgments.

      2.2.1. Select a sample of employees and determine that they acknowledged acceptance of the code.

      2.2.2. Determine that all officers have accepted the code.

      2.2.3. Assess adequacy of procedures for any employees who fail/refuse code acknowledgment.

      2.2.4. Assess adequacy of code acknowledgment records.

   2.3. Assess adequacy of processes for updating code of conduct as required.

   2.4. Assess processes in place to distribute code to all organization stakeholders, including remote locations and foreign sites, vendors, and others.

3. *Hotline/Whistleblower Processes*

   3.1. Develop a general understanding of processes in place and determine they cover all areas including SOA matters.

   3.2. Assess adequacy of processes for logging calls received and documenting interactions.

   3.3. Review process for disposition of calls and select sample of recent calls to determine if processes appear adequate.

   3.4. Review overall security processes in place including protection of key documents and individual whistleblower stakeholders.

(continues)

EXHIBIT 4.7   Auditing the Ethics Function *(Continued)*

> 3.5.   Meet with Human Resources to determine that adequate procedures are in place to protect/encapsulate any whistleblowers.
>
> 4.   *Audit Committee Responsibilities*
>
>   Meet with audit committee representative to determine knowledge and understanding of the ethics and whistleblower programs in place.

NOTES

1. Ethics Officer Association, 30 Church Street, Belmont, MA 02478. This is the major professional organization for professional ethics officers with over 700 companies represented as of 2003.
2. The Wendell H. Ford Aviation Investment and Reform Act for the 21st Century (commonly known as Air 21) protects whistleblowers in the airline industry. A related act is the 1978 Energy Reorganization Act, which protects employees in the nuclear power industry from retaliation for their reporting of safety concerns.

COSO, Section 404, and Control Self-Assessments

"Internal control" or "internal accounting controls" are terms that are used frequently, although a surprising number of business managers may not be able to define them easily. Although internal auditors generally have a good understanding of what is meant by "internal controls," others may respond to the question "Can you define good internal controls?" with answers along these lines:

- "Good internal controls" means everything is well documented.
- "Good internal controls" means strong security.
- "Good internal controls" means the debits equal the credits.

Although each of these terms are components on internal controls, many professionals often have to step back and think about an appropriate answer when asked for a complete definition. Internal controls are necessary for all well-managed and well-functioning business processes and systems. According to a common definition:

"Internal control" comprises the plan of organization and all of the coordinate methods adopted within a business to safeguard its assets, check the accuracy and reliability of its accounting data, promote operational efficiency, and encourage adherence to prescribed managerial policies. This definition recognizes that a system of internal control extends beyond those matters which relate directly to the functions of the accounting and financial departments.

This long and rather academic-sounding definition says that a system or process has good internal controls if it:

1. Accomplishes its stated mission
2. Produces accurate and reliable data
3. Complies with applicable laws and organization policies

4. Provides for economical and efficient uses of resources

5. Provides for appropriate safeguarding of assets

All members of the organization are responsible for the internal controls in their area of operation and for making those internal controls function.

The concept of internal controls is not new. Members of organizations at all levels—and certainly internal auditors—have had an ongoing and long-term responsibility to understand and install effective internal controls in their systems and operations. Concerns about fraudulent financial reporting and the dot-com bust that led to the Sarbanes-Oxley Act (SOA) have made the requirements of an effective system of internal controls very important today.

This chapter discusses the internal control requirements included in SOA; they often are called the Section 404 requirements and represent perhaps one of the more important aspects of the act to a corporation and its internal auditors. The Public Corporation Accounting Oversight Board (PCAOB), the function that sets auditing rules (see Chapter 2), has not yet set the "official" internal control review standards, but these will almost certainly follow the Committee of Sponsoring Organizations (COSO) framework that has been endorsed by all of the major U.S. and other international accounting and auditing professional organizations. This chapter reintroduces COSO in the context of compliance with SOA Section 404.

An introduction to the Organizational Sentencing Guidelines follows the section on COSO. These guidelines are the congressionally mandated penalties for organizations or individuals found guilty of a violation of some federal statute, such as SOA. The sentencing guidelines have reward-type features, such that an organization that has been found guilty can have its judicial punishment or penalty reduced if it has an effective compliance program in place. Conversely, other factors can increase the length of the minimum sentence or fine. The chapter concludes with a discussion of the control self-assessment process of the Institute of Internal Auditors (IIA). This new auditing approach follows the "new rules" theme of this book.

SOA SECTION 404

Although there has been considerable analysis to date and the formal Securities and Exchange Commission (SEC) rules are yet to be issued, Section 404 of SOA simply requires an annual internal controls report, as part of the SEC financial reporting, which shall both:

1. State the responsibility of management for establishing and maintaining an adequate internal control structure and procedures for financial reporting

2. Contain an assessment, as of the end of the most recent fiscal year of the issuer, of the effectiveness of the internal control structure and procedures of the issuer for financial reporting

In addition, the public accounting firm, external auditors, that issued the supporting audit report is required to review and attest to the process that led to management's assessment of internal financial controls. An attestation made under this subsection shall be made in accordance with standards for attestation engagements issued or adopted by the board. Any such attestation shall not be the subject of a separate engagement.

Simply put, management now is required to report on the quality of its internal controls, and the public accounting firm responsible for the financial statements audit must attest to that internal controls report. Management always has been responsible for preparing periodic financial reports; external auditors reviewed those financial numbers and certified that they were fairly stated as part of their audit. With SOA Section 404, management is responsible for documenting and testing its internal financial controls in order to prepare a report on their effectiveness. The external auditors will review the supporting materials leading up to that internal financial controls report to assert that the report is an accurate description of that internal control environment.

To the nonauditor, this requirement might appear to be obscure or almost trivial. However, audit reports on the status of internal controls have been an ongoing and simmering issue between the public accounting community, the SEC, and other interested parties going back to 1974. Over the years since the mid-1970s, initiatives about once every five years have attempted to require public companies to report on the *quality* of their internal controls. Although SEC regulators talked about the need for a formal report on the quality of internal controls, the auditing profession as well as other commentators felt that the quality of internal control evaluations was too subjective, and no one wanted to affirm that their internal controls were adequate. Much of the debate, going through the 1980s, was that there was no recognized definition for what is meant by "internal controls." The release of COSO in 1992, as described below, established a common framework for internal control that has become an accepted standard. SOA Section 404 has ended this debate. Management now is required to report on its internal controls with public accounting firms attesting to those internal controls reports.

Establishing Section 404 Compliance

Section 404 of SOA presents a major challenge to SEC-registered organizations. Although some organizations took a hard look at the COSO internal control framework, described later in this chapter, and evaluated their internal controls using that framework, many did not. The organizations that evaluated their own controls in a COSO context almost certainly have some work ahead, but at least they should have an understanding of their internal controls environment. Organizations that relied on external auditors who issued favorable financial reports, with only limited internal control work, and on internal audit, which reviewed internal controls in various selected areas but often not in totality, face a potentially major challenge in completing their assessment of internal controls. A third group are organizations, often smaller, that have given little attention to their internal controls and have no internal audit function. They are potentially facing a major challenge in establishing Section 404 compliance.

As discussed in Chapter 2, an effective internal audit function should play a major role in helping an organization get ready for SOA and its Section 404 compliance. External auditors who once did some internal financial controls assessment work as part of their annual audits are no longer directly responsible here, according to SOA. Those external auditors can only review and attest to management's internal financial controls assessment report but cannot do this work themselves. In the past, public accounting firms also often recommended that their own consultants help solve any perceived internal control weaknesses, such as a poorly performing financial system. SOA has ended that. Although some very qualified and excellent consulting firms can help an organization to achieve SOA compliance, an effective internal audit function should take a key role in aiding senior management here.

Who should perform these internal financial control reviews, since the external auditors are no longer legally allowed to do the work? Internal audit could be an obvious answer. However, based on the IIA Standards discussed in Chapter 6, internal audit does not necessarily hold itself to be directly responsible for implementing the internal financial controls testing and documentation program that it eventually will be requested to review. Internal audit should review or audit these controls in support of the attestation materials given to the external auditors. However, internal audit should not assume the role as project manager here but only play a participant role in any internal controls implementation. Internal audit's role in auditing new systems under implementation might prove a good example. Typically, internal auditors will serve on the team that is installing a new application and will recommend internal control improvements as the new application is being developed. However, they are not responsible for installing those changes or for the overall new system. Thus, they can return later and review the new system while maintaining their independence.[1]

Protiviti, an internal audit and risk management consulting firm, has suggested that the best approach for establishing SOA Section 404 compliance is to launch a formal, special project to address the issue.[2] The actual project would be somewhat different based on the strength of the organization's internal control processes, but the project could be launched in four steps:

1. *Organize the Section 404 compliance project approach.* Assign a project team to lead the effort. A senior executive, such as the chief financial officer (CFO), should act as the project sponsor with a team of both internal and external resources to participate in the effort. Roles, responsibilities, and resource requirements should be estimated at this time as well.

2. *Develop a project plan.* The internal financial controls compliance project should be well in process prior to the organization's financial year end. Although the existing plan can be updated in subsequent years, there will be a major challenge and time crunch for the first year. The plan should focus on significant areas of organization operations with coverage over all significant business units. There can be many variations here for developing such a plan. Exhibit 5.1 shows one Section 404 compliance review project work breakdown structure for launching the project.[3] Although work breakdown structures are usually fairly high level, the team normally would develop a more detailed document. Based on this high-level approach, the project team would develop a detailed set of plan steps to begin the internal financial controls review.

3. *Identify, document, and test key internal controls.* This step can be a major effort. Using some form of criticality analysis, key organization internal financial control processes should be identified, compliance to control procedures tested, and the results documented. Documentation is very important here, because when external auditors review these processes, they will need to examine this documentation to attest that controls are in place and operating. Internal audit should play a key role in this area in advising the internal financial controls project team.

4. *Review compliance results with key stakeholders.* Senior financial and executive management ultimately will be responsible for the final Section 404 report. The project team should review its progress with senior management on a periodic basis, highlighting review approaches and any short-term corrective actions initiated. Similarly, since they must formally attest to the results of this internal financial control review, external auditors should be kept informed of progress and any outstanding issues in process of resolution.

5. *Complete report on the effectiveness of the internal control structure.* This is the final step to Section 404 compliance. Since this is not a one-time exercise, all work should be documented for follow-up reviews. The documentation process here is similar to a financial audit process where results are documented in workpapers for ongoing periods. This report, plus the external auditor's attest work, will be filed with the SEC as part of the organization's 10-K annual report.

EXHIBIT 5.1 Section 404 Compliance Review Work Breakdown Structure

1. Assemble review team, including sponsor and other review team members, including internal audit.
2. Define project objectives.
    a. Determine if review will cover just financial controls or efficiency and effectiveness areas as well.
    b. Determine organizational units to be covered in review.
    c. Review results from any previous Section 404 or internal audit reviews requiring follow-up.
    d. Establish project time line that allows time for external audit review.
    e. Review planned objectives with CFO and audit committee.
3. Develop detailed project plan covering processes to be reviewed.
4. Establish review approach for each process/system included in review.
    a. Define nature and types of possible errors and omissions.
    b. Define nature, size, and composition of transactions to be reviewed.
    c. Determine volume, size, complexity, and homogeneity of individual transaction processed.
    d. Establish guidelines for materiality and error significance.
    e. Understand process transaction susceptibility to error or omissions.
5. Review approach and timing with external auditors.
6. Establish standards for review of documentation and project progress reporting.
7. Complete preliminary reviews for each identified process or system.
8. Follow up and resolve any items requiring investigation.
9. Consolidate review work and prepare preliminary 404 report.
10. Review 404 report results with CFO and release report.

This Section 404 compliance project can be a major undertaking and certainly will require considerably more time and effort, particularly in the first year, than is expressed in the limited number of work steps described above. Internal audit should play a very significant but advisory role in this compliance project. The level of work required will depend on which of the three groups described previously best fits the organization.

Group 1: Strong Internal Audit Function That Has Reviewed COSO Internal Controls

Many larger major corporations already have embraced the COSO internal control framework discussed below, and have strong internal audit functions in place that have performed audit reviews of those installed internal controls. Often through the leadership of internal audit, these organizations have reviewed, tested, and documented their internal controls following the COSO framework standard. Such organizations will have an easier task in achieving Section 404 compliance. SOA requires that companies evaluate the effectiveness of their internal controls over information reported to the financial markets. In the past, internal audit may have focused on such COSO internal control factors as the effectiveness and efficiency of operations, leaving financial controls to the external auditors. Now the internal control review team may have to make a bit of a shift.

The work involved here may require internal auditors to spend some time in reviewing their past COSO audits and updating program guidance or making changes to broaden scope as required. If the COSO-related review had been just an internal audit project, finance and other members of management should be included and brought up to speed. A major task here will be to document all internal controls and the results of all internal controls' tests performed. This revised process should be reviewed with senior management and the external auditors. If there are no significant problems or concerns, the review should be planned and scheduled with internal auditors as a major component of the process.

Group 2: Limited Overall COSO Internal Financial Control Work

Group 1 organizations here have things relatively easy. They have embraced COSO, its Canadian counterpart the Criteria of Control (CoCo), or some other internal control framework such as control objectives for information and related technology (CobiT) and are regularly performing internal control reviews following one of those frameworks. (CoCo and CobiT will be introduced in Chapter 6) Although no published data are available from the IIA or other sources, there are many more organizations that have not fully embraced a COSO-type framework than those that have. Many if not most medium-size to larger SEC-registered corporations today fit into what we call Group 2. These are organizations whose internal audit functions have performed some internal control reviews but have not otherwise embraced a full COSO-like internal control framework throughout the organization. Often in these organizations, the internal audit function is relatively small with activities focused on reviews related to operational efficiency or financial internal audit work in support of the company's external auditors. It is almost certain that if internal audit has not been involved in such a COSO internal control review program, management in total has not been.

These Group 2 corporations will have a challenge in getting ready for Section 404 compliance. Internal audit functions may have to go through a total reengineering process through training staff, revising audit approaches, and seeking outside control review help. A major task may be the need for the person responsible for the internal audit function, the director of internal audit but not the senior-level chief audit executive (CAE)–type person, to meet with the audit committee and senior financial officers to explain that the internal audit work to date may not really meet SOA Section 404 standards and that adjustments are necessary. Exhibit 5.2 lists planning considerations for this level of SOA Section 404 compliance internal financial controls review.

Based on the information gathered from Exhibit 5.2 and reviews by management, the audit committee, external auditors, and the project team responsible for this Section 404 compliance effort should develop an audit action plan. Because time and resources will not allow them to cover all control areas during a given period, their emphasis should be on areas with potentially high risks for financial misstatements. Exhibit 5.3 illustrates this process. The idea is to look at risks where there is a high possibility of financial misstatement on the horizontal axis and the significance of the transaction on the vertical axis.

The assertion concept used by external auditors is a good way to identify these various risks:

- *Existence.* Assets, liabilities, and ownership rights should exist at the time of the review. Taking a physical inventory shortly before the financial statement date reduces the risk that those assets and other items will not exist at the time of the financial statement.

- *Occurrence.* Recorded transactions must represent the events reported. The risk is that something like a recorded sale has really not taken place at the statement date.

- *Completeness.* All events during the reporting period should have been recognized or considered during that period. The risk is that there may be unrecorded transactions during the period.

- *Rights and Obligations.* The recorded assets and liabilities are bona fide at that point in time. The risk is that some other party may have an interest.

- *Valuations of Accounts.* All transactions should be recorded at appropriate amounts and in correct accounts. The risk here is possible misstatement.

- *Presentations and Disclosures.* Items in the financial statements are properly described and are fairly presented. Again, the risk is possible misstatement.

These risk-based assertions cover financial statement issues. A similar set can be developed for operational issues.

EXHIBIT 5.2 Planning Considerations for Section 404 Compliance Audits

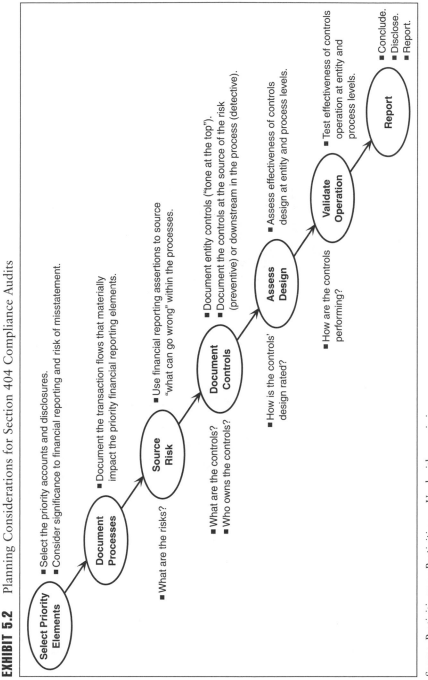

Select Priority Elements
- Select the priority accounts and disclosures.
- Consider significance to financial reporting and risk of misstatement.

Document Processes
- Document the transaction flows that materially impact the priority financial reporting elements.

- What are the risks?

Source Risk
- Use financial reporting assertions to source "what can go wrong" within the processes.

- What are the controls?
- Who owns the controls?

Document Controls
- Document entity controls ("tone at the top").
- Document the controls at the source of the risk (preventive) or downstream in the process (detective).

- How is the controls' design rated?

Assess Design
- Assess effectiveness of controls design at entity and process levels.

- How are the controls performing?

Validate Operation
- Test effectiveness of controls operation at entity and process levels.

Report
- Conclude.
- Disclose.
- Report.

Source: Protiviti, *www.Protiviti.com.* Used with permission.

111

EXHIBIT 5.3   Risk Selection Criteria

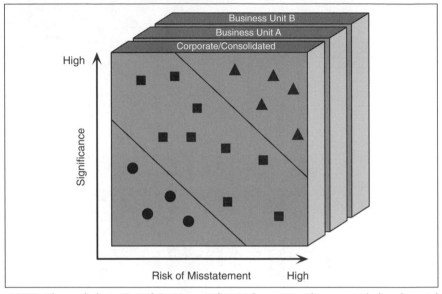

NOTE: The symbols ▲, ■, and ● represent financial reporting elements, including financial statement accounts and disclosure items.

Source: Protiviti, *www.Protiviti.com.* Used with permission.

Group 3: No Internal Audit or Very Limited Internal Audit Functions

Smaller organizations with little or no internal audit resources face the greatest challenge under Section 404. While the typical internal audit professional today may ask "How can this be possible, don't all companies have an internal audit function?" many firms do not. Indeed, while New York Stock Exchange (NYSE)–registered corporations are required to have an internal audit function and Nasdaq and American Stock Exchange (ASE)–listed corporations soon will have similar requirements, many other SEC-registered corporations do not have an internal audit function or have only a very low-level type of internal audit function. These are the many smaller, almost private, corporations whose stock trades on what are called pink sheets. All are subject to SOA requirements. In addition, numerous private organizations have some bond offerings registered with the SEC, making them subject to SOA.

Section 404 represents a major challenge for these Group 3 corporations. They have the same SOA requirement to formally review and document their internal financial controls, to identify any weaknesses, and to take appropriate corrective actions. Such a review can be accomplished by the financial management team with reviews by an internal audit function, if it exists. Otherwise, the CFO and the financial teams can take on this responsibility, if there are sufficient time and other resources. The best solution here may be to contract for outside services. While the external audit firms are barred from helping their own audit clients here, they can consult for other, nonaudit clients. Several internal audit specialist consulting firms can provide help such as Protiviti, Parson Consulting, or Jefferson Wells.

Control Objectives and Risks under Section 404

Regardless of what type of corporations they are—what we have called Group 1, 2, or 3—all SEC-registered organizations are *required* to comply with SOA requirements. Organizations with June 30 fiscal year ending dates in 2004 or later have been the first with others to follow. At the time of this book's publication, some organizations are just beginning their first round of Section 404 compliance reporting. In mid-2003, the SEC extended due dates, giving everyone a bit more breathing space. It is easy for those who already have gone through this first round of Section 404 compliance to say something along the lines of "Wow, we're done with that. Now let's get back to business as usual." However, it will be not that easy. Once an organization has gotten itself through the first hurdle, it should establish processes for a continuous monitoring, evaluation, and improvement.

Going forward, an organization needs to monitor its key systems, determine if there were any changes in subsequent periods, and design control procedures to correct any internal control weaknesses or otherwise fill control gaps. This an ongoing periodic exercise, and the team sponsored by senior management that first implemented the Section 404 compliance project will almost certainly have returned to normal job duties. This is an annual project, and internal audit probably should assume responsibility and get started after the organization's year-end reporting date. The external auditors, as part of their review of the organization's internal financial controls report, may have made recommendations as part of their management letter. Corrective action steps need to be initiated if required. In addition, a Section 404 implementation plan needs to be reviewed and updated on a regular basis. Systems and processes change and acquisitions or corporate reorganizations modify the environment. Internal audit should initiate such an annual review. Exhibit 5.4 summarizes review steps for keeping internal control procedures current and up to date.

While SOA does not designate internal audit as the key function or entity to review Section 404 procedures, in many organizations it can be the best resource to review internal controls and make such things happen. The real challenge here might be for the head of internal audit for what we have described as a Group 2 organization. Here internal audit may be a fairly small function with limited resources. Efforts must be devoted to understanding the organization's overall control environment and helping the overall organization be prepared for ongoing Section 404 compliance

EXHIBIT 5.4   Keeping Compliance Review Procedures Current

1. Develop a documentation standard for all Section 404 reviews setting up minimum requirements for entering materials in documentation files. Documentation should include, at a minimum, a record of:
   - The planning and preparation of SOA review scope and objectives
   - The Section 404 review program
   - The review steps performed and evidence gathered
   - The 404 findings, conclusions, and recommendations
   - Any report issued as a result of the this work
   - Evidence of supervisory reviews

2. Launch procedures to document all significant accounts, processes, risks, and internal controls that conform to standards such as the COSO framework.

3. Launch procedures for the integrity of records with audit trails, document management, version control, and security measures that ensure the protection of data and documentation.

4. For processes and systems included in past Section 404 reviews, establish ongoing procedures to:
   - Keep processes updated on regular basis
   - Follow-up and resolve any issues highlighted from past Section 404 reviews
   - Include results of interim internal reviews and testing for processes

5. Arrange the appropriate custody and retention of the documentation that supports Section 404 conclusions for a time sufficient to satisfy legal, professional, and organizational requirements.

6. Documentation should be organized, stored, and secured in a manner appropriate for the media on which it is retained and should continue to be retrievable for a time sufficient to multiple Section 404 review cycles.

reporting. Smaller Group 3 organizations have an even greater problem. Their external auditors can no longer help them beyond offering general advice, and the actual internal financial control review work will be the responsibility of management. Initially, these smaller organizations may want to seek outside help to establish Section 404 compliance procedures. Going forward, however, this may be an appropriate time to launch a small internal audit function, which has as a major responsibility monitoring and reviewing internal financial control risks and processes. Exhibit 5.5 outlines duties and responsibilities for a smaller internal audit function in the era of SOA Section 404 compliance.

EXHIBIT 5.5   Smaller Internal Audit Function Responsibilities under SOA

Smaller internal audit functions are internal audit groups of 10 or fewer internal auditors headed by an audit director who may also be a hands-on internal auditor. The audit director should:

- Develop an understanding of SOA through personal study, communications with the external auditor, and other approaches.

- Meet with the executive team and audit committee and brief them on SOA requirements.

- Help to assess whether the designated audit committee financial expert meets required experience and expertise.

- Based on complexity of processes, past internal audit activity, and overall resources, work with the CFO and audit committee to determine the approach for Section 404 reviews: internal resources with or without internal audit or through use of external consultant.

- If external Section 404 consultants are used, assist in selection process focusing on ongoing internal audit activities and how they could provide support.

- If internal audit is to participate in Section 404 reviews, modify audit plans and approaches to allow for participation.

- Offer ongoing support to management and the audit committee to maintain SOA compliance.

Review of Internal Accounting Controls under SOA: An Example

This chapter and indeed much of this book discuss the review internal financial accounting controls and assessments of supporting control processes. This section outlines procedures and steps for the internal financial control review for one example process in an organization. We have selected as an example a vendor accounts payable (A/P) process and have considered how such a process might have been selected for review and then tested, evaluated, and documented as part of a Section 404 compliance. These steps should be familiar to the seasoned internal auditor; and they represent the seven steps that financial management needs to follow to achieve Section 404 compliance.

1. *Select key processes.* Every organization uses a wide range of financial and operational processes. We have used the term "process" here as opposed to "system" because we too often think of a system as a computer program–driven set of procedures, while a process includes all of the steps performed, automated or manual, to achieve objectives. The payroll *system,* for example, is a set of automated routines that takes

time and attendance data and produces payroll checks or transfers wages to employee checking accounts. The payroll *process* is much larger, including steps necessary to add a new employee, to process a pay increase, and to communicate with accounting and benefit systems. There can be numerous transaction flows in this overall process.

Internal audit and/or the Section 404 compliance team needs to review all organization processes and select the ones that are financially significant. This key process selection should focus on processes where a failure could cause a major loss or expense to the organization. Consideration should be given to processes in all organization entities, not just headquarter systems. The processes then should be ranked either by the size of assets controlled or some other meaningful measure. Exhibit 5.6 contains some alternatives or guidelines for this key process selection. The organization should have a documented procedure to justify why it felt one process was more worthy or significant for detailed review than another. The external auditors who review selection criteria may ask for such a justification. In this example, the A/P process was one of the key processes selected.

2. *Document selected process transaction flows.* The next step, and an important one, is to prepare transaction flow documentation for the key processes selected. In organizations in which there has been a COSO-type review with key processes previously documented, this can be an easy step. Then the existing documentation should be reviewed to determine that it is still accurate and has been updated as required. Process

EXHIBIT 5.6   Process Review Selection Guidelines

The following questions can serve as a guide for selecting processes to review as part of a SOA Section 404 review exercise.

I.   **Process or System Status**

    A. Nature of the process or system to be reviewed:
- Is the new system or process developed inhouse?
- New purchased application package?
- Have there been major changes over past period affecting functionality?
- Have there been only minor changes?

    B. Past history of process or system changes:
- Have there been significant changes over the past two years?
- Few changes in the the past two years?
- Two years or more since the last change?
- New process or no recent changes?

EXHIBIT 5.6 Process Review Selection Guidelines *(Continued)*

C. Process or system development team:
- Outside contractor development or management?
- Inhouse group responsible for development and management?
- Packaged solution with minor vendor changes?

D. Top management interest in process of project:
- Enterprise level process mandated by senior management?
- System or process responsibility of operating unit?
- Process initiated by middle management?
- Individual user or department responsibility?

II. **Audit and Control Significance**

A. Type of system or process:
- Supports financial statement balances?
- Supports major organizational operations?
- Primarily for logistical or administrative support?
- Statistical or research application?

B. Past internal audit or SOA review involvement:
- Prior audits including recommendations?
- Prior reviews with limited recommendations?
- Audit reviews of related, manual areas?
- Never formally reviewed?

C. System or process control procedures:
- Process-generated internal controls?
- Run-to-run controls with other systems or processes?
- Primarily batch or manual controls?

III. **Impact of Process Failure**

A. Impact of incorrect reported results:
- Potential legal liability?
- Financial statement impact?
- Potential for incorrect management decisions?
- Limited decision support risks?
- Incorrect results passed to other systems?
- Corrupted data requiring reconstruction?
- Corrupted data requiring reprocessing?

B. Impact of application failure on personnel:
- Need for extra management analysis time?
- Need for extra user clerical time?
- Need for systems or programmer efforts?

documentation is much more of a challenge if the organization has never documented its processes or if its documentation only represents old automated system transaction flows.

Various automated tools are available to support documentation protocols that accept a variety of transaction flows. The goal is to select some notation that is easy to prepare and update as well as easily understood by all interested parties. The documentation should show key transaction flows and control points. Exhibit 5.7 shows a transaction flow from the A/P system documentation system example using standard flow chart notation. The real key for any process documentation is to keep it updated. Three-ring notebooks full of process documentation are of little value if they are never updated. Organizations should establish procedures to ensure that all changes are added to previously documented systems. Whoever led the project to document SOA processes may be given the responsibility to maintain this documentation. Internal audit can take a major role here, but this ongoing maintenance task probably would not be an appropriate responsibility for internal audit.

3. *Assess selected process risks.* Once an organization has defined and documented its key processes, the next step is to assess risks to determine what might go wrong. Here the team that first identified key process areas and documented them should go through a detailed "What could go wrong?" type of analysis. As an example, we have identified the A/P process for an organization. What are the potential risks here? For example, could someone gain access to the system and then arrange to cut herself an unauthorized check? Could system controls be so weak that multiple payments are generated simultaneously to the same authorized vendor? Numerous risks of this sort can exist. A management team should go through each of the selected processes and highlight potential risks in such an open-ended set of questions. Internal audit can play a very valuable role by leading or consulting in this type of analysis. Exhibit 5.8 is an example of this type of review and points to a review approach that should be developed for any key process. In many cases, existing internal audit programs can solve this need.

4. *Document key process controls.* After a wide-ranging list of selected process risks has been developed, the analysis team should speculate which risk areas have the greatest likelihood of occurring. Team members may be aware that no check can be generated unless it matches to an authorized vendor file, which makes it more difficult for a system perpetrator to prepare a check to himself. The fact that there must be an authorized vendor set up becomes a key process control in this example. In a similar manner, the team should go through all of these risks and identify any known controls that have been established to limit the

EXHIBIT 5.7 A/P Process Flow Chart Example

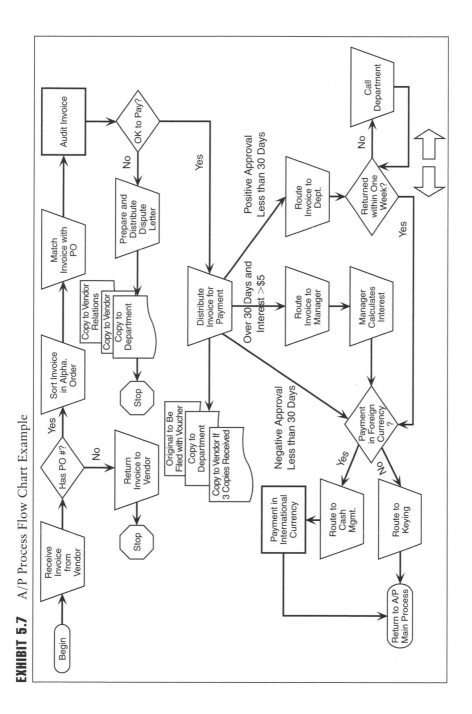

EXHIBIT 5.8   Sample A/P Review Procedures

1. Are accounts payable personnel independent from purchasing and receiving functions? _____
2. Are debit memos, adjustments, and other noncash debits to accounts payable approved and periodically reviewed by supervisory personnel? _____
3. Are there defined cut-off procedures at month end that are monitored continually by supervisory personnel? _____
4. Are month-end accruals and other credit accounts payable estimates and adjustments reviewed by management? _____
5. Are all accounts payable vouchers and debit memos prenumbered? _____
6. Are all vendor invoices date- and time-stamped in sequential order, and is the sequence checked periodically? _____
7. Are all unused forms controlled? _____
8. Are records maintained for all voided forms? _____
9. Are daily runs of total cash disbursed to accounts payable compared to check run? _____
10. Is accounts payable subledger maintenance separate from general ledger maintenance? _____
11. Are accounts payable trial balances and general ledger control accounts reconciled and reviewed periodically by supervisory personnel? _____
12. Are reconciliations of monthly vendor account statements made against unmatched open purchase orders and receiving reports and reviewed by supervisor? _____
13. Is receipt of vendor account statements performed by someone other than the accounts payable bookkeeper? _____

risks from occurring. While there are numerous approaches to developing this documentation, the techniques typically used by internal audit in documenting controls as part of a normal internal audit review might be appropriate. If internal audit does not have consistent control documentation standards in place, it may want to use the approach developed for SOA as a standard for all subsequent internal audit reviews.

5. *Assess control effectiveness through appropriate test procedures.* System controls are of little value if they are not working effectively. Sometimes it can be determined that appropriate controls are not in place or are ineffective. In that case, the conclusions from the assessment should be documented and discussed with the process owners, and an action plan

should be developed to take corrective actions to improve the controls. The reviewer who is told that there is no approval process in place to generate an A/P check beyond initial approval of the invoice will recognize that this is an obvious internal control weakness that should be documented and discussed for planned corrective action.

In most instances, the reviewer's initial assessment of controls will require testing. Audit testing has been a common process for both internal and external auditors in their reviews of controls. These audit tests once were extensive for financial audits, with large attribute and variables sample transactions taken and the sample results evaluated. Attributes sampling is used for evaluating internal controls; variables sampling is used for estimating financial balances. Evaluation of the results of these samples allowed internal or external auditors to draw conclusions regarding whether financial results were fairly stated or internal controls appeared to be working. The use of statistically based audit sampling is less common today for external auditors due to pressures for greater audit efficiencies. Attributes sampling, however, can be a powerful tool to assess internal controls and to state with some measure of statistical confidence that the internal controls tested are working.

Whether using a statistically based sample or not, the SOA process reviewer should always use one or more sample transactions to test a process. If studying a complex but largely paper-based process with many people-based approval steps, the SOA reviewer might borrow from classic internal audit techniques and try a "walk-through" test. The idea is to take a single transaction—such as a vendor invoice requiring approval before the A/P check is generated—and walk that transaction through each of the processing steps prior to cutting the check. Again, this is a test to assess internal controls over a process. If the results of the test are positive, the process reviewer could determine if the process appears to be working correctly, with adequate internal controls. All internal auditors should be familiar with this type of exercise.

6. *Evaluate test results and develop opinion.* The results from this sample will allow SOA reviewers to state whether internal financial controls appear to be working and are adequate for the selected processes reviewed. This exercise will roll in to the final report discussed below. The key task here is for the reviewers to take a good hard look at the results of internal control evaluations and tests. This is the step where the reviewer determines whether internal financial controls over a particular process appear to be adequate. If not, steps should be taken to initiate corrective actions. Doing this may require working with managers responsible for the process reviewed and developing an action plan to establish an implementation plan to correct the internal control weaknesses identified.

A key requirement here is the need for documentation and even more documentation. External auditors may very well review this area, particularly if control weaknesses were identified. They will be seeking more information on the nature of any control weaknesses identified as well as plans for corrective action, if necessary. Because under SOA, the external auditors will be primarily external reviewers and not part of the ongoing internal control review process, they will rely on these documented results.

7. ***Report results and close documentation files.*** The last step here is to report the results of the SOA internal financial control process review. Typically, a report is not prepared for each process; rather, all of the results should be consolidated into the overall internal financial controls assessment for the organization. Under SOA rules, this internal financial controls report will have nearly the same level of importance as the organization's financial statements. Although investors may continue to rely primarily on the financial statements, such as the income statement, balance sheet and related disclosures, internal financial controls reports will have growing significance for financial report users and investors.

We have used the terms "internal financial controls reviewer" and "internal auditor" to describe the person or group performing these internal financial control process reviews. As we have suggested throughout this book, internal audit may not be the designated resource to perform these reviews, particularly if senior management expects someone—probably internal audit—to audit this SOA internal financial control process review work. However, in smaller organizations, internal audit may be the only in-house resource to understand how to review process controls, to test those controls, and to develop audit-related conclusions to support that work. As always, internal auditors review established processes but do not implement them.

Internal Audit and the Disclosure Committee

The SEC has recommended that SOA-impacted organizations create a disclosure committee to consider the materiality of information discovered, to identify relevant disclosure issues, and to ensure that relevant material is disclosed to investors on a timely basis. In other words, someone should be responsible for reviewing the results of the internal control reviews, decide what is important, or "material," and then determine which and if any matters are worthy of formal disclosure to investors. Such a disclosure committee will almost necessarily be composed of a senior CEO or CEO-level group. The sponsor for the SOA internal financial controls project review team should be at least a disclosure committee member; internal audit can potentially serve as a key representative as well.

A major task of this disclosure committee is to consider the materiality of any exception information encountered. This group is looking over the data that will be presented to external auditors for their review and report. Almost certainly there will be a tendency, at least in the early years of SOA, to err on the side of viewing too many matters as material. In the big picture of things in a large corporation, many internal control weaknesses individually or collectively are not all that material. Because the disclosure committee will be going through some very important information, the CAE or another member of the audit team should suggest to management that internal audit could provide valuable information and insights to any newly formed disclosure committee.

COSO INTERNAL CONTROL FRAMEWORK

The worlds of auditing, accounting, and internal controls are filled with acronyms, and we often forget what those acronyms really stand for. The internal control standard COSO is such an example; its letters stand for the Committee of Sponsoring Organizations. Of course, that explanation does not offer much help. To understand how this internal control standard came about, it is necessary to go back to the late 1970s and early 1980s, a period when there also were many major organization failures in the United States due to high inflation, the resultant high interest rates, and high energy costs as a result of excessive government regulation. The scope of these failures seems minor today when compared with the likes of Enron or WorldCom, but they raised major concerns at the time. Several major organizations suffered financial collapse shortly after the release of favorable financial reports, signed by external auditors, showing adequate earnings. Some failures were caused by fraudulent financial reporting, but many others were caused by high inflation or other factors. Although members of Congress drafted legislation to "correct" these business and audit failures and although congressional hearings were held, no legislation was passed. Rather, the National Commission on Fraudulent Financial Reporting was formed to study the issue. Five U.S. professional organizations sponsored the commission: the IIA, the American Institute of Certified Public Accountants (AICPA), the Financial Executives Institute (FEI), the American Accounting Association (AAA), and the Institute of Management Accountants (IMA). These are the Sponsoring Organizations of COSO, which was originally called the Treadway Commission.

The commission's first report, released in 1987, called for management reports on the effectiveness of their internal control systems.[4] It emphasized the key elements of an effective system of internal controls, including a strong control environment, a code of conduct, a competent and involved audit committee, and a strong internal audit function. The report emphasized the need for a consistent definition of internal control and launched the study that developed what is now known as the COSO definition of internal control, now generally recognized as the world's internal accounting control standard. Another alternative framework is the CobiT model discussed in Chapter 6.

The COSO report, *Internal Control–Integrated Framework,* was released in September 1992.[5] (Here it is referred to as the COSO report, its common name.) The report proposes a common framework for the definition of internal control as well as procedures to evaluate those controls.

The following sections describe the COSO definition of internal control in greater detail. An extersion to COSO, called the Enterprise Risk Model (ERM) was released in draft form in the year 2000 and may soon become a risk model for the total enterprise similar to the COSO framework. An understanding of COSO is essential to understand SOA Section 404 requirements of internal controls.

COSO Internal Control Components and Objectives

Virtually every public corporation that comes under SOA requirements has a complex control procedures structure. Following the description of a classic organization chart, there are levels of senior and middle management in multiple operating units or performing different activities. Control procedures may be different at each of these levels and components. For example, one operating unit may operate in a regulated business environment where control processes are very structured, while another unit may be an entrepreneurial start-up operation with a less formal structure. Different levels of management in these organizations will have different control perspectives. The question "How do you describe your system of internal controls?" might receive different answers from persons in different levels or components in the organization.

COSO provides an excellent description of this multidimensional concept of internal control. It defines internal control as:

> *a process, effected by an entity's board of directors, management, and other personnel, designed to provide reasonable assurance regarding the achievement of objectives in the following categories:*
>
> - *Effectiveness and efficiency of operations*
> - *Reliability of financial reporting*
> - *Compliance with applicable laws and regulations*

This COSO definition of internal control can be used as a basis for SOA assessments. The definition should be very familiar to internal auditors. It follows the same theme that Victor Brink used as a definition of internal auditing in his first 1943 edition of *Modern Internal Auditing* and all subsequent editions. Brink defined internal auditing as:

> *an independent appraisal function established within an organization to examine and evaluate its activities as a service to the organization.*

Although SOA focuses on financial reporting controls, Brink used the broader definition of service to management to define what the new profession of internal auditing was then. That definition is still important today.

Using the above general definition of internal control, COSO uses a three-dimensional model to describe an internal control system in an organization. Exhibit 5.9 defines the COSO model of internal control as a pyramid with five layers or interconnected components comprising the overall internal control system. The Control Environment component serves as the foundation for the entire structure. Four of these internal components are described as horizontal layers, with another component of internal control, called communication and information, acting as an interface channel for the other four layers. Each of these components is described in greater detail in the following sections. Exhibit 5.10 shows this same COSO model from a slightly different perspective. Here, the three major components of internal control—effectiveness and efficiency of operations, reliability of financial reporting, and compliance with applicable laws and regulations—give a third dimension to this model. Just as the pyramid structure of Exhibit 5.9 showed the internal control structure as the environment for all internal control processes, the view in Exhibit 5.10 gives equal weight to each of these three components.

EXHIBIT 5.9   COSO Components of Internal Control

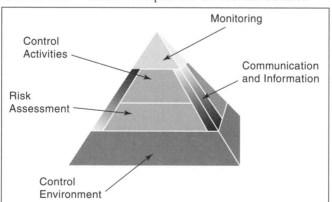

Source: Robert Moeller and Herbert Witt, *Brink's Modern Internal Auditing,* 5th ed. (New York: John Wiley & Sons, 1999).

EXHIBIT 5.10   Relationship between COSO Entities

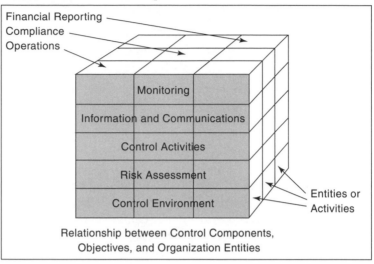

Financial Reporting
Compliance
Operations

Monitoring

Information and Communications

Control Activities

Risk Assessment

Control Environment

Entities or
Activities

Relationship between Control Components,
Objectives, and Organization Entities

Source: Robert Moeller and Herbert Witt, *Brink's Modern Internal Auditing,* 5th ed. (New York: John Wiley & Sons, 1999).

COSO Internal Control Elements: Control Environment

The foundation of the internal control structure for any organization is what COSO calls the *internal control environment.* This is the foundation for all internal controls in the entity. COSO emphasizes that, in any organization, this control environment has a pervasive influence on how business activities are structured and risks are assessed. It serves as a foundation for all other components of internal control and has an influence on each of the three objectives and all activities. The control environment reflects the overall attitude, awareness, and actions by the board of directors, management, and others concerning the importance of internal control in the organization.

Organization history and culture often play a major role in forming this control environment. In an organization that historically has had a strong management emphasis on producing error-free products, where senior management continues to emphasize the importance of high-quality products, and where this message has been communicated to all levels, this becomes a major control environment factor for the organization. However, if senior management has had a reputation of "looking the other way" at policy violations, this is the message communicated to other levels in the organization. A positive tone at the top by senior management establishes the control environment for the organization.

The following sections outline some of the major elements of the COSO control environment component of internal control. Internal auditors always should try to understand this overall control environment when performing reviews of various organization activities or units. In some instances, they may want to perform specific reviews of control environment factors covering the overall organization. In smaller organizations, the control environment factors will be more informal. However, internal audit still should look for the appropriate control environment factors in any entity and consider them as essential components of internal control. Following SOA guidance, if the control environment appears to have major deficiencies, the CAE should discuss these concerns with the audit committee.

Control Environment: Integrity and Ethical Values

The collective integrity and ethical values of an organization are essential elements of its control environment. These factors often are defined by the "tone at the top" message communicated by senior management. If the organization has developed a strong code of conduct that emphasizes integrity and ethical values, and if all stakeholders appear to follow that code, internal audit will have assurances that the organization has a good set of values.

As discussed in Chapter 4, the code of conduct is an important component of organizational governance. Although an organization may have a strong code of conduct, principles of that code often can be violated through ignorance rather than by deliberate employee malfeasance. In many instances, employees may not know that they are doing something wrong or may erroneously believe that their actions are in the organization's best interests. Many times this ignorance is caused by poor moral guidance by senior management rather than by any employee intent to deceive. An organization's policies and values must be communicated to all levels of the organization. Although there always can be "bad apples" in an organization, a strong moral message will encourage everyone to act correctly. When performing a review in a given area, internal auditors should ask questions to determine if appropriate messages or signals have been transmitted throughout the organization.

Internal auditors should have a good understanding of the organization's code of conduct and how it is applied throughout the organization. If the code is out of date, if it does not appear to address important ethical issues facing an organization, or if management does not appear to be communicating the code to all stakeholders on a recurring basis, internal audit should remind management of the significance of this deficiency, both in the course of audits in other areas and as a special message to management. If the organization does not have a formal ethics office function, internal audit may be asked to suggest changes and to help in the dissemination of the organization's code of conduct.

The code of conduct describes the rules for ethical behavior in an organization, and senior members of management should transmit a proper ethical message throughout their organization. However, other incentives and temptations can erode this overall control environment. Individuals may engage in dishonest, illegal, or unethical acts if their organization gives them strong incentives or temptations to do so. For example, an organization may establish very high, unrealistic performance targets for sales or production quotas. If there are strong rewards for the achievement of these performance goals—or worse, strong threats for missed targets—employees may be encouraged to engage in fraudulent or questionable practices to achieve those goals. The kinds of temptations that encourage stakeholders to engage in improper accounting or similar acts include:

- Nonexistent or ineffective controls, such as poor segregation of duties in sensitive areas, that offer temptations to steal or to conceal poor performance

- High decentralization that leaves top management unaware of actions taken at lower organization levels and thereby reduces the chances of getting caught

- A weak internal audit function that has neither the ability nor the authority to detect and report improper behavior

- Penalties for improper behavior that are insignificant or unpublicized and thus lose their value as deterrents

There is a strong message here both for internal auditors performing their various reviews and for the internal audit organization as a whole. First, the internal auditor always should consider control environment factors when performing reviews. A good internal auditor always should be skeptical and perform appropriate levels of tests when reviewing various areas of operations. When things look "too good," auditors might want to look a bit harder, not just to "find something" but to assess whether deficiencies in the control environment may lead to possible fraudulent activities. Procedures for fraud investigations are discussed in Chapter 8.

A strong internal audit function should be a major component of the COSO control environment. If internal audit finds that management is placing constraints on the internal audit function, the CAE should remind management of the importance of internal audit as part of the organization's overall internal control structure and should go to the board of directors' audit committee, if necessary, to achieve corrective action.

Control Environment: Commitment to Competence

An organization's control environment can be seriously eroded if a significant number of positions are filled with persons who lack required job skills. Occasionally internal auditors will encounter situations when a person assigned to a particular job does not seem to have the appropriate skills, training, or intelligence to perform that job. Because all humans have different levels of skills and abilities, adequate supervision and training should be available to help the person until proper skills are acquired.

An organization needs to specify the required competence levels for its various job tasks and to translate those requirements into necessary levels of knowledge and skill. By placing the proper people in appropriate jobs and giving adequate training when required, an organization is making an overall *commitment to competence,* an important element in its overall control environment. When reviewing a functional area, internal auditors often find it valuable to assess whether adequate position descriptions have been created for the various functions under review, whether procedures are in operation to place appropriate people in those positions, and whether training and supervision are adequate.

Although it is an important part of the control environment, assessment of staff competence can be a difficult internal audit review area. How does an internal auditor determine that the staff is "competent" with regard to its assigned work duties? If an internal auditor visits a remote subsidiary operation and finds that no one in the accounting department there seems to know how to record and report financial transactions, and also that no training program exists to help these "accountants," the auditor can easily raise control environment issues for this operating unit. However, the auditor should exercise extreme caution before attempting to check on the background and training of an individual manager at the headquarters facility. A personality conflict or difference of opinion is no reason to question someone's competence.

Control Environment: Board of Directors and Audit Committee

The control environment is very much influenced by the actions of an organization's board of directors and its audit committee. In the years prior to SOA, boards and their audit committees often were dominated by senior management with only limited, minority representation from outside members. Situations were created in which boards were not totally independent of management. Company officers sat on the board and were, in effect, managing themselves with less concern for the outside investors. As discussed in earlier chapters, SOA has changed all of that. Boards now have a more important corporate governance role, and audit committees are required to be composed of independent, outside directors.

An active and independent board and its audit committee are essential components of an organization's control environment. Board members should ask appropriate questions of top management and should give all aspects of the organization detailed scrutiny. By setting high-level policies and by reviewing overall organization conduct, the board and its audit committee have the ultimate responsibility for setting this "tone at the top."

Although not included in SOA, this same principle applies to the board of directors of publicly held organizations or boards of trustees for not-for-profit and other public bodies.

Control Environment: Management's Philosophy and Operating Style

The philosophy and operating style of top management has a considerable influence over an organization's control environment. Often some top-level managers take significant organizational risks in new business or product ventures; others are very cautious or conservative. Some managers seem to operate by the seat of their pants; others insist that everything must be properly approved and documented. Still other managers take very aggressive approaches in their interpretations of tax and financial reporting rules while others go "by the book." One approach is not always good and the other not always bad. A small, entrepreneurial organization may be forced to take certain business risks to remain competitive; an organization in a highly regulated industry would be more risk-averse. The new COSO enterprise risk model discussed in Chapter 9 refers to this attitude as the organization's appetite for risk.

These management philosophy and operational style considerations are all part of the control environment of an organization. Internal auditors and others responsible for assessing internal controls should understand these factors and take them into consideration when evaluating the effectiveness of internal controls. Although no one set of styles and philosophies is always the best for all organizations, it is important to consider these other components of internal control in an organization.

Control Environment: Organization Structure

The organizational structure component provides a framework for planning, executing, controlling, and monitoring activities for achieving overall objectives. This is an aspect of the control environment that relates to the way various functions are managed and organized, following the classic organization chart. Some organizations are highly centralized; others are decentralized by product or geography. Still others are organized in a matrix manner with no single direct lines of reporting. Organizational structure is a very important aspect of the organization's control environment. No one structure provides a preferred environment for internal controls.

The various components of an organization can be assembled in many ways. Organizational control is a part of a larger control process. The term "organization" often is used interchangeably with the term "organizing" and means about the same thing to many people. "Organization" sometimes refers to hierarchical relationships between people but is also used broadly to include all of the problems of management. This book and other sources generally use the term "organization" to refer to the organizational entity, such as a corporation, a not-for-profit association, or any organized group. This section considers the organization as the set of *organizational arrangements* developed as a result of a management process.

An organization can be described as the way individual work efforts are both assigned and subsequently integrated for the achievement of overall goals. Although in a sense this concept could be applied to the manner in which a single individual organizes individual efforts, it is more applicable when a number of people are involved in a group effort. For a large modern corporation, a strong plan of organizational control is an important component of the system of internal control. Individuals and subgroups must have an understanding of the total goals and objectives of the group or entity of which they are a part. Without such an understanding, there can be significant control weaknesses.

Every organization or entity—whether a business, government, philanthropic, or other type of unit—needs an effective plan of organization. The internal auditor needs to have a good understanding of this organizational structure and the resultant reporting relationships. Often a weakness in organizational controls can have a pervasive effect throughout the total control environment. Despite clear lines of authority, organizations have built-in inefficiencies that become greater as the size of the organization expands. These inefficiencies often cause control procedures to break down, and the auditor should be aware of them when evaluating the organizational control environment in the functional organization.

Control Environment: Assignment of Authority and Responsibility

This area of the control environment, as defined by COSO, is similar to the organization structure area. An organization's structure defines the assignment and integration of the total work effort. The assignment of authority is essentially the way responsibilities are defined in terms of job descriptions and structured in terms of organization charts. Although job assignments can never fully escape some overlapping or joint responsibilities, the more precisely these responsibilities can be stated, the better. The decision of how responsibilities will be assigned often is concerned with avoiding confusion and conflict between individual and group work efforts.

Many of today's organizations have streamlined operations and pushed their decision-making authority downward and closer to the front-line personnel. The idea is that these front-line employees should have the knowledge and power to make important decisions in their own area of operations rather than be required to pass the request for a decision up through organizational channels. The critical challenge that goes with this delegation or empowerment is that although it can delegate some authority to achieve some organizational objectives, senior management is ultimately responsible for any decisions made by subordinates. An organization can place itself at risk if too many decisions involving higher-level objectives are assigned at inappropriately lower levels without adequate management review. In addition, each person in the organization must have a good understanding of the organization's overall objectives as well as how individual actions interrelate to achieve those objectives. The framework section of the COSO report describes this very important area of the control environment in this way:

> *The control environment is greatly influenced by the extent to which individuals recognize they will be held accountable. This holds true all the way to the chief executive, who has ultimate responsibility for all activities within an entity, including internal control system.*

Control Environment: Human Resources Policies and Practices

Human resource practices cover such areas as hiring, orientation, training, evaluating, counseling, promoting, compensating, and taking appropriate remedial actions. While the human resources function should have adequate published policies in these areas, its actual practice areas send strong messages to employees regarding their expected levels of ethical behavior and competence. The higher-level employee who openly disregards a human resources policy, such as a plant smoking ban by smoking a cigarette in his private office, quickly sends a message to other levels in the organization. The message grows even louder when a lower-level employee is disciplined for the same unauthorized cigarette while everyone looks the other way at the higher-level violator.

Areas where these human resources policies and practices are particularly important include:

- *Recruitment and Hiring.* The organization should take steps to hire the best, most qualified candidates. Potential employee backgrounds should be checked to verify their education backgrounds and prior work experience. Interviews should be well organized and in-depth. They also should transmit a message to the prospective candidate about the organization's values, culture, and operating style.

- *New Employee Orientation.* A clear signal should be given to new employees regarding the organization's value system and the consequences of not complying with those values. This is the time when new employees are introduced to the code of conduct and asked to acknowledge formally acceptance of that code. Without these messages, new employees may join the organization lacking an appropriate understanding of its values.

- *Evaluation, Promotion, and Compensation.* There should be a fair performance evaluation program in place that is not subject to an excessive amount of managerial discretion. Because issues such as evaluation and compensation can violate employee confidentiality, the overall system should be established in a manner that appears to be fair to all members of the organization. Bonus incentive programs often are useful tools to motivate and reinforce outstanding performance by all employees.

- **Disciplinary Actions.** Consistent and well-understood policies for disciplinary actions should be in place. All employees should know that if they violate certain rules, they will be subject to a progression of disciplinary actions leading up to dismissal. The organization should take care to ensure that no double standard exists for disciplinary actions — or, if any such double standard does exist, it is that higher-level employees are subject to even more severe disciplinary actions.

Effective human resource policies and procedures are a critical component in the overall control environment. Messages from the top regarding strong organization structures will accomplish little if the organization does not have strong human resource policies and procedures in place. Internal audit always should consider this element of the control environment when performing reviews of the internal control framework.

COSO Control Environment in Perspective

Exhibit 5.9 showed the components of internal control as a pyramid, with the control environment as the lowest or foundation component. This concept of the control environment acting as the foundation is very appropriate in today's SOA world. Just as a strong foundation is necessary for a multistory building, the control environment provides the foundation for the other components of internal control. An organization that is building a strong internal control structure should give special attention to placing solid foundation bricks in this control environment foundation.

Internal auditors always should be aware of the control environment components in place when performing reviews. In many instances, internal audit may find internal control exceptions that are attributable to the lack of a strong control environment foundation. For example, they may find that employees in a given unit are violating some travel expense rule that is defined in a company policy statement. The excuse by local management may be that the rule does not apply to them or that "everyone" is doing what the auditors found. Depending on the nature of the issue, internal audit may have to talk with appropriate persons in senior management and point out the control environment problem.

COSO Internal Control Elements: Risk Assessment

The next level in the COSO pyramid in Exhibit 5.9 is risk assessment. An organization's ability to achieve its objectives can be at risk due to a variety of internal and external factors. As part of its overall control structure, an organization should have a process in place to evaluate the potential risks that may impact attainment of its various objectives. This risk assessment process should be performed at all levels and for virtually all activities within the organization. COSO describes risk assessment as a three-step process:

1. Estimate the significance of the risk.

2. Assess the likelihood or frequency of the risk occurring.

3. Consider how the risk should be managed, and assess what actions must be taken.

The COSO risk assessment process puts the responsibility on management to go through the steps to assess whether a risk is significant and then, if so, to take appropriate actions. This process should be familiar to internal auditors. For example, Chapter 7 discusses computer security risk assessment issues, including business continuity planning. In this process an auditor might assess both whether an automated application is critical to the organization and whether it has an adequate disaster-recovery backup plan. Internal audit can assist members of management who are not familiar with this type of a risk assessment process.

COSO emphasizes that although risk analysis is not a theoretical process, often it is critical to an entity's overall success. As part of its overall assessment of internal control, management should take steps to assess the risks that may impact the overall organization as well as the risks over various organization activities or entities. A variety of risks, caused by either internal or external sources, may affect the overall organization. The COSO enterprise risk model framework, recently released in draft and discussed in Chapter 9, will increase our understanding and awareness for risk in the overall enterprise or organization.

COSO Internal Control Elements: Control Activities

The next layer in the COSO internal control model is called control activities. These are the policies and procedures that help ensure that actions identified to address risks are carried out. This internal control component includes a wide range of activities and procedures, from establishing organization standards with appropriate segregation of duties to reviewing and approving key operations reports properly. Control activities should exist at all levels within the organization, and in many cases, they may overlap one another.

The concept of control activities should be familiar to the internal auditor who develops a procedure to sample a set of invoice records from an A/P system to test whether invoices were properly coded and discounts properly calculated. The audit or control activity here is to determine if the invoices were correctly handled. The audit procedure may be to use sampling techniques to review a representative set of these invoice records. Just as an internal auditor performs such control activities, other levels of management should have control activities in place to ascertain that control objectives in various areas are being achieved.

Types of Control Activities

Many different definitions of controls are used, including manual, computer system, or categorizing controls in terms of being preventive, corrective, or detective. No one set of control definitions is correct for all management situations or for all organizations. COSO suggests a series of control activities that might be installed by the organization. While certainly not an all-inclusive list, these control activities represent the range and variety of such activities in the modern organization.

- *Top-level Reviews.* Management at various levels should review the results of their performance, contrasting those results with budgets, competitive statistics, and other benchmark measurements. Management actions to follow up on the results of these top-level reviews and to take corrective action represent a control activity.

- *Direct Functional or Activity Management.* Managers at various levels should review the operational reports from their control systems and take corrective action as appropriate. Many management systems have been built to produce a series of exception reports covering various activities. For example, a computer security system will have a mechanism to report unauthorized access attempts. The control activity here is the management process of following up on these reported events and taking appropriate corrective action.

- *Information Processing.* Information systems contain many controls where systems check for compliance in a variety of areas and then report any exceptions. Those reported exception items should receive corrective action by systems' automated procedures, by operational personnel, or by management. Other control activities here include controls over the development of new systems or over access to data and program files.

- *Physical Controls.* An organization should have appropriate control over its physical assets, including fixtures, inventories, and negotiable securities. An active program of periodic physical inventories represents a major control activity.

- *Performance Indicators.* Management should relate sets of data, both operational and financial, to one another and take appropriate analytical, investigative, or corrective actions. This process represents an important organizational control activity that also can satisfy financial and operational reporting requirements.

- *Segregation of Duties.* Duties should be divided or segregated among different people or functions to reduce the risk of error or inappropriate actions. This is a basic and important internal control procedure.

These control activities, included in the COSO report, represent only a small number of the many such activities performed as part of the normal course of business. These and other activities keep an organization on track toward achieving its many objectives. Control activities usually involve both a policy establishing what should be done and procedures to effect those policies. While these control activities may sometimes only be communicated orally by appropriate levels of management, COSO points out that no matter how they are communicated, the policy should be implemented "thoughtfully, conscientiously, and consistently." This is a strong message for internal auditors who review control activities. Even though an organization may have a published policy covering a given area, an internal auditor should review the established control procedure that supports the policy. Procedures are of little use unless there is a sharp focus on the condition to which the policy is directed. All too often, an organization may establish an exception report as part of an automated system that receives little more than a cursory review by the report recipients. However, depending on the types of conditions reported, those reported exceptions should receive appropriate follow-up actions, which may vary depending on the size of the organization and the activity reported in the exception report.

Integration of Control Activities with Risk Assessment

Control activities should be closely related to the identified risks discussed previously as part of the COSO risk assessment component. Internal control is a process, and appropriate control activities should be installed to address identified risks. Control activities should not be installed just because they seem to be the "right thing to do" if management has identified no significant risks in that area. All too often, management still has in place control activities or procedures that once served some control risk concern, although the concerns now have largely gone away. Although a control activity or procedure should not be discarded merely because there have been no control violation incidents in recent years, management needs to reevaluate the relative risks periodically. All control activities should contribute to the organization's overall control structure.

The comments above refer to what might be called "dumb" control activities that once had a purpose but currently accomplish little. For example, business data processing computer operations centers, up through the 1970s, had input-output clerks who manually checked file-record count reports from various programs in automated systems. Computer operating system facilities effectively automated the need for those control procedures long ago, but some organizations continued to employ these clerks long after they were needed. If there had been a record count exception, the operating system would have flagged the problem and initiated corrective action long before any reports were delivered. This is a "dumb" control because it accomplishes little or nothing in today's control environment. While the need for some controls will cease, other basic controls, such as the importance of strong separation of duties over incompatible functions, should always remain in effect.

Controls over Information Systems

COSO emphasizes that control procedures are needed over all significant information systems—financial, operational, and compliance-related. Information systems controls are a key activity in the overall control environment, and COSO breaks down those controls into general and application controls. General controls apply to much of the information systems function to help ensure adequate control procedures over all applications. A physical security lock on the door to the computer center is such a general control covering all applications running at that data center.

Application controls refer to specific information systems applications. A control in a weekly payroll application program that prevents any employee from being paid for over 100 work hours in a given week is an example of an application reasonableness test control. COSO highlights a series of information systems control areas for evaluating the overall adequacy of internal controls. General controls include all centralized data center or computer systems controls, including job scheduling, storage management, and business continuity planning. These controls typically are the responsibility of operations specialists in centralized computer or server centers. However, with newer, more modern systems connected to one another through telecommunications links, these controls can be distributed across a network of server-based systems.

COSO Internal Control Elements: Communications and Information

The pyramid model of COSO internal controls describes most components as layers, one on top of another. The information and communication component, however, is not a horizontal layer but spans across all of the other components. In the original draft of COSO, information and communication were treated as two separate components. In order to make the final report less complex, they were combined in the final version. Information and communications are related, but are really very distinct internal control components. Both are important portions of the internal control framework. Appropriate information, supported by automated systems, must be communicated up and down the organization in a manner and in a time frame that allow people to carry out their responsibilities. In addition to formal and informal communication systems, organizations must have effective procedures in place to communicate with internal and external parties. As part of any evaluation of internal controls, there is a need to have a good understanding of the information and communication flows or processes in the organization.

Relationship of Information and Internal Control

Various types of information are needed at all levels of the organization in order to achieve operational, financial reporting, and compliance objectives. The organization needs proper information to prepare the financial reports that are communicated to outside investors. It also needs both internal cost information and external market preference information to make correct marketing decisions. This information must flow both from the top levels of the organization on down and upward from lower levels. COSO takes a broad approach to the concept of an information system; it recognizes the importance of automated systems but specifies that information systems can be manual, automated, or conceptual. Any information system can be formal or informal. Regular conversations with customers or suppliers can be highly important sources of information and are an informal type of an information system. The effective organization should have an information system in place to listen to customer requests or complaints and to forward that customer-initiated information to appropriate personnel.

The COSO framework also emphasizes the importance of keeping information and supporting systems consistent with overall organization needs. Information systems adapt to support changes on many levels. Internal auditors often encounter cases where an information system was implemented many years ago to support different needs. Although its application controls may be good, the information system does not support the current needs of the organization. COSO takes a broad view of information systems, both automated and manual, and points to the need to understand both manual information systems processes and computer processing technologies.

Strategic and Integrated Systems

Many organizations have upgraded their automated systems over time, but their basic mix of supporting automated applications may not have changed significantly. An organization will have its general ledger, payroll, inventory, accounts receivable, accounts payable, and related financial-based processes as core information systems, without too much else. COSO suggests that the effective organization should go a step further and implement both strategic and integrated information systems to support the organization's business and help it to carry out its overall mission. Many companies have developed strategic information systems to support their business strategies—systems that moved them even further forward. An example is American Airlines, which developed its SABRE automated reservation system back in the 1960s, greatly enhancing its ability to sell tickets and make more effective use of its resources. The same airline developed the first frequent-flyer program in the early 1980s, again giving it a business edge. Other airlines subsequently developed similar or even better information systems, but American Airlines' systems gave it an initial marketing and customer-acceptance edge for many years.

COSO also emphasizes the importance of processes through integrating automated information systems with other operations. Examples would be a fully automated manufacturing system that controls both production machines and equipment inventories or a highly automated distribution system that controls inventory and schedules shipments. These comments about strategic information systems are a step forward when contrasted with the information systems–related comments from earlier internal control standards. COSO emphasizes, however, that it is a mistake to assume that just because a system is new, it will provide better control. Older systems presumably have been tried and tested through use; a new system can have unknown or untested control weaknesses. The internal auditor can play a significant role in assessing whether controls are adequate in new automated systems by appropriate audit tests and assessments.

Quality of Information

The COSO report has a brief section on the importance of the quality of information. Poor-quality information systems, filled with errors and omissions, affect management's ability to make appropriate decisions. Reports should contain enough data and information to support effective control activities. The quality of information includes ascertaining whether:

- The content of reported information is appropriate
- The information is timely and available when required
- The information is current or at least the latest available
- The data and information are correct
- The information is accessible to appropriate parties

These points all circle back to SOA requirements. Although the COSO framework set up these quality of information points as objectives, SOA effectively makes them requirements. As discussed in the SOA overview in Chapter 2, the chief financial officer is effectively attesting to these points as they pertain to an organization's financial statements.

Internal auditors always should be aware of the quality of the information produced by all manual and automated systems. This concern goes beyond the traditional role of auditors, who historically have looked only at systems controls and given little attention to quality-related issues.

Communications Aspect of Internal Control

Communications is really a separate internal control element, although it is combined with information as one component of COSO's internal control framework. Communication channels provide the details to individuals to carry out their financial reporting, operational, and compliance responsibilities. COSO emphasizes that communication must take place in a broader sense in dealing with various individuals and groups and their expectations. The existence of appropriate channels of communication is an important element in the overall framework of internal control. An organization needs to establish these communication channels throughout its various levels and activities and between the organization and various interested outsiders. Although communication channels can have many dimensions, COSO highlights the separate components of internal and of external communications.

Internal auditors always have looked at communication channels in their reviews and have focused on formal channels of communication, such as procedure manuals or published systems documentation. Internal audit reports frequently cite entities for a lack of documentation in their reviews. While that documentation is a very important element of communication, COSO takes an expanded view when considering internal control.

Communications: Internal Components

According to COSO, perhaps the most important component of communication is that all personnel should receive periodic messages from senior management reminding them that their internal control responsibilities must be taken seriously. The clarity of this message is important to ensure that the overall organization follows effective internal control principles. This message is part of the "tone at the top" discussed earlier as part of the control environment, and it should be communicated throughout the organization.

In addition to these overall messages, all organization stakeholders need to understand how their specific duties and actions fit into the total internal control system. If this understanding is not present, various parties in the organization will ignore errors and make decisions thinking no one cares. This is really the result of an organization lacking a mission statement, as discussed in Chapter 4.

All stakeholders need to know the types of activities that may be unethical, illegal, or otherwise improper. People also need to know how to respond to errors or other unexpected events in the course of performing their duties. They typically require communication in terms of messages from management, procedure documentation, and adequate training. Internal auditors often encounter these issues in the course of their review. While auditors historically may have presented some findings about the lack of documentation as a fairly minor point, both COSO and SOA emphasize that this lack of documentation may point to a lack of appropriate internal control communication channels.

Communication must flow in two directions, and COSO emphasizes that stakeholders must have a mechanism to report matters upward throughout the organization. This upward communication has two components: communication through normal channels and special, confidential reporting channels. Normal reporting refers to the process in which members of the organizations are expected to report status information, errors, or problems up through their supervisors. This communication should be freely encouraged, and the organization should avoid "shooting the messenger" when bad news is reported. Otherwise, it will soon be understood throughout the organization that employees should report only good news, and managers may not become aware of significant problems. Because personnel sometimes may be reluctant to report matters to their immediate supervisors, the whistleblower programs discussed in Chapter 4 are essential. This section of COSO concludes with the importance of communication channels between top management and the board of directors. According to the COSO framework of over 20 years ago, management should take care to inform the board of major developments, risks, and occurrences. The board, in turn, must review operations independently and communicate their concerns and decisions to management. These recommendations were part of the original COSO framework that did not receive sufficient attention until they became legal requirements through SOA.

External Communications

Organizations need to establish appropriate communication channels with interested outside parties including customers, suppliers, shareholders, bankers, regulators, and others. This communication should go beyond the public relations–type of function that large organizations often establish to talk about themselves. Similar to internal communication channels, external information must flow in two directions. The information provided to outside parties should be relevant to their needs so they can better understand an organization and the challenges it faces. The organization that sends out highly optimistic reports to outsiders when many inside the organization realize there are problems is also giving an inappropriate message to its own employees. This is what was occurring in the events leading up to SOA, when some organizations were reporting fraudulent results.

Means and Methods of Communication

There is no one correct means of communicating internal control information within the organization. The modern organization can communicate its messages through many vehicles, including web pages, bulletin board announcements, procedure manuals, videotaped presentation, or speeches by members of management. Often, however, the action taken by the communicator either before or after the message will give a stronger signal to the recipients of that communication. COSO summarizes this internal control element:

> *An entity with a long and rich history of operating with integrity, and whose culture is well understood by people through the organization, will likely find little difficulty in communicating its message. An entity without such a tradition will likely need to put more into the way the messages are communicated.*

COSO Internal Control Elements: Monitoring

The capstone of the pyramid internal control framework model, as shown in Exhibit 5.9, is the monitoring component. Although internal control systems will work effectively with proper support from management, control procedures, and both information and communication linkages, a process must be in place to monitor these activities. Monitoring activities has long been the role of internal auditors, who perform reviews to assess compliance with established procedures; however, COSO takes a broader view of monitoring while still reserving a significant portion of that activity to internal audit.

COSO recognizes that control procedures and other systems change over time. What appeared to be effective when it was first installed may not be that effective in the future due to changing external conditions, new personnel, new systems and procedures, and other factors. A process should be in place to assess the effectiveness of established internal control components and to take corrective action when appropriate. While this certainly points to the role of internal audit, this internal control component cannot be relegated to the auditors while management remains somewhat oblivious to potential control problems. An organization needs to establish a variety of monitoring activities to measure the effectiveness of its internal controls.

Monitoring can be accomplished through a series of separate evaluations as well as through ongoing activities. The latter—ongoing activities— refer to processes that monitor performance and make corrective action when required.

Ongoing Monitoring Activities

Many routine business functions can be characterized as monitoring activities. Although auditors and others do not always think of these in that sense, COSO gives the following examples of the ongoing monitoring component of internal control:

- *Operating Management Normal Functions.* Normal management reviews over operations and financial reports constitute an important ongoing monitoring activity. However, special attention should be given to reported exceptions and potential internal control deviations. Internal control is enhanced if reports are reviewed on a regular basis and corrective action initiated for any reported exceptions.

- *Communications from External Parties.* This element of monitoring is closely related to the component of communication from external parties discussed earlier. External communication measuring monitors, such as a customer complaint telephone number, are important; however, the organization needs to monitor closely these calls and then initiate corrective action when appropriate.

- *Organization Structure and Supervisory Activities.* Although more senior management should review summary reports and take corrective action, the first level of supervision and the related organization structure often plays an even more significant role in monitoring. Direct supervision of clerical activities, for example, should routinely review and correct lower-level errors and ensure improved clerical employee performance. COSO emphasizes the importance of an adequate separation of duties in this review. Separation of duties between employees allows them to serve as a monitoring check on one another.

- *Physical Inventories and Asset Reconciliation.* Periodic physical inventories, whether of storeroom stock or negotiable securities, are an important monitoring activity. An annual inventory in a retail store, for example, may indicate a significant merchandise loss. A possible reason for this loss could be theft, pointing to the need for better security controls.

These are examples from a longer list in the COSO report. They illustrate procedures that are often in place in organizations but are not thought of as ongoing monitoring activities. Any activity that reviews organization activities on a regular basis and suggests potential corrective actions can be thought of as a monitoring activity.

Separate Internal Control Evaluation

COSO points out the importance of ongoing monitoring activities to support the internal control framework and also suggests that "it may be useful to take a fresh look from time to time" at the effectiveness of internal controls through separate evaluations. The frequency and nature of these separate special reviews will depend greatly on the nature of the organization and the significance of the risks it must control. Although management may want to initiate periodically an evaluation of its entire internal control system, most reviews should be initiated to assess a specific area of control. These reviews may be initiated when there has been an acquisition, a significant change in business, or some other significant activity.

COSO also emphasizes that these evaluations can be performed by direct line management through self-assessment types of reviews. Internal audit is not required to perform the review unless requested by senior management; the scheduling of these reviews will depend on audit's risk assessment process and the resources available to schedule and perform reviews. Considerable time may pass before internal audit may have scheduled a normal review in a given area of operation. However, responsible management in that area should consider scheduling and performing self-assessments on a more regular basis. The internally generated review can point out potential control problems and cause operating management to implement corrective action. Because these self-assessment reviews typically will not be as comprehensive as a normal internal audit, internal audit can be requested to perform a more comprehensive review over the same general area if potentially significant problems are encountered through such a limited review.

Internal Control Evaluation Process

COSO talks about the evaluation process for reviewing a system of internal controls. The controls evaluator first should develop an understanding of the system design, identify its controls, test those controls, and then develop conclusions on the basis of the test results. This is really the internal audit process. COSO mentions another approach for evaluation called *benchmarking,* an approach that is common for process improvement exercises and is occasionally used by internal auditors. Benchmarking is the process of comparing an organization's processes, control procedures, and other activities with those of peer organizations. Comparisons may be made with specific similar organizations or against published statistics from similar industry groups. This approach is convenient for some types of measures but filled with dangers for others. For example, it is fairly easy to benchmark the organization size, staffing levels, and average compensations of a sales function against comparable organizations in the same general industry; however, the evaluator may encounter difficulties in trying to compare other factors due to the many small differences that make all organizations unique. The control self-assessment process described later in this chapter is an alternative approach that may achieve some of the benefits of benchmarking without going through an extended analysis.

Reporting Internal Control Deficiencies

Whether internal control deficiencies are identified through processes in the internal control system itself, through monitoring activities, or through other external events, these internal control deficiencies should be reported to appropriate levels of management. The key questions for the evaluator—such as internal audit or the SOA review team—is to determine what should be reported, given the large body of details that may be encountered, and to whom the reports should be directed. COSO states that "all internal control deficiencies that can affect the entity's attaining its objectives should be reported to those who can take necessary action." Although this statement initially makes sense, the experienced internal auditor will realize that this directive is difficult to implement. The modern organization, no matter how well organized, will be guilty of a variety of internal control errors or omissions. COSO suggests that all of these should be identified and reported and that even the most minor of errors should be investigated to understand if they were caused by any overall control deficiencies. The report uses the example of an employee's taking a few dollars from the petty cash fund.

Even though the amount may not be significant, COSO urges that the matter be investigated rather than ignored, since "such apparent condoning personal use of the entity's money might send an unintended message to employees." External auditors regularly apply the concept of materiality when performing their reviews. That is, they may decide that some errors and irregularities are so small that they are not material to the overall conclusion that they will reach. The operational efficiency of administrative control is of prime importance; however, materiality also should be considered when evaluating internal controls in general. SOA does not really discuss materiality issues, but it certainly should be a major factor in any enforcement actions.

COSO concludes by discussing to whom internal control deficiencies in the organization should be reported. In one paragraph, COSO provides guidance that is useful for evaluations:

> *Findings on internal control deficiencies usually should be reported not only to the individual responsible for the function or activity involved, who is in the position to take corrective action, but also to at least one level of management above the directly responsible person. This process enables that individual to provide needed support or oversight for taking corrective action, and to communicate with others in the organization whose activities may be affected. Where findings cut across organizational boundaries, the reporting should cross over as well and be directed to a sufficiently high level to ensure appropriate action.*

SOA has tightened up this COSO reporting guidance. Matters that appear to be of a material nature become an almost immediate chief financial officer and audit committee reporting issue. The organization also should develop reporting procedures such that all internal financial control deficiencies, whether encountered through a Section 404 review or through internal audit reviews of ongoing operations, are reported to appropriate levels of the organization. Management reporting and monitoring is a highly important aspect of internal control.

COSO and SOA Section 404 Compliance

Understanding and following the COSO framework is almost essential for achieving Section 404 compliance. Although SOA does not specifically mandate the COSO framework at this time, it is a very useful framework to guide an organization to achieve a strong system of internal financial system controls. Other frameworks such as CobiT, discussed in Chapter 6, can be used. However, COSO has become an almost internationally accepted internal control framework standard that will allow an organization to assess its internal control processes in an effective and consistent manner. The yet-to–be-issued PCAOB internal control standards will almost certainly reflect COSO.

COSO internal control standards have been in use for some years now; almost ten years have past since the AICPA adopted the COSO model in its internal controls review standards. However, as evidenced by the accounting and financial fraud scandals of the late 1990s and beyond, the controls and controls procedures described as part of the COSO framework were not always fully accepted. Had the practices and procedures in the COSO framework been more aggressively adopted earlier, there perhaps would never have been the need for SOA. But this is speculation and all organizations now have a heightened need under SOA Section 404 to establish effective internal financial controls that follow the COSO framework or some very similar substitute.

VIOLATION PENALTIES: ORGANIZATIONAL SENTENCING GUIDELINES

SOA legislation is filled with penalties for the failure to comply with its outlined rules. Those penalties can be levied against the corporation and an individual officer or board member. Usually they are described as fines of not more than some dollar maximum and/or imprisonment up to some number of years. Historically, our society has viewed these as white-collar crimes and has treated violators somewhat gently. With a tradition going back to English common law that a corporation could not be held criminally liable, organizations often have gotten off somewhat easy, with fines that were not that significant compared to corporation assets or with a penalty along the lines of community service.

The U.S. Organizational Sentencing Guidelines have changed this for organizations that violate most federal laws. Established by an act of Congress in 1991, the guidelines allow federal judges to rationalize penalties for violating corporations. The guidelines are:

> *designed so that sanctions imposed upon organizations . . . will provide just punishment, adequate deterrence, and incentives for organizations to maintain internal mechanisms for preventing, detecting and reporting criminal conduct.*

Although certainly not a new rule, the guidelines are an important set of legal requirements that encourage good corporate governance practices. The guidelines provide judges with a carrot-and-stick approach for assessing fines and penalties for organizations found guilty of violating applicable federal laws.

The guidelines are a strong reason to encourage good corporate governance. This section describes the risk and reward aspects of the guidelines. Although they are not a tool for an internal auditor to use when evaluating internal controls systems or assessing risk, they become a very compelling reason or rationale for an organization to install good compliance systems, whether for adherence to SOA or many other federal laws.

Scope

Today a corporation can be held to be criminally liable for the acts of even the lowest-level employee, and even if that employee was acting contrary to express employer directions. This legal standard has become increasingly tough over the years, and a corporation can be held criminally liable for the acts of its employees or agents through what is called the "Scope of Authority" or the "For the Benefit of the Corporation" doctrines.

The first of these says that the corporation can be held liable for any employee or agent who committed an illegal act in the course of ordinary or authorized duties. It really says that corporations are responsible for the acts of their agents and employees. If an employee in an automotive assembly plant installed an incorrect part in error and subsequently that automobile caused damages and loss of life, the corporation would be held liable for damages. For obvious reasons, the corporation could not say that it is not its fault, find the employee who made the error, and then allow the injured parties to seek damages from that employee. Likewise, if an employee made fraudulent account transactions under SOA rules, the action of the employee or agent obligates the corporation.

The "For the Benefit of the Corporation" doctrine says that a corporation can be held liable even if the employee or agent was committing the act for personal gain, if the employee's illegal action *could have* conferred some benefit to the corporation. This doctrine applies even if the illegal action was primarily for personal gain and even if the employee or agent never realized the intended benefits of the act. A scheme to record fictitious sales transactions for personal employee gain might an example here. The corporation could be held liable simply because the fictitious reported sales, designed to aid the fraudulent employee scheme, benefited the corporation because it was reporting better performance in the eyes of investors.

We have used the words "employee or agent" for these doctrines. For purposes of corporate liability, a "corporate agent" could be any of these actors:

- *Officers and Directors.* Although not employees, their actions are sufficient to hold the corporation liable.

- *Middle Managers and Supervisors.* The principles of accountability impute corporate liability to the acts of these middle managers.

- *Lower-level Employees.* Acts may be imputed to the corporation provided they occurred within the scope of the employee's authority and responsibility.

- *Subsidiaries.* The parent corporation has an obligation to supervise any subsidiary. Actions of a lower-level employee in an unaffiliated subsidiary could impute liability to the parent corporation.

- *Independent Contractors.* The illegal acts of anyone working on a contract for a corporation puts that parent corporation in legal jeopardy.

There also can be a personal criminal penalty for officers, directors, and employees. Individuals are not allowed to hide behind the corporate shield if they actually participated in the crime. Also, an employee can facilitate the commission of a crime by either taking some affirmative action that indicates knowledge or knowingly failing to act. Thus, an employee or agent that knows about some corporate criminal activity but does nothing about it could be held criminally liable as well as the corporation itself. Finally, by simply being the "responsible officer," an individual can be held liable for failing to prevent or correct some action. This does not say that individuals always are held criminally liable when their corporation is charged; nor are corporations always charged because of the criminal actions of persons who happen to be employees or agents. Depending on circumstances and the decisions of prosecutors, however, the criminal legal action can apply to both.

The Process: A Potentially Illegal Act

The federal legal process generally follows the same six steps before completion. Here we list that process and use the Arthur Andersen paper-shredding matter of early 2002 to explain how this process works.

1. *Discovery of the Criminal or Illegal Act.* Whether someone gives a tip to a federal prosecutor or a matter is encountered by regulators,

someone has to discover the illegal act and report it to prosecutors. In the case of Arthur Andersen's actions at Enron, the potential accounting fraud had been reported initially by Enron as a reason to restate its reported earnings. There were rumors that the SEC was coming to investigate the affair, and several Enron employees tipped authorities that Andersen appeared to be shredding all of its documentation covering this audit work.

2. ***Investigation by Federal Prosecutors.*** Random tips are of no value unless they are found to be credible. Some reported tips may have no substance because someone may report something without a full understanding or perhaps only because he or she has an ax to grind. The Andersen paper shredding initially received press attention and was correctly halted after the SEC arrived. The Enron failure was big and received considerable attention. Andersen claimed to the press and eventually to a congressional hearing that it had done nothing wrong and was just following normal good auditing procedures. It was unclear what specific laws, if any, had been violated, but federal prosecutors along with the SEC announced a detailed investigation of the affair.

3. ***Decision to Seek Indictment.*** This step is not always automatic. The entire organization, just some representative "bad apples," or both can be the investigative target. Prosecution decisions must be made, and in some instances nothing happens beyond the investigation. Before too long in the Enron matter, Andersen announced that the entire shredding activity was the fault of a rogue partner whom it had fired. One of the major public accounting firms at that time, Andersen had just gone through a peer review by another Big 5 counterpart, Deloitte & Touche, which had given the company a clean report on its audit quality standards. However, Andersen also had paid a large fine as a result of an out-of-court settlement regarding poor accounting at Waste Management. As part of that settlement, Andersen promised the SEC to clean up its auditing practices, but the Enron matter seemed to indicate that not much had changed.

4. ***Pretrial Negotiations.*** The Andersen case is again representative of how this process works. The supposed rogue partner was indicted first, but he quickly agreed to plead guilty and to testify against Andersen in exchange for reduced charges. Prosecutors often start at a lower level getting employees to testify against the persons or the organization the next level up. This phase often is settled before the trial occurs. An organization or individual will not admit to any fault but will pay a fine or agree to some remedial action as if it were found guilty. Andersen here was indicted for obstruction of justice, and the firm started unwinding even before being found guilty. Audit clients left in droves, and international affiliates moved to other firms.

5. *Formal Trial for Offense.* As the above paragraphs indicate, there is considerable activity and negotiation before a formal jury trial. If it goes that far, a jury is assembled, witnesses are called, and the trial takes place. Andersen did not settle with prosecutors and allowed the matter to go to trial. This was unusual behavior, making the news almost daily at the time. In the end, a jury found Andersen guilty of obstruction of justice. Although appeals were filed, the game was essentially over for Anderson with that guilty verdict.

6. *If Guilty, Determine Punishment through Organizational Sentencing Guidelines.* In this formal process, a judge determines the guilty party's culpability score and decides on the punishment based on those guidelines. Andersen's fine and probation might appear to be a minor punishment here, but all public confidence in the firm had been destroyed, and soon it essentially ceased to exist.

This prosecution process outlines all of the steps necessary before the Organizational Sentencing Guidelines are taken into consideration. An organization or individual must have been accused of violating some federal law, must have let the matter go to prosecution, and then will have to contend with the provisions of the guidelines if found guilty. We have used the Andersen and Enron situation as an example primarily because it involved what was once a well-respected public accounting firm, and the affair there was one of the reasons for the enactment of SOA. The guidelines and their requirements for an effective compliance program, as described in the sections following, are much more typical.

Culpability Scores under the Guidelines

If an organization is found guilty of a violation of some federal law, whether SOA or any one of many other statutes, the federal prosecutor responsible makes a recommendation to the sentencing judge. There are three general principles in this process:

1. *Establish a remedy for the harm.* In some instances, the matter can be settled here with an agreement for restitution or even community service. This remedy can apply to either individuals or an organization.

2. *Use probation or formal sanctions to prevent future criminal conduct.* In the end in our Enron example, Andersen was given three years' probation plus a fine that was not that crippling, given the firm's size.

3. *Penalize the organization, using the Sentencing Guidelines.* The penalty here is based on the seriousness of the offense and the culpability of the organization.

If we end up at step 3, the matter starts to get more complex. First, prosecutors will determine what is called a base fine. That base fine is the *greater* of: (1) the pecuniary gain to the corporation from the violation, (2) the pecuniary loss caused by the offense, or (3) an amount based on the statutory offense. Number 3 here goes back to the actual law, which may say that a fine in a given area shall be no greater than some value. Further, the overall minimum base fine in the Guidelines is $5,000 with a maximum of $72,500,000. Given the total losses to employees' 401-K plans that some prosecutors could have attributed to Andersen's actions at Enron, the firm got off easy with a $500,000 fine.

Matters now get even more complex. That base fine is multiplied by something called a *culpability score* to determine the actual fine to the organization. The process seems to have been designed by federal regulators who previously had drafted our Internal Revenue Service tax laws. Exhibit 5.11 shows the range of culpability scores. Each organization starts with a base score of 5 points, which can go up to a maximum of 17 points or down to below 0 points depending on the characteristics of the organization and its past history. The guidelines then have a fairly extensive set of tables to determine these score increments and decrements. If the CEO is involved in the criminal act and if the organization has more than 10,000 employees, another 5 points is added to the culpability score. If the organization has only 25 to 200 employees, 3 points are awarded. These added points increase the fine multiplier for the total fine to the organization.

EXHIBIT 5.11　　Sentencing Guidelines Culpability Scores

Base Score	5 Points	
add　Level of Authority and Size of Organization		+5, +4, +3, +2, or +1
add　Prior Sentencing History		+1 or +2
add　Violation of Court Order		+1 or +2
add　Obstruction of Justice Ruling		+3
less　Effective Program to Prevent and Detect Violations		−3
less　Self-Reporting, Cooperation, Acceptance of Responsibility		−5, −4, −3, −2, or −1
Highest Maximum Score:		9
Lowest Possible Score:		−3

An organization can have either of two programs in place to reduce the number of points calculated for determining a fine. If an organization has an "Effective Program to Prevent and Detect Violations of the Law," the base fine can be reduced by 3 points. This "Effective Program" could be just a whistleblower program, such as was discussed in Chapter 4. Even if an organization was found blatantly guilty of some offense, its fine at conviction could be reduced significantly if it could convince the judge that it had a program in place that was just not working at the time of the offense. Similarly, that culpability score could be reduced by 5 points if the organization voluntarily reported the matter, by 2 points if the charged organization fully cooperated with the investigation, or by 1 point if the organization exhibited acceptance of the charges through a guilty plea prior to the trial.

In the next level of complexity, the calculated culpability score is used to determine a fine multiplier through the minimum and maximums listed in Exhibit 5.12. Based on the nature of the offense, the judge and prosecutor then will determine whether minimum or maximum multiplier factors will be applied. An organization could be fined from a trifling less than $1 million to a maximum of $290 million, a fatal penalty no matter the size of the organization.

Several examples may better explain this process. First, assume that the XXX Corporation, a relatively small consumer products distributor, was found guilty of an accounting fraud with a total loss of $10 million, the base fine. XXX receives a starting 5 point culpability score with an additional

EXHIBIT 5.12   Sentencing Guidelines
Minimum and Maximum Multipliers

Culpability Multiplier	Minimum Multiplier	Maximum Multiplier
10 or more	2.0	4.0
9	1.8	3.6
8	1.6	3.2
7	1.4	2.8
6	1.2	2.4
5	1.0	2.0
4	0.8	1.6
3	0.6	1.2
2	0.4	0.8
1	0.2	0.4
0 or less	0.05	0.2

2 points for its smaller size. It has no history of legal convictions and has never been accused of any obstruction of justice charges. XXX has never established an effective compliance program, nor had it taken any steps to self-report this matter. Based on the minimum fine ranges, its culpability score of 5 + 2 + 0 = 7 would result in a fine of $10 million × 1.4, or $14 million.

A second much larger corporation, YYY, was found guilty of an accounting fraud of $50 million. YYY receives a starting 5 point culpability score with an additional 5 points for its size. It was involved in a similar accounting fraud problem in the past, for an additional 1 point. However, prior to that first fraud, YYY established a very effective ethics and compliance program, for a 3 point reduction. Also, when this fraud was first discovered, YYY organized an internal task force to cooperate with prosecutors, for a 2 point reduction. Based on the minimum fine ranges, YYY's culpability score of 5 + 5 + 1 − 3 − 2 = 6 would result in a fine of $50 million × 1.2, or $60 million.

The much smaller XXX, which did not have a past history of such illegal acts but also had no effective compliance program, would be subject to a comparatively much larger fine than YYY, which had an effective compliance program in place and cooperated with prosecutors. While no organization and its stockholders expects to be found guilty of an illegal federal offense involving a significant fine, organizations can establish processes to shield themselves from more severe consequences.

Requirements for an Effective Compliance Program

SOA, as discussed in Chapter 2, legally mandates that a corporation must establish an effective compliance program for its senior officers. Chapter 4 discussed why an effective ethics and compliance program is important to essentially every organization. Organizations also should develop ethics and compliance programs as an insurance measure from Organizational Sentencing Guidelines penalties. This is another very powerful reason for organizations to establish effective compliance programs.

The guidelines outline seven very specific minimum requirements for what would be considered an effective compliance program:

1. Compliance program standards and procedures should be reasonably capable of preventing criminal conduct. Codes of conduct and guidance materials should communicate the overall rules to all employees.

2. The program should have the oversight of higher-level personnel. A program does little good if managers are monitoring employee performance against that program. Employees will soon realize that situation.

3. Care should be taken in delegating substantial discretionary authority to individuals. Depending on the nature of the matter, approval levels

always should be established at appropriate levels, whether they pertain to the administrative assistant who must secure approval when ordering office supplies above a certain but fairly low monetary limit to large transactions that will require board approval.

4. There must be an effective procedure for the communication of standards and procedures to all employees. This goes beyond codes of conduct and includes other mechanisms to explain rules and procedures to everyone.

5. Reasonable steps must be taken to achieve compliance. Action can be taken at all levels here, but certain internal audit monitoring programs can be very important here.

6. Disciplinary mechanisms must be in place to enforce compliance to rules and procedures. Actions here can take a variety of forms, but potential penalties should be communicated with the penalties or actions applied consistently.

7. There should be appropriate responses after the detection of any offense. These responses include reporting the matter to proper levels and taking all reasonable steps to prevent further similar offenses. Action here could result in the very favorable 3 point culpability score downward adjustment as discussed above.

Based only on the rewards and punishments in the Organizational Sentencing Guidelines, there are very strong reasons for an organization to establish an effective ethics and compliance program. Of course, even the best programs will not eliminate misconduct. If employees engage in conduct to violate the law, the compliance program may detect that activity.

Why Are Sentencing Guidelines Important for Auditors?

The Organization Sentencing Guidelines represent a fairly new rule for many internal auditors. Most internal auditors do not envision getting trapped by violating a federal law and facing prosecution, but the effective compliance programs mandated here are another reason auditors should help to establish an effective compliance program and to review it periodically to assess effectiveness. The guidelines bring home the fact that there can be severe penalties for the organization and certain individuals if they are prosecuted for some criminal act.

While SOA focuses primarily on larger corporations today, U.S. Sentencing Commission data show that a very large number (around 74 percent) of prosecutions under the guidelines have been directed toward organizations of 100 employees or less. An effective compliance and ethics program can be initiated for any size organization; this is not a large-corporation issue. No matter how small the organization or its organizational structure, the responsible internal auditor has a strong reason to encourage the implementation of effective compliance and ethics programs. The Organizational Sentencing Guidelines provides another level of support here.

CONTROL SELF-ASSESSMENTS

One of COSO's recommendations is that organizations "should report on the effectiveness and efficiency of the system of internal control." That internal control reporting can be at a total organization level or can be limited to individual departments or functions within the organization. The concept of an internal audit function looking at its own controls or helping others to review their controls has evolved into the IIA's formal control self-assessment (CSA) methodology. Based on the Total Quality Management (TQM) approaches of the early 1990s as well as COSO, the CSA methodology has become a powerful new tool for internal auditors and others to better understand an organization's internal control environment by assembling a team to assess those internal controls.

CSA was first initiated at Gulf Oil of Canada in 1987 as a tool to assess its control effectiveness and business processes. Facing both a legal consent decree requiring Gulf Canada to report on its internal controls and the difficulty resolving oil and gas measurement issues through the traditional audit process, its internal audit group launched a *facilitated meeting* self-assessment approach that involved gathering management and staff for interviews relating to, and discussions of, specific issues or processes. The process became a successful mechanism to assess informal, or soft, controls as well as traditional hard controls.

CSA has been adopted by a number of major corporations and has become part of the IIA Standards of Professional Practice. This section discusses how internal audit can launch CSA and evaluate the data and results from a CSA project.

Launching the CSA Process

CSA is a process through which internal control effectiveness is examined and assessed. The objective is to provide reasonable assurance that all business objectives will be met. Earlier we discussed organizations and their internal audit functions by size, ranging from the larger Group 1 organization with a strong COSO internal controls review process in place to the much smaller Group 3 organizations with essentially no formal internal audit capability. Although larger organizations have the tools and resources to launch CSA more easily, this internal controls assessment review process might be particularly valuable for the more midsize Group 2 sized organization that has not launched a formal COSO-based internal controls assessment yet but needs to evaluate controls for SOA compliance.

The CSA concept requires gathering management and staff for interviews to assess the internal controls environment. CSA can be facilitated by any function in an organization, but the two key groups usually are internal audit with its internal control review background and the quality function for its understanding of CSA-type processes. Quality functions refer to an organization's quality assurance process, as is briefly introduced in Chapter 6. Regardless of who acts as leader or facilitator, a CSA project should improve the control environment of an organization by making involved stakeholders more aware of organizational objectives and the role of internal control in achieving goals and objectives. Going forward, it should motivate employees to design, implement, and continually improve control processes. A CSA review is particularly effective if the internal control system reviewed is a large enterprise resource planning (ERP) system that covers all or most aspects of operations. This is the case where one basic automated system covers accounting, human resources, production, marketing, and more. Vendors such as SAP, PeopleSoft, and Oracle supply these all-encompassing applications.

The first step to launch CSA is for the CAE or some other person leading the initiative to "sell" the concept to senior management. In a Group 2 organization, the message may be that CSA should help the organization to improve its internal control procedures and SOA compliance while not embarking on a time-consuming, expensive exercise. Other potential benefits from CSA are to:

- Increase the scope of internal control reporting during a given year
- Target audit work by focusing on high-risk and unusual items discovered in CSA reviews
- Increase the effectiveness of corrective actions by transferring ownership to operating employees

The CSA team leader then needs to decide what portion of the entity will use CSA, what functions or objectives to consider, and what level of stakeholders should be included in the assessments. The number and level of stakeholders will depend on the CSA approach selected. The three primary CSA approaches are:

- Facilitated team meetings or workshops
- Questionnaires
- Management-produced analysis

Organizations often combine more than one approach to accommodate their self-assessment.

Facilitated team meetings gather internal control information from work teams that may represent multiple levels within an organization. A facilitator, trained in internal control system design, should lead the sessions. A questionnaire-based approach uses a survey that usually is based on simple yes/no or have/have not responses. Process owners use the survey results to assess their control structure. The third approach, a management produced analysis, is really an internal audit type of analysis. A CSA specialist—probably an internal auditor—combines the results of a study produced by management or staff of the business process with information gathered from sources such as interviews with other managers and key personnel. By synthesizing this material, the CSA specialist develops an analysis that process owners can use to better understand and improve internal controls for the given process area.

The CSA approach and format used here will depend on the overall organizational culture as well as senior management decisions. In the event a corporate culture does not support a participative CSA approach, questionnaire responses and internal control analysis can enhance the control environment.

Just as internal audit should be the reviewer and not the implementer in SOA Section 404 reviews, the same is true for CSA processes. There must be a decision as to whether internal audit or operating management will drive the CSA process. Some CSA practitioners believe that internal audit, as the arm of management responsible for internal control oversight, may be the appropriate driver for CSA. The presence of internal auditors in CSA facilitated meetings is, in and of itself, an oversight control. Other practitioners believe that self-assessment can be performed effectively only by operating management and/or work units. The involvement of internal audit, in this view, means that management will be less accountable for its internal controls improvements.

Performing the Facilitated CSA Review

The basic concept behind a CSA review of an internal control process is to gather a group of people, across multiple levels of the organization and from multiple units, and then to gather extensive information about internal controls for that selected process. The idea is to select representative samples of stakeholders throughout the organization to meet and discuss the selected system's operations and controls. An internal auditor or some other communications specialist is designated to head these workshops, lead discussions, and help draw conclusions.

Facilitated team workshops gather information from work teams representing different levels in the business unit or function. The format of the workshop may be based on objectives, risks, controls, or processes. Each has distinct advantages depending on the internal controls area reviewed. Assume as an example that an organization has installed a large, comprehensive ERP system that encompasses many major operations areas. Management has requested an internal control risk assessment of this major application. Because the ERP system covers many aspects of business operations, a decision is made to review systems controls through a series of focus group users gathering to discuss and review systems operations. Planning steps for organizing these CSA reviews should be developed into a CSA organization plan. Based on the extensive set of CSA materials published by the IIA, this plan and a facilitated CSA session can follow any of four meeting formats:

1. *Objective-based CSA facilitated sessions* focus on the best way to accomplish a business objective, such as accurate financial reporting. The workshop begins by the team identifying the controls currently in place to support the system objectives and then determining any residual risks remaining if controls are not working. The aim of this workshop format is to decide whether the control procedures are working effectively and whether any remaining risks are within an acceptable level.

2. *Risk-based CSA facilitated sessions* focus on the CSA teams listing risks to achieve internal control objectives. The workshop begins by listing all possible barriers, obstacles, threats, and exposures that might prevent achieving an objective and then examining the control procedures to determine if they are sufficient to manage any identified key risks. The aim of the workshop is to determine significant residual risks. This format takes the work team through the entire set of objective-risks-controls surrounding the entity reviewed.

3. *Control-based CSA facilitated sessions* focus on how well the controls in place are working. This format is different from the two sessions above because the facilitator identifies the key risks and controls before the beginning of the workshop. During the CSA session, the work team assesses how well the controls mitigate risks and promote the achievement of objectives. The aim of the workshop is to produce an analysis of the gap between how controls are working and how well management expects those controls to work.

4. *Process-based CSA facilitated sessions* focus on selected activities that are elements of a chain of processes. Processes are a series of related activities that go from some beginning point to an end, such as the various steps in purchasing, product development, or revenue generation. This type of workshop usually covers the identification of the objectives of the whole process and the various intermediate steps. The aim of the workshop is to evaluate, update, validate, improve, and even streamline the whole process and its component activities. This session format may have a greater breadth of analysis than a control-based approach by covering multiple objectives within the process and by supporting concurrent management efforts, such as reengineering, quality improvement, and continuous improvement initiatives.[6]

Each of these formats can be effective for developing and understanding hard and soft controls as well as the risks surrounding any significant internal control process. The keys to success here are to have knowledgeable and well-prepared meeting facilitators ask appropriate questions and get all of the selected team members to participate. The other major key is to take detailed transcriptions of the meeting sessions. While not every word spoken has to be recorded, strong meeting highlights are needed. Recording major discussion points through the facilitator's large notepad in the front of the room often works well.

Although the facilitator is a major driver here, CSA sessions can easily turn into disasters with the wrong people mix. Lower-level stakeholders may feel reluctant to discuss control weaknesses if people who are more senior are in the session. Comments about risks or control weaknesses can get very personal if some team members have major responsibilities for the systems or process discussed. Despite all of this, the CSA process can be a very worthwhile, but expensive, tool to look at a comprehensive system or process from multiple perspectives and to understand any internal control weaknesses.

Performing the Questionnaire-Based CSA Review

A CSA facilitated review can be difficult and time-consuming, no matter whether risk control or process based. In many cases, a questionnaire format can be an effective way to gather control information. A questionnaire is prepared covering the process or system of interest and then distributed to a selected group of stakeholders to gain an understanding of the risks and controls in that area. Exhibit 5.13 is an example CSA questionnaire for planning and budgeting processes. It was developed by the IIA, which has an extensive set of sample CSA questionnaires on its web site (*www.theiia.org*).

The CSA team would circulate these questionnaires, with the respondent's name attached, to a selected group of stakeholders, monitor results

EXHIBIT 5.13   CSA Specific Function Questionnaire:
Planning and Budgeting

The following questions might be used for a Planning and Budgeting CSA review.

1. Do you ensure that completed budgets are consistent with the strategic plan of the company?

2. Are policies and procedures in place to avoid understatement of expenditures?

3. Do you investigate all variances between actual expenditures and budgeted amounts, and, for all variances, are explanations required?

(continues)

EXHIBIT 5.13 CSA Specific Function Questionnaire *(Continued)*

4. Do you ensure that the finalized budget and all revisions are properly documented and approved?

5. Have you assigned a person to receive all information regarding changes to the company that may affect the budget?

6. Is the budget preparation procedure (including approval level requirements) fully documented, and is it distributed to all management involved in the budget process?

7. Are procedures in place to provide adequate information to departmental management for their use in developing a budget?

8. Do you monitor trends in expenses?

9. Are calculations methods for expenses (including new categories) adequately explained?

10. Do you ensure that departments are given adequate time to complete and submit their budgets?

11. Have you identified one individual within each department who has the responsibility for completing the budget, and is assistance provided as needed?

12. Do you advise departments on what and how expenses are to be charged for acquisitions or disposed operations?

13. Are procedures in place to ensure that a limited number of authorized individuals have access to the budgets and that any additions, changes, and deletions are approved and traceable? If the budget is online, are all transactions identified by user ID, date, and transaction type?

14. Do you review the initial budgets and identify areas of possible cost reductions?

15. Are procedures in place to identify departments that consistently incur large expenditures at year-end to bring actual costs up to budget?

16. Are procedures in place to handle cash forecasts?

17. Do you monitor and require approvals for all capital expenditures?

18. Have you identified all of the documentation required of departments when submitting numbers for budgets, return on investments calculation, etc.?

19. Do you monitor project breakdown to ensure that large projects are not broken down into smaller projects to avoid approval requirements?

Source: Reproduced by permission of The Institute of Internal Auditors, Altamonte Springs, Florida.

to ensure that an appropriate number have been returned, and then compile the results. Questionnaires will not yield the discovery-type comments that would come out of focus groups but will give an overall assessment of the soundness of processes and internal controls. This is an effective way to gather basic CSA background data.

Performing the Management-Produced Analysis CSA Review

As an alternative to a survey or a facilitated workshop, a management-produced analysis is very similar to the type of operational review that an internal auditor would perform. This is one of the three CSA analysis approaches suggested by the IIA. Using this approach, management produces a staff study of the business process—almost a research study. The CSA specialist, who may be an internal auditor, combines the results of the study with information gathered from sources such as other managers and key personnel. By synthesizing this material, the CSA specialist develops an analysis that process owners can use in their CSA efforts.

The management-produced analysis approach is difficult for the typical organization to accomplish. It suggests an almost "academic" review by someone in the organization followed by some comparative research for subsequent analysis. We generally do not suggest this approach.

The IIA believes all the above formats strengthen the entity's control structure. Each entity should perform an analysis of external opportunities or threats as well as internal strengths and weaknesses to determine which format is most appropriate in the organization. Many CSA users combine one or more formats within a given facilitated meeting to best meet their needs.

Evaluating CSA Results

A CSA analysis, particularly if it covered multiple processes or systems, will result in a large amount of data. Some may support existing process strengths, others will point to internal control weaknesses in need of correction, and still others may point to areas in need of further research. In many cases, the work will validate the integrity and controls of the systems and processes reviewed.

The results of this CSA review will be similar to the COSO review of internal accounting controls—a disciplined and thorough method for evaluating significant internal controls. CSA provides a way for reviewers to gain a better understanding of the soft controls that surround many processes or systems. Published documentation or focused controls review interviews may indicate that some controls exist. However, the back and forth from a facilitated session may reveal that control processes are described in the organization's systems documentation, but personnel always push the escape key to ignore the control warning messages. These sessions can be effective ways to expose such internal control vulnerabilities.

Future of CSA

CSAs were introduced to the internal audit community in the late 1980s and subsequently were embraced by the IIA. Many private-sector organizations worldwide initiated successful CSA programs, and several state governments within the United States began requiring CSA-oriented internal control assessments. The auditing and accounting departments within those states complied with the regulations via questionnaires or management-produced analysis processes. The Federal Deposit Insurance Corporation (FDIC) and the Canadian Deposit Insurance Corporation (CDIC) now require financial institutions throughout the United States and Canada to assess internal controls with specific CSA guidance compliance.

In recent years, the IIA has launched its first specialty certification, the Certification in Control Self-Assessment (CCSA). This examination-based certificate is designed to enhance senior management's confidence of a reviewer's understanding, knowledge, and training of the CSA process. CSA is a "new rule" within the profession of internal auditing.

The IIA believes that CSA effectively augments internal auditing. One of the primary responsibilities of the board and officers of any organization is providing stakeholder assurance through oversight of the organization's activities. Internal auditing, by definition, assists members of the organization in the effective discharge of their responsibilities. Through CSA, internal auditing and operating staff collaborate to produce an assessment of an operation. This synergy helps internal auditing assist in management's oversight function by improving the quantity and quality of available information. The quantity is increased as internal auditing relies on operating employees to participate actively in CSA, thus reducing time spent in information gathering and validation procedures performed during an audit. The quality is increased since participating employees have a more thorough understanding of the process than an internal auditor can develop in a relatively short period of time.

NOTES

1. Chapter 18 of *Brink's Modern Internal Auditing* discusses internal audit's role in reviewing new systems under development.
2. Protiviti, Inc., of Menlo Park, California, is a U.S. and international risk management and internal audit consulting firm.

3. A work breakdown structure is an initial step that a Project Management Profession (PMP) will use to develop and execute a project plan. See the glossary for more information on the PMP designation.

4. Report of the National Commission on Fraudulent Financial Reporting (National Commission on Fraudulent Financial Reporting, 1987)

5. Committee of Sponsoring Organizations of the Treadway Committee, *Internal Control–Integrated Framework* (Jersey City, NJ: AICPA, 1992).

6. IIA, *Control Self-Assessment: Experience, Current Thinking, and Best Practices* (Altamonte Springs, FL: Institute of Internal Auditors Research Foundation, 1996).

CHAPTER 6

IIA, CobiT, and Other Professional Internal Audit Standards

Every profession requires standards to govern its practices, general procedures, and ethics. The standards allow specialists performing similar work to call themselves professionals. The key internal auditor standard is the Professional Standards for the Practice of Internal Auditing of the Institute of Internal Auditors (IIA), a set of guidance materials known as the Red Book by many internal auditors. The older IIA Standards were lengthy and difficult to embrace. The IIA revised these standards in 2001 with a series of additional proposed changes currently in process. This chapter summarizes the current IIA Standards and some of the "exposure draft" proposed changes currently in process.

It also looks at the control objectives for information and related technology (CobiT) framework from the Information Systems Audit and Control Association (ISACA) and its related professional group, the IT Governance Institute. CobiT's focus is on information technology (IT) processes and controls. The chapter concludes with an introduction to the American Society for Quality (ASQ) audit standards. ASQ's internal audit standards and its quality auditors represent a different dimension and discipline when contrasted with the IIA's approaches and standards. They also represent a group or sector of professionals who should be better understood in the overall world of internal auditing.

INSTITUTE OF INTERNAL AUDITORS STANDARDS FOR PROFESSIONAL PRACTICE

As the primary internal audit professional organization worldwide, the IIA has had a code of ethics as well as a set of standards to support its definition of internal auditing:

> *Internal auditing is an independent, objective assurance and consulting activity designed to add value and improve an organization's operations.*

165

> *It helps an organization accomplish its objectives by bringing a systematic, disciplined approach to evaluate and improve the effectiveness of risk management, control, and governance processes.*

This definition is not part of the new rules discussed throughout this book, as it has been established for some time and describes the internal auditing profession.

There have been changes in recent years to the IIA's Code of Ethics and its Standards for the Professional Practice of Internal Auditing. In many respects, the IIA has made changes to reflect the reality of changes in business processes and internal control procedures. This section discusses both the current IIA Code of Ethics and the Standards. These IIA Standards can change over time; an international IIA committee proposes changes through the release of an exposure draft to the IIA membership. Based on comments received, new or revised standards then are released. The professional internal auditor is obligated to be aware of any changes to internal audit standards and to modify practices, if necessary, based on those standards changes.

IIA's Code of Ethics

The IIA's Code of Ethics promotes an ethical culture in the profession of internal auditing. This code is displayed in Exhibit 6.1. It is necessary and appropriate for a profession that depends on the trust placed on users of internal audit services to have guidance on such matters as objective assurances about risk management, control, and governance. The IIA's current Code of Ethics was released in 2000 and is based on the principles of internal auditor integrity, objectivity, confidentiality, and competency. The code lists the behavior norms expected of internal auditors and is intended to guide the ethical conduct of internal auditors.

The current IIA Code of Ethics replaces a 1988 version. That earlier version, which had 11 specific articles defining preferred practices, replaced a 1968 version consisting of 8 articles. The current version, with its highlighted emphasis on integrity, objectivity, confidentiality, and competency, is much easier to understand and apply than the detailed articles in the 1988 version. As a minor note, the 1988 version used the term "Members and CIA's" throughout, while the current code simply says "Internal Auditors," a better term. Any person performing internal audit services, whether a member of the IIA or not, should be able to follow this Code of Ethics.

The IIA Code of Ethics applies to both individuals and entities that provide internal auditing services. For IIA members and recipients of or candidates for IIA professional certifications, breaches of the Code of Ethics will be evaluated and administered according to IIA Bylaws and Administrative Guidelines. The IIA goes on to state that even if a particular conduct is not mentioned in this code, this does not prevent the conduct or practice from

EXHIBIT 6.1   Institute of Internal Auditors Code of Ethics

1. **Integrity**

    Internal auditors:

    1.1   Shall perform their work with honesty, diligence, and responsibility.

    1.2   Shall observe the law and make disclosures expected by the law and the profession.

    1.3   Shall not knowingly be a party to any illegal activity, or engage in acts that are discreditable to the profession of internal auditing or to the organization.

    1.4   Shall respect and contribute to the legitimate and ethical objectives of the organization.

2. **Objectivity**

    Internal auditors:

    2.1   Shall not participate in any activity or relationship that may impair or be presumed to impair their unbiased assessment. This participation includes those activities or relationships that may be in conflict with the interests of the organization.

    2.2   Shall not accept anything that may impair or be presumed to impair their professional judgment.

    2.3   Shall disclose all material facts known to them that, if not disclosed, may distort the reporting of activities under review.

3. **Confidentiality**

    Internal auditors:

    3.1   Shall be prudent in the use and protection of information acquired in the course of their duties.

    3.2   Shall not use information for any personal gain or in any manner that would be contrary to the law or detrimental to the legitimate and ethical objectives of the organization.

4. **Competency**

    Internal auditors:

    4.1   Shall engage only in those services for which they have the necessary knowledge, skills, and experience.

    4.2   Shall perform internal auditing services in accordance with the *Standards for the Professional Practice of Internal Auditing*.

    4.3   Shall continually improve their proficiency and the effectiveness and quality of their services.

    Adopted by The IIA Board of Directors, June 17, 2000

being unacceptable or discreditable. Violators of this code, whether IIA members, certification holders, or candidates, can be held liable for disciplinary action.

Internal Auditing's Professional Practice Standards

As the key internal audit professional organization, the IIA's Internal Auditing Standards Board develops and issues standards that define the basic practice of internal auditing. These standards, known as the Standards for the Professional Practice of Internal Auditing, are designed to:

- Delineate basic principles that represent the practice of internal auditing as it should be
- Provide a framework for performing and promoting a broad range of value-added internal audit activities
- Establish the basis for the measurement of internal audit performance
- Foster improved processes and operations

As mentioned, the IIA historically had published these standards, with the above title, in a small publication known as the Red Book. With a changing world and roles for internal auditors, these standards have changed over the years. There was a major update in 2001 and, at the time of publication here, an exposure draft is outstanding for additional changes to the standards.

This section discusses the overall framework of the current Standards and upcoming exposure draft changes. For any internal auditor who has attempted to follow and understand the old standards, the current and forthcoming releases are refreshing in their simplification. The older standards were released in an almost impossible level of detail. An example of the new as well as the old standards explains this.

Current Standard: 2500 on Monitoring Progress

One general Attribute and Performance standard states that the chief audit executive (CAE) should establish a system to monitor the disposition of the results of audits. This one general standard has one related assurance activity and one consulting substandard. As will be discussed, the standards recognize that internal auditors will be involved in audit assurance as well as in consulting related activities.

Previous Standard 440 on Following Up

Starting with a general standard similar to the current Section 2500, this older standard had 23 individual sub- or sub-sub clarifying standards following it. There perhaps is good guidance here, but this older standard was far too specific. As an example, Substandard 440.01.12.a states that the

"Director of Internal Audit" should establish the procedures for the time frame in which audit report responses are required. Although certainly a valid guideline, it does little good to tell an auditee that IIA Standards "require" that their audit report responses must be delivered in perhaps seven days if their response is that it will take ten days.

This is just one small example. The older standards were too detailed for effective internal audit management. The current standards provide a much more realistic set of guidance materials to allow internal audit to perform effectively and efficiently.

The past standards were divided into five broad sections, ranging from old Section 100 on overall standards for internal audit independence to Section 500, which contained very detailed standards for managing the internal audit department. The current standards consist of two broad sections, the 1000 Series of Attribute Standards and the 2000 Series of Performance Standards. Under each of these series are detailed Implementation Standards further split between standards covering internal audit assurance activities and others for internal audit consulting work.

Recognizing that internal auditors may be asked to just review internal controls or to sometimes act more as internal consultants, there are multiple sets of Implementation Standards for each of these types of internal audit activity. Implementation Standards established for assurance activities are coded with an "A" following the standard number (e.g., 1130.A1), and those covering consulting activities are noted by a "C" following the standard number (e.g., nnnn.C1). The objective here is not just to reproduce these IIA-published standards but to describe how they have changed or have evolved over recent years. All internal auditors should obtain these standards from the IIA or at least gain access to them and develop an understanding of their contents.

Internal Audit Attribute Standards

The IIA standards address the characteristics of organizations and individuals performing internal audit activities and cover 13 broad areas listed by their standards paragraph numbers:

- *1000—Purpose, Authority, and Responsibility.* The purpose, authority, and responsibility of the internal audit activity should be formally defined in a charter, consistent with the standards, and approved by the board of directors. Separate Implementation Standards here state that internal auditing assurance and consulting services should be defined in the internal audit charter.

- *1100—Independence and Objectivity.* The internal audit activity should be independent, and internal auditors should be objective in performing their work. Subsections discuss the importance of both individual and organizational objectivity as well as the need to disclose any impairment to internal audit independence or objectivity.

- *1200—Proficiency and Due Professional Care.* Engagements should be performed with proficiency and due professional care. There is an important proposed new implementation standard here:

  □ *1210.A3:* Internal auditors should have general knowledge of key information technology risks and controls available technology-based audit techniques. However, not all internal auditors are expected to have the expertise of an internal auditor whose primary responsibility is information technology.

This is an important change to internal auditing standards. Recognizing that there is a need for information systems audit specialists, the standard states that *all* internal auditors *should* have an understanding of information systems risks and controls. In addition, a proposed new sub-standard here on due professional care specifies that internal auditors should consider the "Use of computer-assisted audit tools and techniques." Computer-assisted audit techniques have been part of the tool kits of many but certainly not all internal auditors.[1] A good idea for years, they now have risen to the level of internal audit standard.

- *1300—Quality Assurance and Improvement Program.* The CAE should develop and maintain a quality assurance and improvement program that covers all aspects of the internal audit activity and continuously monitors its effectiveness. The program should be designed to help internal audit add value and improve the organization's operations and provide assurance that the internal audit activity is in conformity with the standards and the Code of Ethics. A proposed change here is the insertion of the sentence, "This program includes periodic internal and external quality assessments and ongoing internal monitoring." This sentence emphasizes the importance of quality assurance internal audit processes.

Internal Audit Performance Standards

These standards describe the nature of internal audit activities and provide quality criteria against which their performance can be measured. There are six Performance Standards, outlined below, along with substandards and Implementation Standards that apply to compliance audits, fraud investigations, and control self-assessment projects.

- *2000—Managing the Internal Audit Activity:* The CAE should manage the internal audit activity effectively to ensure it adds value to the organization. This standard covers six substandards: Planning, Communication and Approval, Resource Management, Policies and Procedures, Coordination, and Reporting to the Board and Senior Management.

These substandards describe such good internal audit management practices as 2040 on Policies and Procedures, which states that the CAE should establish such guides.

Substandard 2060 on Reporting to the Board and Senior Management contains guidance applicable to today's SOA rules: "The CAE should report periodically to the board and senior management on the internal audit activity's purpose, authority, responsibility, and performance relative to its plan. Reporting should also include significant risk exposures and control issues, corporate governance issues, and other matters needed or requested by the board and senior management."

- **2100—*Nature of Work:*** Internal audit activity includes evaluations and contributions to the improvement of risk management, control, and governance systems. One of the proposed changes here adds that work processes should use "a systematic and disciplined approach." Previous IIA Standards did not really address the important area of risk management, which is discussed in Chapter 9.

- **2110—*Risk Management:*** Internal audit should assist the organization by identifying and evaluating significant exposures to risk and contributing to the improvement of risk management and control systems.

  □ **2110.A1:** Internal audit activity should monitor and evaluate the effectiveness of the organization's risk management system.

  □ **2110.A2:** The internal audit activity should evaluate risk exposures relating to the organization's governance, operations, and information systems regarding the COSO standards of internal control.

  □ **2110.C1:** During consulting engagements, internal auditors should address risks consistent with the engagement's objectives and be alert to the existence of other significant risks.

  □ **2110.C2:** Internal auditors should incorporate knowledge of risks gained from consulting engagements into the process of identifying and evaluating significant risk exposures of the organization.

The 2120 and 2130 substandards cover Control and Governance. This proposed standard change on Governance is very appropriate and timely, given the Sarbanes-Oxley Act:

- **2130—*Governance:*** Internal audit activity, consistent with the organization's structure, should contribute to governance processes by proactively assisting management and the board in fulfilling their responsibilities by:

  □ Assessing and promoting strong ethics and values within the organization

  □ Assessing and improving the process by which accountability is ensured

□ Assessing the adequacy of communications about significant residual risks within the organization

□ Helping to improve the board's interaction with management and the external and internal auditors

□ Serving as an educational resource regarding changes and trends in the business and regulatory environment

As discussed in the next section, IIA Standards are *very consistent* with SOA requirements. Internal auditors who follow these proposed new standards should be consistant with SOA principles of good corporate governance.

■ *2200—Engagement Planning:* Internal auditors should develop and record a plan for each engagement. There are standards sections here for Planning Considerations, Engagement Objectives, Engagement Scope, Resource Allocation, and the Work Program. These standards describe the necessary steps to plan and execute an effective internal audit with words such as "The engagement's objectives should address the risks, controls, and governance processes associated with the activities under review," all proper procedures for any effective internal audit.

□ *2201.A1 and 2201.A2:* These two new proposed Engagement Standards for Planning state that when planning an audit that includes clients outside of the organization or where the results will be released to outsiders, internal audit should establish a written understanding with the outsiders regarding the objectives, scope, responsibilities, and expectations. This proposed change would have been a good additional standard when internal auditors were doing extensive work for their external auditors. SOA has changed all of that, but this still is an appropriate clarifying engagement planning standard for other forms of internal audit work.

■ *2300—Performing the Engagement:* Internal auditors should identify, analyze, evaluate, and record sufficient information to achieve the engagement's objectives. A proposed change to this standard adds that internal auditors should "use a disciplined approach in identifying, analyzing, evaluating, and recording" that audit information. Substandards here are 2310 on Identifying Information, 2320 on Analysis and Evaluation, 2330 on Recording Information and, finally, 2340 on Engagement Supervision. The 2300 series of Performance Standards discusses the steps necessary to plan and perform an effective internal audit. This section is a simplification compared to the lengthy old standards.

■ *2400—Communicating Results:* Internal auditors should communicate their engagement results promptly. Several sections here cover the criteria and quality of audit report information. Two substandards here are important:

- ☐ *2421—Errors and Omissions:* If a final audit report contains a significant error or omission, the CAE should communicate that corrected information to all who received the original report. This is a matter that may be missed in some current internal audit functions.

- ☐ *2430—Engagement Disclosure of Noncompliance with the Standards:* If full compliance was not achieved for any of the standards in an audit report, that matter should be disclosed along with the reasons for and the impact of this noncompliance.

With our increasing need for privacy and confidentiality of information, there are several new Engagement Standards in the standards exposure draft:

- ■ *3410.A3:* When releasing results to clients or other parties outside the organization, the communication should include limitations on distribution and use of the results. If the internal audit activity meets the conditions for use, the results should state that "the engagement was conducted in accordance with the Standards for the Professional Practice of Internal Auditing."

- ■ *3440.A2:* When releasing results to parties outside the organization, the CAE should:
  - ☐ Assess the potential risk to the organization
  - ☐ Control dissemination of the results
  - ☐ Obtain the approval of senior management and/or legal counsel prior to release

In many respects, these proposed or exposure draft standards changes represent good internal audit practices. An internal auditor is performing work at the request of one or another management group and ultimately for the audit committee. The results of internal audit work should not be freely and openly distributed to other parties. This leads to the next performance standard on the CAE's responsibility for the findings and recommendations included in audit reports.

- ■ *2500—Monitoring Progress:* The CAE should establish and maintain a system to monitor the disposition of results communicated to management. Assurance and consulting implementation standards here state that the CAE should establish procedures for monitoring and following up on the recommendations in issued audit reports. These good internal audit practices also were reflected in the previous standards.

- *2600—Resolution of Management's Acceptance of Risks:* When the CAE believes some auditee manager has accepted a level of residual risk that may be unacceptable to the overall organization, the matter should be discussed with senior management. If the decision regarding residual risk is not resolved, the CAE and senior management should report this to the board for resolution. These are the yet-to-be-approved words from the exposure draft. They emphasize that the CAE should seek resolution through proper channels of senior management and the audit committee.

The current IIA Standards, along with their outstanding proposed changes, represent a significant improvement over the older and very lengthy standards that were in place through the 1990s. Both the existing standards and the proposed changes conclude with a glossary of terms to better define the roles and responsibilities of internal auditors. Some of these glossary terms will be introduced later, but one is important for the introduction of internal audit new rules, the definition of "independence." The word frequently appears in internal auditing literature, but the exposure draft adds a revised definition that should soon become official:

> *Independence is the freedom from significant conflicts of interest that threaten objectivity. Such threats to objectivity must be managed at the individual auditor level, the engagement level, and the organizational level.*

These are important concepts for today.

IIA Standards in Today's SOA World

Professional standards almost always tend to be reactive. We tend to find a problem or issue in some area, realize that we do not have any rules to cover the problem area, and then eventually establish standards or rules to cover the matter. SOA is an example of this phenomenon. High-level concepts were in place in the old standards regarding external auditor independence and audit committee objectivity. However, the financial scandals of the late 1990s proved that these standards were not working. The result was SOA in mid-2002.

SOA has made internal auditors much more important in today's world of strong corporate governance and effective internal controls. Internal auditors need a strong set of standards to operate effectively under these rules, and the current IIA Standards, along with the draft changes in process, seem to very much satisfy those needs. The older Red Book Standards were so detailed that they tended to overwhelm the internal auditor. While the basic concepts behind internal auditing have really not changed, the current Standards for the Professional Practice of Internal Auditing provide important guidance and direction in the post-SOA world. Today's experienced internal auditor should examine the current IIA Standards and make certain that all internal audit activities are consistent with these standards. The CAE should review the standards with the audit committee to help them to better understand and appreciate internal audit's role in the organization.

COBIT AND INFORMATION TECHNOLOGY GOVERNANCE

The professional and business world is filled with acronyms or initials that have become words themselves. We use the acronym "IBM" not thinking that it stands for the corporation's original name, International Business Machines. While hardly at the same level of recognition, CobiT is an acronym that stands for *c*ontrol *ob*jectives for *i*nformation and related *t*echnology. Because of its emphasis on controls and technology, the first and last letters are usually capitalized. This is another important audit and control framework that can stand by itself or serve as a supplement to both the COSO and IIA Standards. Although its emphasis is more on information technology (IT), all internal auditors should at least have an understanding of CobiT and its use as a tool for reviewing and understanding internal controls with an emphasis on information systems controls.

The CobiT standards and framework are issued and maintained by the Information Systems Audit and Control Association (ISACA) as well as its affiliated research arm, the IT Governance Institute. ISACA is also the professional organization that administers the CISA (Certified Information Systems Auditor) examination and program. ISACA was originally known as the EDP Auditor's Association (EDPAA), a professional group that was founded in 1969 by internal auditors who felt the IIA was not giving sufficient attention to the importance of computer systems and related technology controls. It is almost forgotten today that "EDP" stands for electronic data processing, an almost archaic term. ISACA is still leading the IIA on technology-related issues. As discussed, the IIA has just now released a Proficiency Standard stating that all internal auditors should have a general understanding of information technology risks and controls.

ISACA began to develop IT professional control standards shortly after its formation. Just as the EDPAA evolved into ISACA, its initial standards became an excellent set of control objectives that evolved to CobiT, now in its third edition.[2] CobiT's stated mission is a good introduction to the next sections:

> *The CobiT Mission: To research, develop, publicize and promote an authoritative, up-to-date, international set of generally accepted information technology control objectives for day-to-day use by business managers and auditors.*

CobiT has been enhanced with existing and emerging international technical, professional, regulatory, and industry-specific standards. CobiT is designed to be both pragmatic and responsive to business needs while being independent of the technical IT platforms adopted in an organization. To the first-time reader, however, CobiT's third-edition materials may appear formidable. The guidance material is scattered over multiple volumes of charts, tables, and diagrams. At times terminology can be inconsistent. For example, "processes" are defined as a subset of "IT processes," whatever that is supposed to mean. Nevertheless, CobiT is an excellent tool for understanding and auditing IT systems in general, and the following sections provide an overview to CobiT's third edition.

CobiT Framework

Information is an extremely valuable asset for virtually all organizations, and management has a major responsibility to safeguard these assets, including supporting IT assets, such as automated information systems. A combination of management, users of IT, and auditors all need to understand the information-related processes and the controls that support them. This combination is concerned about the effectiveness and efficiency of their IT resources, the IT processes, and overall business requirements, as shown in Exhibit 6.2. The idea is that each these three groups has somewhat differing concerns regarding the business requirements of the IT systems, the supporting IT resources, and IT processes. Management is interested in the quality, cost, and appropriate delivery of resources. These relate to a component of well-controlled IT resources whose control components are the three COSO internal control elements discussed in Chapter 5. The third leg of this framework consists of the IT processes that require appropriate levels of confidentiality, availability, and integrity controls. Internal controls over IT resources are very much based on the interdependencies of these three components.

In addition to the three interconnected groups, CobiT looks at controls in three IT dimensions: resources, processes, and information criteria. Resources represent all of an organization's IT assets, including its people, application systems, installed technology, IT facilities, and the value of data. Risks and control concerns can be associated with each of these groups—that is, there may be many applications, some of which are more critical than others, or there may be multiple types or versions of data.

The second CobiT dimension, called IT Processes, consists of domains, processes, and activities. Domains are the natural grouping of processes and often match an organizational domain of responsibility. Within an IT organization, CobiT lists an IT function's domains as its planning and organization processes, procedures for acquisition and implementation, delivery and support operations, and monitoring activities. Within the IT organization,

EXHIBIT 6.2   CobiT Framework Principles

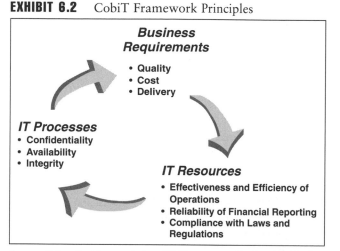

Source: Printed with permission, IT Governance Institute and Information Systems Audit and Control Foundation.

the installed systems development life cycle (SDLC) procedures could be viewed as part of the implementation domain, and quality assurance could be a part of the monitoring domain. The CobiT materials describe each of these in greater detail. For planning and organization, it suggests these specific process steps:

- Define a strategic IT plan.
- Define the information architecture.
- Determine technological direction.
- Define the IT organization and relationships.
- Manage the IT investment.
- Communicate management aims and direction.
- Manage human resources.
- Ensure compliance with external requirements.
- Assess risks.
- Manage projects.
- Manage quality.

Individual processes are the next level down. They are a series of joined activities with natural, logical breaks. Finally, activities are the actions needed to achieve measurable results. Activities have a life cycle, whereas tasks are discreet. We have used what we called the A/P process as an example in Chapter 4 and 5 discussions. The CobiT framework would view A/P as an activity within the purchasing process and within the manufacturing domain.

The third dimension of the CobiT model is what is described as the Information Criteria, consisting of quality, fiduciary, and security. That is, all IT overall systems or processes should be evaluated with consideration given to these three areas. Exhibit 6.2 describes these quality, cost, and delivery management concern factors. For example, management is concerned about such factors as financial integrity—fiduciary criteria—covering all of the IT resources as well as all of the IT processes.

CobiT combines these factors into a three-dimensional model called the CobiT Cube. This model, shown in Exhibit 6.3, is very similar to the COSO model of Exhibits 5.9 and 5.10. Like the COSO approach, controls should be considered in a three-dimensional environment. While controls and procedures may be strong in one respect or dimension, they may need improvements in another. This becomes a very realistic way to evaluate IT controls and processes. CobiT uses this model as the basis to establish control objectives and audit, management, and implementation guidelines, as discussed in the next sections.

Control Objectives under CobiT

The term "control objectives" is familiar to most internal auditors. When reviewing any area of operations, the auditor needs to have some type of objective to determine or guide the audit review. When performing a financial audit, an auditor may establish a control objective that the transactions reviewed must be authorized and correctly classified, and that total balances should tie to the proper general ledger account. These objectives might be

EXHIBIT 6.3   CobiT Cube

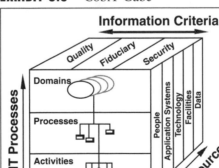

Source: Printed with permission, IT Governance Institute and Information Systems Audit and Control Foundation.

considered the auditor's major control objectives here. An auditor also could be concerned with other control objectives, such as whether the documentation covering the financial system reviewed was current or whether the staff preparing the accounting transactions received proper vendor training on use of the financial system. These are all areas for an internal auditor to review, but priority in a financial review would be given to the more important control objectives, such as determining that the transactions reviewed were authorized.

Whether done formally or informally, establishing control objectives is an important part of the audit process. CobiT starts with the proposition that in order to provide the information that the organization needs to achieve its objectives, IT resources need to be managed by a set of naturally grouped processes. The published CobiT material defines such a set of detailed processes and control objectives to support each process. Earlier we discussed the process of planning and organization as part of the CobiT framework. That process was followed by a list of specific detailed processes starting with "Define a strategic IT plan," a process an auditor would want to see in place for any IT function. A series of subprocesses are defined under this heading as well as a control objective for each. Exhibit 6.4 lists these subprocesses and examples of the detailed control objectives. Not every process and its related control objective will fit for every organization, but the CobiT material provides excellent guidance for establishing effective controls in an IT environment.

The next step is to consider each of these IT processes and to define the business requirements that they satisfy. For example, controls over managing an organization's IT investments will satisfy a business requirement for controls over the disbursement of financial resources. The step is enabled by an operational budget established and approved by appropriate levels in the organization with consideration given to funding alternatives, clear budget ownership, controls over the actual spending, and a cost justification and awareness of total cost of ownership among other factors.

Exhibit 6.5 shows this process flow. The published CobiT materials are filled with these factors to consider for each process. The CobiT framework materials can appear formidable, with 4 identified domains each consisting of 34 defined processes for each. Within each process, there are from 3 to 30 detailed IT control objectives defining controls that should be in place. Although complex, the domains format forms a systematic and logical method for defining and communicating IT control objectives. It leads to the CobiT audit and management guidelines discussed in the following sections.

CobiT Audit Guidelines

Information technology controls reviews have presented challenges to auditors ever since automated systems became major components of business

EXHIBIT 6.4   CobiT Control Objectives Example:
Define a Strategic IT Plan

1.1 IT Should Be Part of the Organization's Long- and Short-Range Plan

Supporting Control Objective: Senior management is responsible for developing and implementing long- and short-range plans that fulfill the organization's mission and goals. In this respect, senior management should ensure that IT issues as well as opportunities are adequately assessed and reflected in the organization's long- and short-range plans. IT long- and short-range plans should be developed to help ensure that the use of IT is aligned with the mission and business strategies of the organization.

1.2 IT Long-Range Plan Process

Supporting Control Objective: IT management and business process owners are responsible for regularly developing IT long-range plans supporting the achievement of the organization's overall missions and goals. The planning approach should include mechanisms to solicit input from relevant internal and external stakeholders impacted by the IT strategic plans. Accordingly, management should implement a long-range planning process, adopt a structured approach, and set up a standard plan structure.

1.3 IT Long-Range Planning—Approach and Structure

Supporting Control Objective: (Published as part of CobiT materials.)

1.4 IT Long-Range Plan Changes

Supporting Control Objective: (Published as part of CobiT materials.)

1.5 Short-Range Planning for the IT Function

Supporting Control Objective: (Published as part of CobiT materials.)

1.6 Communication of IT Plans

Supporting Control Objective: (Published as part of CobiT materials.)

1.7 Monitoring and Evaluating IT Plans

Supporting Control Objective: (Published as part of CobiT materials.)

1.8 Assessment of Existing Systems

Supporting Control Objective: (Published as part of CobiT materials.)

Note: This is an example of CobiT's definition of processes and subprocesses. The CobiT guidance material includes a detailed supporting control objective for each.

Source: Printed with permission, IT Governance Institute and Information Systems Audit and Control Foundation.

EXHIBIT 6.5   CobiT Process to Control Practices Linkages

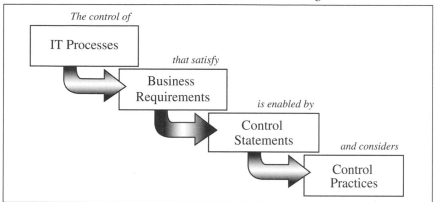

The control of

IT Processes

that satisfy

Business Requirements

is enabled by

Control Statements

and considers

Control Practices

Source: Printed with permission, IT Governance Institute and Information Systems Audit and Control Foundation.

processes. CobiT tries to improve this IT audit process with a set of generic and high-level Audit Guidelines to help with reviews of processes against IT control objectives. The CobiT audit process is built on several generic guidelines that can be used for all processes as well as specific audit procedures oriented to each of the defined CobiT processes.

The CobiT generic guidelines are just that, *guidelines,* to identify tasks to be performed in assessing control objective. There are also process-specific guidelines with suggested audit steps to provide assurances that a control is in place and working. Generic audit guidelines cover four areas:

1. *Obtaining an Understanding.* This guideline describes the audit steps to be performed to document activities underlying the control objectives and to identify the control procedures in place.

2. *Evaluating the Controls.* The guideline outlines audit steps for assessing the effectiveness of control measures in place and the degree to which the control objectives are achieved. This guidance is to help an auditor decide what, whether and how to test.

3. *Assessing Compliance.* A guideline stating that audit steps should be performed to ensure that the control measures established are working as prescribed, consistently and continuously, and to conclude on the appropriateness of the control environment.

4. *Substantiating the Risk.* This guideline outlines steps to be performed to substantiate the risk of a control objective not being met, including using analytical techniques and/or consulting alternative sources. The objective here is to support the opinion and to "shock" management

into action (CobiT's words). Auditors have to be creative in finding and presenting often sensitive and confidential information.

CobiT suggests that each of these four generic guidelines should be used for *every process* reviewed. Each also contains guidance for obtaining direct or indirect evidence for selected items/periods, suggestions for limited reviews of the adequacy of the process deliverables, and general guidance on the level of substantive testing and additional work needed to provide assurance that the IT process is adequate.

CobiT also includes specific audit procedures for each of the detailed processes. These are very generic documents with guidance along the lines of "Consider whether . . . " followed by lists of items specific to that process area. The general structure of these detailed processes follows four steps:

1. Items or areas to consider when evaluating controls

2. Items to examine or test to assess compliance to control procedures

3. Steps to perform to substantiate the risk of control objectives not being met

4. The identification of such matters as IT failures to meet the organization's missions and goals, IT failures to meet cost and time guidelines, or missed business or IT opportunities

These materials provide excellent guidance for assessing controls over IT processes. There is sufficient material to allow any internal auditor and an IT audit specialist in particular to review and assess controls for all aspects of an organization. Although CobiT is heavily oriented to IT, these same procedures can be used as a basis for internal control reviews in many other areas.

CobiT, IIA Professional Standards, and SOA

CobiT fits in an interesting position when compared to the IIA Standards discussed earlier in this chapter and with SOA with its reliance, at present, on the COSO framework. IIA Standards have been part of the practice of internal auditing for many years and have changed recently to become more workable and to better emphasize corporate governance issues. The IIA Standards, however, historically have been deficient in covering much more than minimal IT audit standards. CobiT, which has come from a different direction, provides a framework that is much more oriented to IT issues, important in today's organization.

The CobiT framework is documented in a very general manner with many review steps that the auditor should "consider." That is, auditors using CobiT to perform a review are not operating in violation of good audit procedures if they do not follow some suggested CobiT procedure. Internal auditors should use professional judgment to consider a suggested CobiT step and, if they bypass one, should document why they did not perform the step. The IIA Standards are different. Rather than providing a long list of things that auditors should consider, IIA Standards cover a much more limited set of audit activities and are filled with words stating that auditors "should" follow some procedure. There is a big difference between "should" do something and should "consider" doing something. CobiT covers auditing procedures while the IIA Standards cover more specific audit professional practices. There is a lot less flexibility for internal auditors when the standard says "should."

Can an internal audit function use CobiT as its professional standards in place of the IIA Standards? Probably not. The IIA Standards cover professional performance issues—not covered in CobiT—such as objectivity, independence, and due professional care. However, an organization highly dependent on IT processes would have trouble performing effective and efficient review of its IT resources without CobiT. An organization would do well to adopt the CobiT model for audits of its information systems resources.

SOA is the third element to consider here. While the Public Corporation Accounting Oversight Board (PCAOB) has not defined an internal control audit framework as yet, it will almost certainly mandate the COSO framework. As we have discussed, the multidimensional COSO internal control model is very similar to the CobiT Cube shown in Exhibit 6.3. Even if an internal audit organization has not fully embraced the COSO framework yet, it would do well to adopt CobiT as audit guidance for its IT processes and procedures. CobiT allows an internal auditor to think in the same multidimensional control environment as defined in COSO.

As mentioned, CobiT still has some rough edges. Terminology problems include processes being defined as part of processes, and CobiT Management Guidance materials do not seem to blend that well with the rest of the CobiT framework. All in all, however, CobiT represents an excellent set of audit materials to consider for auditing in an IT environment.

ASQ AUDIT STANDARDS: A DIFFERENT APPROACH

Although we often think of only the CPA-type external or IIA internal as auditors, many other professionals also call themselves auditors. Examples include federal government contract auditors or others who audit healthcare standards. These auditors typically do not work in the corporations where external or internal auditors work, and the internal audit professional typically has little contact with them. Another group of auditors that typically works within the organization are quality auditors. They make up an internal audit-like professional group that has its own audit standards and professional certifications. Quality auditors have responsibilities to review a wide range of processes relating to standards compliance, work simplification, and quality in the organization. Quality auditors historically have operated "on the shop floor" and often have had little contact with the IIA-type internal auditors in their organization.

Although separate from the IIA type of internal auditor on which this book is focused, today's classic quality auditor is moving closer to the IIA internal auditor. More accurately, objectives and approaches of both of these types of auditors are changing to bring them closer together. The IIA-oriented internal auditor should gain a better understanding of the activities of quality auditors and how their work fits in the overall environment of corporate controls and governance.

Quality Auditor Standards and Practices

We use the term "quality auditor" to describe this audit professional, even though many in this group just call themselves internal auditors. Quality auditors may belong to the IIA, but they have their own professional organization, the Quality Audit Division (QAD) of the American Society for Quality (ASQ). The ASQ is the leading proponent of the quality movement in the United States with a wide range of publications, professional certifications, and separate divisions covering industries such as aerospace or pharmaceuticals as well as professional practices. ASQ is very involved with the International Standards Organization (ISO) worldwide quality standards, and its QAD provides audit guidance for compliance reviews of the ISO standards discussed in Chapter 10.

QAD's mission is "[t]o support auditors and other stakeholders by defining and promoting auditing as a management tool to achieve continuous improvement, effective communication, and increased customer satisfaction." Its use of the word "auditor" with no qualifications often causes some confusion. Although members of QAD historically called themselves quality auditors, today they usually call themselves just auditors. In addition, there are both internal and external quality auditors. While a quality auditor may be a member of the IIA in addition to the ASQ, the external quality auditor has no relationship with the American Institute of Certified Public Accountants (AICPA) and its certified public accountant (CPA) designation. Exhibit 6.6 shows these different classifications or functions of quality auditors.

As shown in the exhibit, first-party audits are performed by an internal quality auditor within the organization to measure its strengths and weaknesses against its own procedures or standards as well as any external standards that the organization has adopted. Besides ISO standards, numerous industry or specialty standards apply as well, such as the automotive industry's quality-related standards. There may be a separate quality audit function

EXHIBIT 6.6   Classifications of Quality Auditors

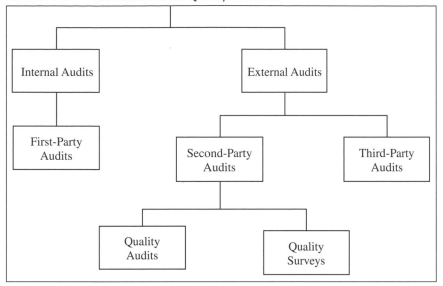

within the organization, or these audits may be performed by regular employees who have appropriate training and certification.

An outside team performs a second-party audit. Frequently, in the quality audit world, a second-party audit takes place when an organization sends its quality auditors out to a supplier or vendor to perform the quality audit of their performance against a contract. These types of reviews often are structured as quality survey reviews or quality audits/assessments. In general, a quality survey is performed prior to the award of a contract to a prospective supplier to ensure that the proper capabilities and quality systems are in place. The quality audit/assessment is a comprehensive evaluation that analyzes such things as the facilities, resources, technical capabilities, and other factors. Second-party external audits are not at all like financial statement external audits. They are used when an organization wants to review the quality practices or other operations at a supplier. For example, if an organization contracts with some supplier to build a product, that contract may contain the right for the contracting organization to audit those production facilities. Suppliers that want repeat business with the organization sending the auditors may have little choice as to whether they want to be audited. Second-party quality audits may be performed by the customer requesting the audit or through outside contracted consulting services.

Finally, external participants other than the customer may perform third-party external quality audits on a supplier. Such audits are performed by a recognized or registered authority to allow the supplier to attest that it meets some audited and attested standard. As an example, a government unit may perform mandatory audits on regulated industries, such as nuclear power facilities. The supplier being audited in a mandated audit situation has no real opportunity to select the audit or auditing organization.

The ASQ currently has 11 separate certification programs covering various industry or specialty areas. One of these is the CQA (certified quality auditor) certification. Within the CQA are specialty designations for hazard analysis or biomedical auditing. These certifications require auditors to have designated levels of work experience and to pass an examination.

ASQ quality auditors are involved in similar professional activities and standards as can be found with IIA internal auditors, particularly those with the CIA certification. In addition to specialized professional publications, the ASQ has a series of national meetings and conferences for ASQ quality auditors.

Role of the Quality Auditor

Many of various standards and guidance materials covering quality auditing are very similar to the tools and techniques of the IIA internal auditor. Quality auditors follow the same general procedures as "regular" internal auditors in their procedures for developing audit programs, reporting findings, and the like. Quality auditors often are not involved with the financial issues that come with reviews of financial statement integrity. Quality audit procedures often follow published standards, such as ISO 9000 discussed in Chapter 10, and such audits often tend to be more quantitative and mathematical than those of typical internal auditors. The work of quality auditors often is closely aligned with the classic tools used by quality assurance manufacturing production specialists.

An example might help explain some quality auditor tools and techniques. Exhibit 6.7 shows a Pareto chart, a common diagram in quality-related groups. The idea here is to rank types of errors or problems on the vertical axis with the most severe problems listed first. In this example, there were 62 cases of defect 1 during the period reviewed. Similarly, there were 58 cases of defect 2 with increasingly fewer cases for the other defects. The numbers of cumulative defects are plotted on the vertical axis. The line goes from 62 to (62 + 58 = 120) for the second point and continues. The idea behind a Pareto chart is to see which defects require the most attention. The less than 10 instances of defect 6 should require less management attention.

Although quality auditors have used tools such as Pareto charts to review defects and make recommendations over the years, the worldwide movement to ISO 9000 quality standards has expanded the role of quality auditors in recent years. The ISO 9000 family of quality management standards was adopted in 1987, and sector-specific derivatives followed in the automotive,

EXHIBIT 6.7   Pareto Chart Example

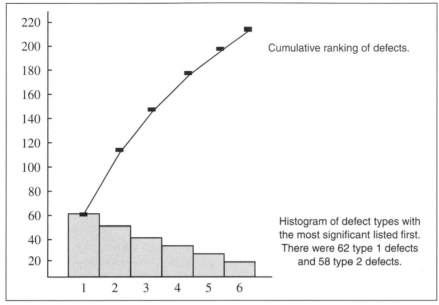

Cumulative ranking of defects.

Histogram of defect types with
the most significant listed first.
There were 62 type 1 defects
and 58 type 2 defects.

aviation, and telecommunications industries. Thousands of organizations have become registered or certified under these standards. Chapter 10 discusses ISO standards and their impact on all internal auditors. Organizations traditionally apply ISO quality standards in areas such as manufacturing, research, and distribution logistics. Over time, quality auditors became the owners of these ISO 9000 assessments.

ISO 9000 standards require more than just having effective controls in place at the time of an audit. They demand examples of continual improvement, with the quality auditor given the responsibility to assess whether such improvement programs are in place. Doing this can be a challenge. A system or process *must be* changed to improve it. This is just not a matter of working harder or being more careful. If there is no change in some aspect of a system or process, the outcomes always will be the same.

Quality auditors often are involved with tests for process or efficiency improvements. To accomplish this, the data must be analyzed for trends and identification of weaknesses. The quality auditor then compares results to goals and objectives and analyzes process data to identify risks, inefficiencies, opportunities for improvement, and negative trends. The results may be recommendations for changes in procedures or in other elements of the process, such as the acceptance criteria or method of monitoring. Recommended changes in equipment or technology also may be among the quality auditor's recommendations for continual improvement. In many respects, quality auditors often recommend more significant changes to the improvement cycle than many IIA internal auditors do.

Quality Auditors and the IIA Internal Auditor

Although the two professional groups have had little in common in the past, there is an evolving level of integration of IIA internal auditing with ASQ quality auditing. The term "quality auditing" is being replaced by just "auditing" in ASQ publications and in some ISO standards. The terminology in both IIA and ISO standards is becoming increasingly consistent with revisions to each over recent years. The ISO has defined an audit as a "systematic, independent and documented process for obtaining audit evidence and evaluating it objectively to determine the extent to which audit criteria are fulfilled."[3] The IIA's 1999 revised definition of internal auditing, discussed earlier, contains some quality-related words, such as assurance, adding value, risk management, systematic, disciplined, control, and process orientation. There appears to be some integration of quality auditing and internal auditing terminology into a generic assessment and business process improvement model.

There will probably be a growing convergence of internal auditing and quality auditing over the coming years. An increasing number of organizations worldwide are seeking ISO registrations, and ISO 9000 standards are becoming more process oriented, customer focused, and business driven. As an example, the AICPA has recently become ISO certified. An ISO 9000–registered company must demonstrate quality system effectiveness.

In some organizations today, the CAE is involved with the organization's quality audit function on at least a courtesy level. In the future, internal audit functions should become more acquainted with their quality audit counterparts and should give consideration to sharing resources. Although their historical roots are different, both audit functions should become involved with value-added audit functions in the modern organization.

NOTES

1. See Robert R. Moeller, *Computer Audit, Control, and Security* (New York: John Wiley & Sons, 1989). Although the 1989 current edition is out of print, a new edition is in preparation.
2. *CobiT—Governance, Control and Audit for Information and Related Technology*, 3rd ed. (Rolling Meadows, IL: IT Governance Institute, 2000).
3. *ISO CD2/ISO 19011* (Milwaukee: ASQ Quality Press, 2000).

CHAPTER 7

Disaster Recovery and Continuity Planning after 9/11

Organizations today are totally dependent on their computer systems and supporting information technology (IT) personnel, communication networks, files, and programs. With today's larger-scale integrated enterprise resource planning (ERP) systems, backup and recovery has become a complex process. Going beyond just keeping sets of backup files for individual applications, IT professionals and certainly auditors raised questions in the past of what would happen to an organization if it lost its IT resources. Starting in the 1980s, IT disaster recovery planning and backup processing strategies included arrangements with remote disaster recovery data processing facilities. Key backup files and programs were stored at off-site locations, with plans for the IT staff to shift to that alternate facility in the event of a disaster event. Professionals usually thought of information systems disasters in terms of fires, floods, or bad weather. In those early mainframe systems days, organizations took what today sounds like rather bizarre actions to develop their IT disaster recovery plans. These included signing reciprocal agreements with nearby sites with similar IT resources so that each could move to that other location in the event of an emergency at either. Others established raised-floor vacant-space facilities with an agreement with their mainframe hardware providers to move in an emergency replacement system quickly. Although hardware vendors still will agree to emergency replacements, computer hardware today is usually available off-the-shelf. Reciprocal agreements sounded good in theory, but never really worked beyond low-level, almost humanitarian help. That nearby reciprocal agreement site might be out of service for the same weather-related disaster or probably would not be interested in someone else running its systems in off-shift time periods. As a final impediment, corporate legal consul would have a dozen reasons to say no.

Those disaster recovery plans of the 1980s and early 1990s were not that sound, and a series of specialized disaster recovery vendors arose with fully equipped computer systems sites operating at idle, or "hot." Organizations contracted to use those sites in the event of a disaster at their own IT operations, and both ran periodic tests there and kept key backup files there. These "hot site" vendors provided the primary IT backup solution for many organizations moving into the twenty-first century.

September 11, 2001—frequently referred to as 9/11—changed everything. Several terrorist-led airliners crashed into the two 100-plus stories New York World Trade Center towers, among other targets, causing those buildings to collapse. In addition to a massive loss of life and property, these events triggered activation of a series of organization IT disaster recovery plans. The World Trade Center was populated with a large number of IT-based financial institutions, most with what were thought to be effective IT disaster recovery plans in place. Later most of those disaster recovery plans were found to be wanting. In the immediate aftermath of 9/11, telephone lines were clogged, bridges to get out of Manhattan were closed, and airlines were shut down. Many of the IT disaster recovery plans just did not work. Only a few impacted firms had effective disaster recovery plans.

This chapter discusses building an effective IT continuity and disaster recovery plan in the wake of what we learned after the 9/11 disaster. The focus today is on business recovery rather than just the recovery of IT systems and operations. Disaster recovery or business continuity is an important aspect of the internal control environment today, and information systems continuity programs are increasingly becoming part of U.S. federal regulations and requirements. Internal audit should play a key role in building, testing and evaluating such continuity plans. These newer approaches to IT continuity planning are among the "new rules" impacting internal auditors.

BUSINESS CONTINUITY PLANNING AND THE NEW LANGUAGE OF RECOVERY PLANNING

An organization today faces numerous risks around its IT assets. Typically there is not one major or central computer facility for handling major automated applications, but a range of desktop devices including servers and other systems connected through complex communications and storage management networks. Organizations do not have all of their information systems resources tied around one or several central data centers, and management is more interested in keeping its information systems up and running rather than worrying about the risk of losing a central computer systems facility. The language and approaches to IT disaster recovery planning have changed. Although we certainly cannot deny that the events of 9/11 represented a major disaster, professionals today think in terms of a business continuity plan (BCP), which encompasses the processes necessary to restore business operations. The user of an online order processing system cares less about whether the server is operating than whether a customer order, often submitted through an Internet site, can be processed properly and efficiently. Even though IT resources should be restored and operating as quickly and efficiently as possible, the key objective is to support and restore the business processes.

Emergency Response Planning

Older IT disaster recovery plans often were published in thick books and located on the desks of key managers. The idea was that in the event of an emergency event, people would pull out their disaster recovery manuals and look up such data as the designated backup site telephone number to report the emergency or to secure instructions for other emergency procedures. These disaster recovery books worked in theory, assuming the manuals were kept up to date and the nature of the crisis event gave people time to review the plan first and then react. Yet actual crises offer little time to dig out and read the disaster recovery manual. When the building is on fire, human nature says that one should get out as soon as possible and not spend time studying the published evacuation instructions. Organizations need to think through these situations in advance. They need an emergency response plan.

Two types of emergency incidents are significant. The first is the fire in the building type of emergency with an emergency response plan that includes posted fire exits and frequent fire drills. This type of emergency response plan covers all operations, not just information systems. The second type of emergency response plan covers specific individual incidents that must be corrected at once followed by an investigation and a plan of corrective action to prevent further incidents. These matters are called emergency *incidents,* and they include such matters as security breaches or the theft of hardware or software. A good emergency incident response plan should be addressed quickly to minimize the possibility of further breaches. An emergency incident response plan can be separated into four sections:

1. *Immediate Response Activities.* Whether a security breach, theft of assets, or physical intrusion, resources should be in place to take immediate corrective action.

2. *Incident Investigation.* All reported matters should be investigated fully to determine the situation that caused the emergency and possible future corrective actions going forward.

3. *Correction or Restoration.* Resources should be available to correct or restore things as necessary. Since emergency incidents can cover a wide variety of areas, the resources may include information systems security specialists, building security managers, or others.

4. *Emergency Incident Reporting.* The entire emergency incident and actions taken subsequently should be documented along with an analysis of lessons learned and any further plans for corrective actions.

Emergency incident responses must be decisive and executed quickly. We initially put water on a fire, not develop strategies to prevent it from burning further. Quick actions are needed with little room for error in most cases. By staging practice emergencies similar to fire drills and measuring response times, a methodology should be developed that fosters speed and accuracy. Reacting quickly may minimize the impact of resource unavailability and the potential damage caused by any future systems or facility compromises. We have mentioned emergency incidents to highlight that an organization faces many other threats beyond the 9/11 type of emergency or overall failure of its computer systems resources. Although our focus is more on major contingency planning issues, an organization needs to have mechanisms in place to respond to every level of unexpected emergency event.

Business Continuity Planning

A business continuity plan should help an organization recover from major service disruptions, whether a fire type of emergency, a computer equipment or network equipment failure, or any other form of major disruption. The goal of a BCP is to reduce the impact of a disaster or extended service interruption to an acceptable level and to bring business operations back. A BCP represents a change in emphasis from what IT professionals formerly called a disaster recovery plan. That older emphasis was to get data processing operations working; the BCP emphasizes overall needs of the business unit.

This section outlines some of the steps necessary to build such a BCP. Although information systems organizations long have had disaster recovery plans in place, those older approaches often were not effective in getting key business processes operating again. Just as there are key separate steps necessary for planning and for conducting an internal audit, there are some key steps necessary for an effective BCP. Several professional organizations, such as the U.S.-based Disaster Recovery Institute[1] and the London, England-based Business Continuity Institute, have adopted a frequently published and well-recognized set of 10 BCP-recommended professional practices, as outlined in Exhibit 7.1. These have become *the* universally accepted standards in the industry for the key components of a BCP. The next sections discuss these steps in greater detail. An effective BCP is critical for an organization, and management is responsible for the survivability and sustainability of total operations to serve customers and service recipients. Companies and government units are increasingly required by law to develop these continuity and contingency plans.

EXHIBIT 7.1   Disaster Recovery Business Continuity Planning
Professional Practices

The following recommended professional practices or steps were initially
developed by the Disaster Recovery Institute:

1. *Project Initiation and Management.* BCP processes should be managed
   through formal project management processes and within agreed time
   and budget limits.

2. *Risk Evaluation and Control.* A formal BCP risk evaluation process
   should be used to determine events that can adversely affect the organization and its facilities with disruptions as well as major disasters, the
   damage such events can cause, and the controls needed to prevent or
   minimize the effects of potential loss. This should include a cost-benefit
   analysis to justify investments in controls to mitigate these risks.

3. *Business Impact Analysis.* Managers should understand the overall impacts resulting from disruptions and disaster events that can affect the
   organization as well as techniques that can be used to quantify and qualify them. This requires identifying critical functions, their recovery priorities, and interdependencies such that recovery time objectives can
   be set.

4. *Developing Business Continuity Strategies.* One single BCP is not applicable for all circumstances, and management should develop an
   appropriate strategy to determine and guide the selection of alternative
   business recovery operating strategies for recovery of business and information resources within the recovery time objective, while maintaining
   the organization's critical functions.

5. *Emergency Response and Operations.* Emergency procedures should be
   in place to respond to and stabilize the situation following an incident
   or event, including establishing and managing an Emergency Operations
   Center to be used as a command center during the emergency.

6. *Developing and Implementing Business Continuity Plans.* The BCP
   should be developed, documented and implemented using a formal, best
   practices based process that provides recovery within established recovery time objectives.

7. *Awareness and Training Programs.* Processes should be in place to make
   all appropriate members of the organization aware of the appropriate
   BCP procedures in place with training programs in place on their usage.

8. *Maintaining and Exercising Business Continuity Plans.* The BCP and its
   key elements should be kept up to date with periodic testing of critical
   plan elements. Processes should be implemented to maintain and update
   the BCP in accordance with the organization's strategic direction.

9. *Public Relations and Crisis Coordination.* Processes should be in place
   to communicate all events surrounding a contingency event and to

(continues)

EXHIBIT 7.1   Disaster Recovery Business Continuity Planning Professional Practices *(Continued)*

> communicate with and, as appropriate, provide trauma counseling for employees and their families, key customers, critical suppliers, owners/stockholders, and corporate management during crisis. All stakeholders should kept informed on an as-needed basis.
>
> 10. ***Coordination with Public Authorities.*** Processes should be in place for coordinating continuity and restoration activities with local authorities while ensuring compliance with applicable statutes or regulations.

CONTINUITY PLANNING AND SERVICE-LEVEL AGREEMENTS

Information technology cannot just arbitrarily establish BCP guidelines for various application areas and stop there. The IT organization and its management must have a strong buy-in from the users and application owners including joint assurances of expectations and service delivery. If a senior executive in a specific user department feels that some business process *always* must be operational with a full backup capability for all significant transactions, the department should negotiate with IT to provide that level of continuity service and must recognize the necessary costs of additional hardware and software. In the past days of application backups based on downloaded tape copies periodically shipped to a remote location, anything close to an immediate backup was only a theoretical concept. A transaction had to be written first in the main system and its database and then copied to a backup facility. There was always a delay, ranging from weekly or daily backup files to almost immediate real-time systems approaches. Newer storage management approaches today, called mirroring, provide immediate backups. They are very effective but certainly more expensive.

While the details of the BCP must be established, key user departments should negotiate their recovery expectations through formal service-level agreements (SLAs). An SLA is a contract between the business process owner and the provider of IT services for specified service objectives. SLAs are part of an evolving set of IT service delivery best practices and are fundamental to business continuity activities. SLAs define minimum levels of expected computer systems backup and recovery. They are a contract between IT and key user areas to support both normal, day-to-day operations and the actions to be taken in the event of a serious service disruption. SLAs describe expected and promised levels of continuity services and are basic building blocks for establishing an effective BCP.

SLAs are encountered most frequently when a contract is made for the services of an outside provider. For example, a computer services vendor may agree to handle the processing of some application at a rate of x cents per transaction and also will agree to process these transactions within a specified turnaround time. The organization pays for these services based on the transaction rate and recognizes adjustments if expected turnaround time standards are missed. For a BCP-related SLA, the benefiting user business function will specify its backup needs and will accept a periodic budget charge for those IT and related services. If IT misses its promised SLA targets, a budget credit would be issued. Even though these SLA debit and credit amounts are often based on internal "funny money," they can become an important measure of management performance.

Business recovery SLAs frequently are structured to cover most if not all departments or functions in the organization. As part of these IT charges, functions that have negotiated such a SLA also are receiving an IT commitment or promise to provide an agreed-on level of continuity services. When a business area has specific needs, special or unique SLAs should be created.

NEW TECHNOLOGIES: CRITICAL DATA MIRRORING TECHNIQUES

Systems backup techniques to download copies of critical transactions to tapes or disk files are not effective in today's world of constant streams of real-time transactions. Full file or database backups taken every week, every day, or even every hour along with captured streams of interim transactions also are not effective. When a system shuts down, it is necessary to go back to the most recent database backup as a benchmark or starting point and then reprocess all of the transactions that had been submitted after the last backup to the present. However, when the business process is very active — such as for high-volume trading or ordering — it is almost impossible to get caught up reprocessing past transactions without shutting down the actual application. An airline ticketing and scheduling system is an example. In order for the enterprise to survive, the system must be operational virtually at all times around the clock and at a high-level availability rate. For an organization to state that it is operating and available at 99.99 percent, it only can be out of operation less than one hour per year.

Legal and regulatory mandates for business continuity often make high availability a top priority, and an organization needs to move and copy its data in order to rapidly recover critical business operations in the event of data loss, data corruption, or disaster. Fortunately, there have been many technology advancements over recent years that allow rapid and frequent backups. A technology known as RAID (Rapid Array of Independent Disks) often is used where data is copied simultaneously to multiple locations on one or more disk files to create redundancy. Exhibit 7.2 shows this concept in a configuration called RAID 1. Numerous variations of the technology exist, with names of RAID 0, 1, 2, and more. Our objective is not to provide a detailed technical description here but to describe this general concept known as mirroring.

RAID technology provides 100 percent redundancy of the application data such that there will be no need to rebuild the disk files structure in the event of a disk failure. We encounter RAID at a very basic level on a desktop computer using Microsoft's XP operating system where, in the event of a power failure or the like, a restored version of disk files is retained. While of no help in a total disk "crash," this technology provides a fairly efficient level of backup and recovery for desktop computer systems.

While RAID technology allows the data center to have multiple disks side by side to provide recovery from any crash-type failures, the technique is particularly valuable when transaction data is mirrored to a remote facility, connected through a wide area network (WAN). The solution to managing this multiple-disk, multiple-locations backup and recovery is really a storage vendor hardware and software solution. Although several vendors have efficient storage management products on the market, we are highlighting one here as an example, EMC Corporation's SRDF solution.[2] The letter S in the SRDF name stands for EMC's Symmetrix high-speed multiple disk storage device, a component the size of a kitchen refrigerator that holds thousands of individual linked disk drives with a capacity of many terabytes of storage data. This mirroring storage device allows the transfer of data between multiple Symmetrix storage management systems at very high speed using public or private networks. Mirroring is just what the name implies. If we set two glass mirrors on the table in front of us at 45-degree angles, we will see two images of ourselves at once. Mirroring data achieve

EXHIBIT 7.2   RAID I: Mirroring and Duplexing

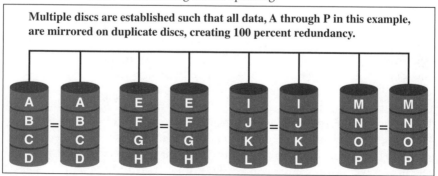

Multiple discs are established such that all data, A through P in this example, are mirrored on duplicate discs, creating 100 percent redundancy.

the same results. Pressing the enter key for a computer transaction immediately writes it to two more mirrored storage devices.

Exhibit 7.3 shows this type of configuration. A computer system uses a
Symmetrix DMX storage device for regular processing with all transactions
that are recorded on the prime storage device also mirrored over high-speed
lines to another Symmetrix storage system. The exhibit shows two redun-
dant systems. This mirrored operation creates multiple copies of the same
data configurations, making it easy to restore services in the event of an
emergency. We have highlighted this product because it distinguished itself
during the 9/11 World Trade Center terrorist attacks. It was reported to have
worked better than its competitors, and essentially lost no data on computer
systems when the two buildings were destroyed. Business picked up on operations at remote sites as soon as employees were able to get to those sites.

ESTABLISHING EFFECTIVE CONTINGENCY POLICIES: WHAT ARE WE PROTECTING?

Effective policies should underpin an organization's whole approach to contingency and disaster recovery and determine the fundamental practices and
culture throughout the organization. A BCP should be linked closely with

EXHIBIT 7.3   EMC SRDF Data Mirroring Example

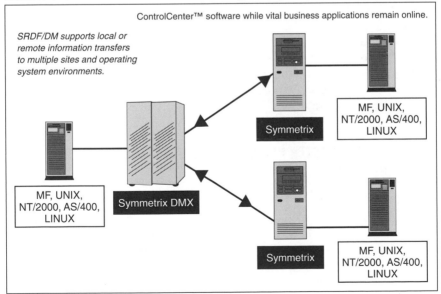

Source: Copyright 2000 EMC Corporation, Hopkinton, Massachusetts. Reprinted with
permission.

information security IT policies, as both address the basic defense requirements to ensure the stability and continuity of the organization. It is essential that BCP policies exist, are up to date, are comprehensive in their coverage, and are understood by all interested parties. In the old days of centralized computer systems and primarily batch processing, it was fairly easy to delineate IT contingency and recovery responsibilities. User transactions were delivered to input/output (I/O) desks, and IT handled all required tasks including building controls in the systems, backing up files, and initiating recovery efforts in the event of some contingency event. Today the world has very much changed. Many "dotted line" functions or groups exist in today's organization, and stakeholders often are not sure who is responsible for contingency procedures. Effective contingency policies are needed to define these relationships and responsibilities.

One level of policy may be simply to state that *the owners* of an application are responsible for making arrangements for backups and contingency processing. That said, arrangements are made through a formal SLA that outlines IT's contingency processing capabilities and the relative costs for each option. If an application owner wants full transaction mirroring, as discussed above, that owner will have to absorb the cost of this value-added service. That is, if the sales department wants one-hour backup recovery for its sales transactions, IT should agree to provide that level of service at a designated cost, and sales would charge this back to other benefiting users, such as marketing or the controller's function. This sounds easy but can become a complex accounting issue coupled with much negotiation. SLA agreements become the basis for establishing a contingency planning policy.

In our era of strong ethical standards and SOA requirements, these SLAs should be shared with key levels of management and the board to outline the overall plans for reacting to a contingency event. All parties should be aware of these arrangements as well as the plans to build an effective business contingency plan.

BUILDING THE DISASTER PLANNING BUSINESS CONTINUITY PLAN

As mentioned, BCPs, or what were once called disaster recovery plans, often were published in thick notebooks that were out of date almost as soon as they were distributed. In addition, they focused on recovering IT operations from a disaster event but not on recovering the business and its key operations. Many organizations have established some form of disaster recovery plan for good business and internal control reasons, and government regulations now require disaster recovery plans in an increasing number of areas.

However, established IT disaster recovery plans following the old rules may not be effective as a BCP.

This section outlines steps to build an effective BCP for an organization. Internal auditors can play a key role in this process with their knowledge of business systems, IT, and the internal control requirements. Although the words "disaster recovery" or "BCP" are not found specifically in SOA legislation, the astute board audit committee or chief financial officer (CFO) should realize that an organization must have an effective BCP in place and working in order to attest that internal controls are effective as required in Section 404 of SOA.

Existing BCPs for part of or all business activities should be reviewed to determine whether those plans are current and can effectively meet projected *business* contingency needs. All plans should have a detailed section on incident and risk assessment and a strategy for recovery of all significant business processes including IT applications, communications resources, and other assets. The BCPs should contain detailed instructions for the business recovery process, including the overall project organization and both notification and reporting procedures.

If no BCP exists or if the current version is very much in need of help, a project should be launched to create a new BCP with a designated project manager appointed to lead the effort. This individual should have good leadership qualities, an understanding of business processes, skills with IT information security management, and strong project management capabilities. An ideal candidate might have Project Manager Professional (PMP) credentials.[3] For some organizations, the information security officer may be an ideal candidate for this role. The objectives and deliverables for such a BCP project need to be clearly defined to enable the overall BCP project team to ensure that their work is consistent with original project expectations.

A BCP project's principle objective should be for the development and testing of a well-structured and coherent plan that will enable the organization to recover normal business operations as quickly and effectively as possible from any unforeseen disaster or emergency which interrupts normal IT services. Subobjectives should ensure that all employees fully understand their duties in implementing the BCP, that information security policies are adhered to within all planned activities, and that the proposed contingency arrangements are cost effective. The BCP deliverables should consist of:

- Business risk and impact analysis
- Documented activities to prepare the organization for various emergencies
- Detailed activities for initially responding to a disaster event

- Procedures for managing business recovery processes, including testing plans
- Plans for BCP training at multiple levels in the organization
- Procedures for keeping the BCP up to date

Each of these BCP major components is discussed in the following sections. A major objective here is to allow the organization to restore business operations as quickly and effectively as possible in light of a disaster event. This is an activity that requires active participation on many levels, and one where internal audit can take a major role in helping to ensure the effectiveness of the BCP.

Risks, Business Impact Analysis, and the Impact of Potential Emergencies

The identification and analysis of risks is an important tool, particularly for many internal audit projects. The overall process of risk analysis was briefly discussed in Chapter 5. Risk or business impact analysis is a particularly important process for determining what applications and processes to include in the overall BCP. The thinking here is different from the old days, when recovery analysts and internal auditors focused too much on the subjective probabilities of some event occurring. That is, there were extensive discussions on the potential probability of a tornado, an earthquake, or some other catastrophic event at a data center location but not on recovery of business applications.

The BCP should include a descriptive list of the organization's key business areas, typically ranked in order of importance to the business, as well as a brief description of the business process and its main dependencies on systems, communications, personnel, and information/data. If the organization already has prepared an assessment of its key business processes, this can be an excellent time for the BCP team to update that documentation and to evaluate the relative importance of each. It should be noted that this is an inventory of *business processes,* not critical application systems. The two are often one and the same and should be considered as the key processes to keep the business operating.

A next step here is to look at those key business processes in terms of potential outage failure impacts. Exhibit 7.4 shows this type of analysis in an Excel worksheet. Each separate key business process would be listed in the column on the left with risk of failure factors considered for each key business process, such as the Impact on Customer Services, Loss of Customers, and the like. Within each of these risk factors, the criticality impacts of various levels of outages should be considered. Factors such as a specified application failure of less than two hours that will impact customer services but cause a minimal loss of customers and essentially no risk of

EXHIBIT 7.4 Business Criticality Analysis Schedule

Loss of Key Information	Possible Litigation	Penalty Clause Exposures	Loss of Additional Recovery Revised Cost	Loss of Customers	Customer Service Impact		
> 6 days							
2–5 days							
24–48 hours							
2–24 hours							
< 2 hours							
	> 6 days						
	2–5 days						
	24–48 hours						
	2–24 hours						
	< 2 hours						
		> 6 days					
		2–5 days					
		24–48 hours					
		2–24 hours					
		< 2 hours					
			> 6 days				
			2–5 days				
			24–48 hours				
			2–24 hours				
			< 2 hours				
				> 6 days			
				2–5 days			
				24–48 hours			
				2–24 hours			
				< 2 hours			
					> 6 days		
					2–5 days		
					24–48 hours		
					2–24 hours		
					< 2 hours		
Business Process							

exposure to possible litigation could be noted on the chart. While monetary values can be added to such a worksheet, this worksheet can be equally effective just to highlight key time-based exposures. The concept behind this analysis table and the steps necessary to get back in operation are components of what is usually called a business impact analysis (BIA). A newer term in the world of disaster recovery and continuity planning, BIA is an approach for defining key process risks that will impact business operations as a result of a loss of services.

Based on the outage risks, the BCP team should study and document its recovery requirements for key business processes. This includes business process procedures, automated systems, and hardware plus software requirements. In addition, existing backup and recovery procedures should be documented within the BCP, including any off-site data storage arrangements or existing arrangements with disaster recovery hot site vendors or empty room cold sites (often internal locations). This data and information will give the organization background material to construct an effective BCP. Again, the emphasis here should be on recovering business operations, not just on getting the automated systems reloaded and operating again.

Preparing for Possible Contingencies

Once the BCP project team has reviewed business processes, completed its initial processes, and assessed the business risks, it should take steps to minimize the effects of potential emergencies. An objective here is to identify ways of preventing an emergency situation from turning into an even more severe disaster due to the lack of preparedness. The BCP project team should focus on activities that are essential to the continued viability of the business and the types of backup and preventive strategies appropriate for these key business activities. The BCP team needs to next develop appropriate backup and recovery procedures for the identified critical applications. The complexity and related cost of these backup continuity procedures will depend on the identified business process restoration needs, as outlined in Exhibit 7.4.

Organizations have a variety of options for establishing a backup strategy. Larger organizations often have the resources to do much of this on their own, although many rely on outside vendors to provide backup processing services. An organization will generally commit to one of these strategies:

1. *Fully Mirrored Recovery Operations.* This is the new rules approach discussed earlier in this chapter. It calls for a fully mirrored duplicate site with mirrored linkages between the live site and the backup site over broadband lines. This approach requires specialized storage management hardware and software but is almost always the most expensive option. Fully mirrored strategies provide the greatest level of recovery assurance.

2. ***Switchable Hot Site Facility.*** Here arrangements are made with a vendor that will guarantee to maintain an identical site with communications to enable the transfer of all IT operations to this hot recovery site within an agreed time period, usually less than one to two hours. Because of the need to keep the equivalent of an exact duplicate site in waiting, the costs here can be almost as high as a fully mirrored arrangement.

3. ***Traditional Hot Site.*** Here the organization will contract with a disaster recovery vendor that will guarantee to maintain a compatible site to enable the switching of IT operations to that site within an agreed time period, usually less than eight hours after notification. This very common recovery approach caused problems in the aftermath of 9/11. Too many organizations in distress were contacting the same hot site vendors, which did not expect to have to handle so many disaster events simultaneously.

4. ***Cold Site Facility.*** This approach was more common when disaster recovery sites were viewed as being very expensive and organization IT management wanted some possible solution. The strategy involves establishing emergency site space to allow the organization to begin processing as well as a standby arrangement with a vendor to deliver minimum hardware configuration. This strategy also goes back to the days of classic mainframe computers, which required air-conditioning and water-cooling operations located under raised-floor computer room sites. In theory, the organization's cold site can be operational within two to three days.

5. ***Relocate and Restore.*** This is the weakest level of backup strategy. It involves the identification of a suitable location, hardware, and peripherals, and the reinstallation of systems and backed-up software and data *after* an emergency has occurred. Some managers have been guilty of advocating this approach. They have backed up their software and data but have no firm plans beyond making arrangements if something happens. This strategy is inadequate for today's business processes.

6. ***No Strategy.*** Some organizations still have no backup-and-restore strategy for their data processing operations. This approach is based on the organization claiming to be "too busy right now" to build its BCP type of approach. This approach carries the highest risk of all, as there are no regular off-site backups of systems or data. In the event of some disaster, this option usually ends up with the organization going out of business. The internal auditor who encounters this situation should warn the audit committee strongly about this business risk.

One of the most important aspects of the BCP is the selection of an appropriate strategy for the backup and recovery of IT-based systems. The strategy should include procedures, especially for key business processes, designed to get systems back in operation per management requirements.

Although in some instances an organizational decision to go to a hot site strategy will be the major direction for almost all applications, an individual but highly critical process may require full mirroring capabilities. Such a mixed mode of backup strategies can be appropriate if the organization decides that full mirroring is justified only for one highly critical process while the others can rely on an adequate but appropriate hot site strategy.

An organization may have a mixed set of backup strategies with some being stronger than others. However, all key processes in an organization should have some level of backup and restoration policy that allows the overall business to remain in operation. Although not all processes may require full mirroring, for example, all should be part of a consistent, comprehensive approach that will allow the overall business to get back in business in the event of a serious disruption. The cost of recovery can be a major factor here, and the BCP team should outline cost options and get the application owners to buy in to an option through an appropriate SLA. Internal audit, in its reviews of BCP procedures throughout the organization, should highlight any discrepancies here.

The BCP should have a high-priority objective to provide an adequate level of service to all customers throughout an emergency. Critical customer service activities should be included in the BCP, ordered in a priority sequence with restoration steps outlined in some level of detail. Business managers who understand customer needs may not necessarily be part of the recovery site BCP team, particularly if it would be operating at a remote hot site. Documentation describing key customers and customer service activities are essential BCP components. The emphasis always is on getting the business back in operation.

No matter what backup strategy used, key files and documents always should be stored in secure off-site locations. Disaster and business recovery teams should be designated and trained, with periodic tests to ensure their ongoing familiarity with processes. Most important, the BCP implementation team should reflect, in general, on the lessons learned from the 9/11 World Trade Center event or from other disaster events. A search of material from the previously referenced Disaster Recovery Institute can be of help. Although a small number of sites with full mirroring capabilities were able to get back in operation quickly after 9/11, many had severe problems. It was a difficult environment that hopefully will not be repeated any time soon.

Disaster Recovery: Handling the Emergency

Building a BCP is a relatively easy process when the team sits in a closed room, brainstorms, talks through, and plots a contingency recovery strategy. It becomes more difficult when alarm bells ring signifying that an emergency event has occurred. One of the first tasks is to determine to what level the emergency situation requires activation of the full BCP and notification of the emergency response team. This notification normally should be communicated through a pre-agreed call list-driven format with members of the disaster recovery team instructed to assemble at a designated off-site location. In addition, management and key employees should be kept informed of developments affecting the BCP activation and its impact on their areas of responsibility. The BCP project team leader would be responsible for this notification activity.

The objective of this phase of the BCP is to get the organization back in operation. Doing so almost always involves contacting the designated alternate processing site, activating communications lines, making arrangements to get the team to that site, and otherwise taking steps to restore operations. Assuming the team is using a hot site vendor, the disaster recovery team should arrive at the backup site, get operating systems versions and key databases loaded, and begin production operations. These steps are often far easier said than done, and it is sometimes a challenge to get communications lines connected and up and running in the new environment. These steps must be handled in a tight time frame and under considerable organizational pressure. But the objective is to have as many as possible critical business processes restored and operating quickly.

For the BCP and its resultant recovery to be effective, the recovery team must carefully consider and plan for the potentially complex series of activities needed to recover from a serious emergency. A planned approach is likely to result in a more coherent and structured recovery. It is likely that a serious disruptive event will produce unexpected results that may differ in some ways from the BCP-predicted outcomes. After the emergency, the recovery team should review any predefined procedures or strategies in light of the actual situation that arose and modify these procedures as appropriate.

Training Staff for the BCP

Extensive BCP processes and published documents are of little value unless the people responsible for executing those processes are regularly trained in their use. Many traditional disaster recovery plans were published with the idea that team members would look up critical references after a disaster event, an approach that is not practical in a 9/11 type of disaster, where the entire building suddenly is collapsing. Secure, online plans will provide some help here, but what is needed is a BCP team trained in the general processes necessary in the event of an emergency. Certain BCP team members must know enough about the plan so they will react almost instinctively in the event of a severe emergency situation.

So that members of the organization can act without having to flip through a published plan to decide the next step, the BCP project team needs to launch a training program on four need-to-know levels.

- *BCP Level 1 Training: General Management Overview.* This training should provide a broad understanding throughout senior levels of the organization that a BCP exists, how it will work, and how it is maintained and tested. This type of training would be given to a wide range of people, starting with the audit committee, to outline the overall strategy for recovery in the event of an emergency event and to describe expectations of how the organization would operate in a contingency environment.

- *BCP Level 2 Training: Key Application Systems Users.* Beyond the senior-level overviews, training should be focused on recovery procedures for critical applications. In many instances, critical applications should function in a business-as-usual sense except that processing will take place at the alternate hot site. However, often some normal resources, such as user help desks, will not work in the same manner. The training here should be oriented to the designated critical applications and how they are planned to operate. This training should operate in a case analysis mode where users can review BCP processes for their applications and ask detailed questions or point out areas where corrective action may be needed.

- *BCP Level 3 Training: IT Operations and Systems Staffs.* The IT staff, both operations and systems, are the persons who usually will be most impacted by a contingency that requires operations in a recovery mode. Training here should emphasize and reemphasize key elements of the BCP; it should take the format of regular and periodic fire drills. In some instances, this training can be based on actual BCP tests, while game-type simulation may be effective in others.

- *BCP Level 4 Training: BCP Team Members.* The smaller team that launched and is responsible for the business continuity plan development, testing, and other related activities has the greatest familiarity with the established BCP. Nevertheless, team members' knowledge of these processes needs to be refreshed and updated on an ongoing basis. The BCP project manager typically would be charged with leading a training effort to review BCP status to date, changes in process, and potential future strategy changes.

TESTING, MAINTAINING, AND AUDITING THE CONTINUITY PLAN

A published BCP is of little value until it receives an appropriate level of testing. Organizations will assemble a team and implement a BCP, as discussed. Often these documents are comprehensive and well thought out, but the plan is of little value unless it is both well maintained and current and is periodically tested. This BCP maintenance challenge is relatively easy. It means that every time there is a change to a critical—or any—element in the BCP, the plan must be updated to reflect those changes. In the "old days" when disaster recovery plans were thick published documents, plan maintenance was difficult as resources were just not available to keep the BCP current. Today, with well-thought-out automated office procedures and IT asset control processes, BCP maintenance should be relatively easy and can be prepared and conducted at three levels:

1. *Software-, Hardware-, and People-level BCP Maintenance.* The equipment environment supporting any set of information systems is almost constantly changing. New equipment is added while other gear is retired, and other technology changes or updates impact such areas as communications facilities. BCP maintenance changes here should take place almost automatically with the maintenance links described previously. That is, the upgrade of a software component or the addition of a new staff member should flow in to the BCP's automated links as described previously. However, those changes must be reassessed and reevaluated constantly. That someone has accepted a new position as an analyst to cover for someone who resigned does not mean that that new person will understand the BCP and his or her responsibilities.

   The BCP team should review all changes to the plan on a regular basis, with a more detailed review perhaps quarterly. Hardware and communications links should be evaluated to determine that they still work in the same manner as identified in the initial BCP, with changes made to the plan as appropriate. That same effort is true for software, and critical elements should be tested as required. New or different people who have been added to the BCP should be interviewed to ascertain they understand their roles and responsibilities. In some instances, repeats of training sessions as described above will be necessary.

2. *BCP Changes to Contingency and Recovery Arrangements.* An organization usually will have made arrangements with outside vendors, including the hot site vendor and communications provider, to support its BCP. These arrangements should be reviewed and updated on a quarterly basis. Changes are not frequent in this portion of the overall BCP, but there is value in determining that all terms and conditions are up to date. A hot site vendor, for example, may have made a small change in its arrangements that did not get included in the organization's BCP. This quarterly review allows the BCP team to affirm that everything is still up to date.

3. *Business Criticality BCP Maintenance.* This portion of BCP maintenance focuses on the key business processes that were identified and described following the Exhibit 7.4 worksheet. That original exercise required a review of all critical business processes and an analysis of recovery requirements including relative priorities. The BCP team should

go through this schedule probably once per quarter to add or delete new applications, to rethink recovery needs, and generally to reorganize this set of critical applications.

Potential changes to this business criticality document may cause substantive changes in the overall recovery plan. The BCP team should be aware of the types of issues that can cause changes here. As an example, the evolving set of SOA rules may increase the Exposure to Possible Litigation as listed in the exhibit.

BCP Testing

All of the effort that goes in to building a BCP, arranging for backup processing, training team members, and planning for business recovery may be of little value unless the BCP, or at least portions of it, is tested on a regular basis. The tests must be planned carefully and often work best when only a component of the overall environment is tested. A BCP test is somewhat like a fire drill in an office building, where security management plans the drill, clears it with appropriate levels of management, and schedules the fire drill for a designated time. Although an actual fire could happen at any time, it is not a good idea to set off the fire alarms concurrent with the chief executive's quarterly employee meeting to report results or on the afternoon before a long holiday weekend. Otherwise, the test can be a career-limiting factor for the manager who instigated the unannounced test. This author recalls a time in the legacy system mainframe days when an IT manager of a European unit decided to "test" his IT disaster recovery operation by personally cutting off power to the computer systems operations center and announcing that, although this was just a test, everyone had two minutes to clear out of the facility. His test proved that his unit's disaster recovery plan was not working; and it also ended his career.

BCP tests should be planned well in advance and structured as rehearsals for portions of the plan. Some test portions are relatively easy, such as operations at a remote hot site. Vendors offer testing time as part of their contracts, and organizations should use their allotted time slots regularly to make certain the operating software, database backups and other supporting programs can be brought up to operations at the remote site. Usually these types of tests are planned well in advance with the hot site vendor and with the IT staff.

A more realistic dimension of the BCP hot site test would be for the responsible organization manager to inform the IT staff that at some time in the next month there will be a hot site test and then make confidential arrangements with the vendor for the test. The BCP manager then could announce the test on a "surprise" basis for a certain segment of operations, with the BCP team required to access backups from off-site storage, initiate arrangements to travel to the hot site, and begin operations. Computer systems operations would continue as normal, but the BCP team would be charged to determine that certain portions of systems can be loaded and brought in to operation at the hot site. The ongoing results of such a test should be documented, and internal audit might be informed in advance to observe and help document the testing process here.

A much more difficult—but very important—aspect of BCP testing is business systems recovery. It is difficult because often what is being tested are key operational systems, such as an online order processing operation that is expected to be up and in operation 24/7. A test of this sort would require loading supporting systems at the hot site and working with the telecommunications provider to set up a dummy network for starting up operations at a test site. A selected group of operations people would be involved here as well to process test orders and other transactions. An objective of this type of test would be to measure how long it takes for the business to be restored for the key business processes. Although organizations have multiple key business processes, such a test should focus on restoration of operations in a very limited number of them.

Testing can be a very important portion of the BCP training discussed previously. It also can be a useful process for internal audit to evaluate the effectiveness of the organization's BCP readiness. Although a BCP test will never totally simulate an actual disaster condition, such as the actual 9/11 events, an effective program of testing will allow the organization to assess its readiness for a potential contingency event. This testing can be expensive and take staff away from important regular activities. Before embarking on any such type of test, the BCP project manager along with senior IT management should define the specific objectives for each test, establish a set of operating rules, and involve a limited set or participants and observers for each test scenario. The results should be documented for a lessons-learned analysis and a program of continuous BCP improvements.

Auditing the BCP

Internal audit can and should play an important role in the BCP development as well as its testing processes. It might offer resources to observe and comment on the results of BCP tests, suggest testing scenarios, or offer consultative advice on the progress of the BCP development. Internal audit personnel can be part of these BCP processes, but they should remember to step back, assert their independence, and schedule periodic audits regarding the adequacy of BCP processes and business recovery procedures. Audits should be planned and scheduled as part of internal audit's regular risk assessment and audit planning process.

Formal internal audit reviews should be scheduled periodically to assess whether all aspects of BCP readiness and the adequacy processes are in place. Internal audit must be careful of the fine line between acting as an advisor to the BCP team and auditing its processes in cases in which the audit committee is the party interested in the overall adequacy of the BCP process for the continuance of the corporation. Internal audit's review of organization BCP processes should be based on such matters as the adequacy and currency of its BCP documentation, the results of scheduled tests, and a host of other issues. Exhibit 7.5 summarizes review points for an internal audit review of organization BCP processes. Every organization is different, but the exhibit points out some general areas that should be considered. These focus on an audit of one self-contained set of resources and processes but could be expanded for a larger, multilocation organization.

The establishment of adequate contingency processes is an important component of an organization's internal control structure. That internal control structure was discussed in Chapter 5 on COSO and SOA Section 404 internal controls. Internal audit should communicate the results of its reviews here with senior organization management, the audit committee, and the external auditors. The results of the BCP audit should be included in the internal control assessment materials given to external auditors for their assessment of internal controls.

EXHIBIT 7.5   Review Points for an Internal Audit of a Business
Contingency Plan

1. Review the existing BCP with the responsible manager.
    1.1. Does the plan appear to be current and up to date?
    1.2. Does the BCP cover all areas of the organization or just IT operations?
    1.3. Are there open BCP issues to be resolved?
    1.4. Has the BCP been reviewed with key members of management?
    1.5. Has the plan been reviewed with external auditors?
2. Examine the contents and format of the BCP.
    2.1. Based on the internal understanding of organization operations, does the BCP appear to cover key business processes?
    2.2. Are there adequate levels of business impact analysis and risk assessments as part of the BCP documentation?
    2.3. Does the plan appear to cover appropriate procedures for backups and off-site storage?
    2.4. Does the BCP carry step-by-step outlined procedures for executing it in the event of an emergency?
    2.5. Are call list chains included in the BCP?
    2.6. Does the BCP include key vendor and emergency supply contacts?

EXHIBIT 7.5 Review Points for an Internal Audit of a Business
Contingency Plan *(Continued)*

  2.7. Does the BCP document contacts for fire, police, and external media contacts?

  2.8. Is there a process in place to provide for regular and automatic updates of the BCP?

3. Determine overall training and understanding of the BCP.

  3.1. Discuss the BCP with several members of the team designated to execute the plan to determine their understanding.

  3.2. Do members in IT operations and systems appear to understand their roles and responsibilities?

  3.3. Based on discussions with key persons in critical business process areas, do they appear to have a general understanding of their business recovery roles?

  3.4. Based on an interview with the CFO or designee, assess whether there is adequate understanding of the BCP and how it will operate.

  3.5. Review BCP training records to determine if the training appears to be adequate, timely, and regularly scheduled.

4. Review the results of recent BCP tests.

  4.1. Is there a formal program of testing critical BCP elements?

  4.2. Are testing results documented in a lessons-learned format?

  4.3. Does BCP testing cover both business recovery as well as IT functions?

5. Review of BCP backup procedures.

  5.1. If a remote hot-site vendor is used, review the contract and related documentation for currency.

  5.2. Review the documented results of hot-site tests.

  5.3. Review the adequacy of other backup vendor or location procedures.

6. Prepare internal audit documentation assessing the overall adequacy of the organization's BCP.

CONTINUITY PLANNING GOING FORWARD

As organizations become ever more dependent on their automated business processes, procedures to keep those processes in operation after some emergency or other disaster have become increasingly important. Business staff members can no longer get by pulling out their No. 2 pencils and completing old paper forms as backup processes. Our automated systems today are tied to complex in-house and Internet-based databases, where those old procedures are no longer applicable. The 9/11 World Trade Center terrorist event proved that these older contingency procedures were just not applicable. The mirroring processes discussed earlier in this chapter point to a direction for future continuity planning.

The old "disaster recovery" rules have changed as well. It is no longer sufficient for IT operations to move to a hot site backup location to begin processing and assume the organization soon will be back in operations. Processes must focus on restoring business operations in light of an extended interruption in information systems services. Business requires the ability to get all of its processes back in operation with minimal delay. Internal auditors have an important role here in helping management to implement effective BCP processes and regularly assess their operations and controls.

NOTES

1. Disaster Recovery Institute International, Falls Church, Virginia, *www.dri.org.*
2. In interest of full disclosure, Robert Moeller, the author, previously worked for EMC Corporation helping to launch its Operations Management Consulting group.
3. PMP is an examination and experience-based qualification administered by the Project Management Institute, *www.omi.org.*

CHAPTER 8

Internal Audit Fraud Detection and Prevention

The accounting scandals that motivated the enactment of the Sarbanes-Oxley Act (SOA) were all examples of financial fraud. Fraudulent activity perpetrated by individual employees can occur at all levels of the organization, but in the days just before and after the mid-2002 enactment of SOA, corporate officers appeared to be real troublemakers in a slew of financial frauds. However, fraud can take place at many levels. Just as a chief executive officer (CEO), in cooperation with the chief financial officer (CFO), has had the ability to fraudulently manipulate earnings to boost corporate reported profits, a manager or even staff-level employee may take some fraudulent action for personal gain or just to get even with someone because of job frustration. Perhaps this is because of an everybody-does-it attitude in the aftermath of the publicity surrounding many fraud-related scandals; incidents of fraud have been increasing in recent years. The public accounting firm Ernst & Young, in its 2003 Global Fraud Survey, reported that 85 percent of the worst frauds were caused by insiders on the payroll and over half of those frauds were initiated by members of management.[1]

An internal auditor needs to understand the concepts surrounding fraud in order to effectively perform audits that search for fraudulent activities. The common-law definition of fraud is "the obtaining of money or property by means of false token, symbol, or device." In other words, someone improperly authorizes some document that causes an illegal transfer of money. Fraud can be costly to any victim organization, and effective internal controls are an organization's first line of defense. A comprehensive, fully implemented, and regularly monitored system of internal controls is essential for the prevention and detection of losses that arise from fraud. Internal auditors often find themselves very involved in fraud-related issues today. When a fraud is discovered in the organization, many times internal audit is called first to conduct an investigation to help determine the extent of the fraud. In other situations, internal auditors may discover a fraud through a scheduled audit and then investigate and report the matter to corporate legal consul or to outside legal authorities. However, internal auditors typically should not regularly look for fraud as part of their scheduled audit reviews.

Auditors, both internal and external, today are being asked to play a more important role in the detection and prevention of fraud. For years, both the American Institute of Certified Public Accountants (AICPA) and the Institute of Internal Auditors (IIA) have asserted that their members did not have the skills to detect fraud and, therefore, could not be held accountable. Given the impetus from recent corporate scandals and SOA, the AICPA has released a tough new auditing standard on the auditor's responsibility to detect fraud, and seven professional associations have developed recommendations to help boards of directors, audit committees and management prevent and root out fraud.[2] These recommendations are a part of Statements of Auditing Standards (SAS) No. 99, "Consideration of Fraud in a Financial Statement Audit," discussed later in this chapter. The recommendation is that appropriate internal controls should become more fraud-specific active controls, including personnel identification tools, physical restraints, or document safeguards. Passive controls to deter fraud should be designed to increase the risk of discovery, including audit trails, surveillance of key activities, and the rotation of key personnel.

This chapter discusses controls to prevent and detect fraud and introduces the new AICPA auditing standard on fraud as well as both IIA initiatives and procedures to detect and prevent computer systems fraud. Fraud has been with us from time immemorial, but auditors in the past have claimed that detecting fraud was beyond their responsibility. They claimed that fraud detection was for law enforcement people even though those persons often did not have the accounting, information technology (IT), or internal controls skills to detect fraud. Today auditors have an increasing responsibility to detect fraud as well as to recommend controls to prevent future frauds.

RED FLAGS: FRAUD DETECTION FOR AUDITORS

Fraudulent activities often are easy to identify *after* the fraud has been uncovered. An employee who has been embezzling money over an extended period will be caught through some slip-up that revealed the fraud. After the fraud is discovered, many times it is easy to look back at the situation and say such things as "But she was such a good employee—she has not missed a day of work for nearly two years! How could she have done this?" or "Now that I think about it, I wondered how he could afford all of those long weekend trips to expensive places!" or "That's why those transactions were processed without a second approval." It is easy to analyze the facts after a fraud has been discovered as a "lessons learned" exercise, but auditors should use a skeptical eye to look for indicators of possible fraudulent activities in advance. They should look for what are called "red flags."

Although there is still much to be resolved as this book was released, the first corporation and CFO to be indicted for accounting fraud under SOA was a healthcare provider called HealthSouth Corporation. The mid-2003 largest U.S. provider of outpatient surgery, diagnostic, and rehabilitative services, HealthSouth operated in approximately 1,900 locations in 50 states and internationally. It reported in excess of $1.4 billion of *fictitious* earnings over a six-year period in order to meet ongoing analyst estimates and to keep stock price high. As matters are now evolving, several financial and other officers have pleaded guilty, and the CEO has been indicted on some 85 counts of fraud. While this accounting fraud had been happening since the early 1990s, external auditors and others evidently ignored numerous signs of possible fraud:

- HealthSouth's year 2000 pretax earnings more than doubled to $559 million, although its sales grew only 3 percent. Pretax earnings for 2001 were nearly twice 1999 levels, although sales rose just 8 percent. Although there is nothing wrong with fantastic earnings growth, analysts and others might have asked some hard questions.

- In late 2002 HealthSouth's internal auditors were denied access to key corporate financial records. Internal audit reported this to their outside auditors, who took no action. The audit committee evidently did not get involved.

- The CEO seemed to be spending an excessive amount of attention on sports and popular music performers, flying his management staff off to events and bringing others in to the company.

These are examples of the kinds of signals that were raised around the company suggesting possible fraud. An ex-employee even sent an e-mail to the external auditors suggesting they look at three specific accounts for fraudulent activity. The external auditors launched some level of investigation but found "nothing." Internal management finally put pressure on the normally dominant CEO to back off from some fictitious financial reports, and that action started a chain of events that subsequently exposed the fraud.

Red flags, such as the ones outlined for HealthSouth, are normally the first indications of a potential fraud. Someone sees something that does not look right and then instigates what is often a low-level investigation. Many times internal auditors are the first people to become involved. Exhibit 8.1 lists a series of red flags that may point to potential financial fraud activities. None of these is an absolute indicator of fraud, but auditors should always be skeptical in their reviews and be aware of such warning signals. When an auditor sees evidence of one or more of these or other red flags,

EXHIBIT 8.1 Financial Fraud Potential Red Flags

This list contains "red flags" that may be warning signals for evidence of financial fraud.

- Lack of written corporate policies or standard operating procedures.
- Based on interviews at multiple levels, lack of compliance with organization internal control policies.
- Weak internal control policies, especially in the division of duties.
- Disorganized operations in such areas as purchasing, receiving, warehousing, or regional offices.
- Unrecorded transactions or missing records.
- Counterfeit or evidence of alterations to documents.
- Photocopied or questionable handwriting on documents.
- Sales records with excessive voids or credits.
- Bank accounts not reconciled on a timely basis or stale items on bank reconciliations.
- Continuous out-of-balance conditions on subsidiary ledgers.
- Unusual financial statement relationships.
- Continuous unexplained differences between physical inventory counts and perpetual inventory records.
- Bank checks written to cash in large amounts.
- Handwritten checks in an otherwise automated environment
- Continuous or unusual fund transfers among company bank accounts.
- Fund transfers to offshore banks.
- Transactions not consistent with the entity's business.
- Poor screening procedures for new employees including no background or reference checks.
- Reluctance by management to report criminal wrongdoing.
- Unusual transfers of personal assets.
- Officers or employees with lifestyles apparently beyond their means.
- Unused vacation time.
- Frequent or unusual related-party transactions.
- Employees in close association with suppliers.
- Employees in close relationship with one another in areas where separation of duties could be circumvented.
- Expense account abuse such as managers not following established rules.
- Business assets dissipating without explanation.

Source: Adapted from the AICPA website, *www.aicpa.org.*

it is time to dig a little deeper. Unfortunately, internal auditors often fail to detect frauds for several reasons:

- *Auditors have an unwillingness to look for fraud.* Due to limited fraud training or the lack of experience with past fraud incidents, auditors historically have not looked that hard for fraud. They have tended to view fraud investigation as a police detective type of activity, not their prime responsibility.

- *Too much trust is placed on auditees.* Internal auditors, in particular, try to maintain a friendly, cordial attitude toward people in their organization. Because they encounter these same people in the company cafeteria or at an annual company picnic, there is usually a level of trust here. Internal auditors quite correctly try to give their auditees the benefit of the doubt.

- *Not enough emphasis is placed on audit quality.* Internal audit findings often encounter some of the same red flags mentioned in Exhibit 8.1. Audit report findings may point out such matters as missing records or accounts that were not reconciled. However, quality reviews of the auditor's work often do not raise potential fraud-related issues.

- *Fraud concerns receive inadequate support from management.* The hint of a possible fraud requires auditors to extend procedures and dig a bit deeper. However, audit management may be reluctant to give an auditor extra time to dig deeper. Unless there are strong suspicions, audit managers may want the audit team to move on and stop spending time in what they feel is an extremely low risk area.

- *Auditors sometimes fail to focus on high-risk fraud areas.* Fraud can occur in many areas, from employee travel expense reporting to treasury function relations with offshore banks. There may be a much greater risk of significant financial fraud in the latter, auditors often tend to focus on the former. Although there can be many possibilities for fraud in employee travel expense reporting, amounts often are not too significant. There is always a need to focus on higher-risk areas.

Fraud is a word that can have many meanings, but we are referring to it in terms of fraud as a criminal act. There are over 300 references to fraud in federal criminal statutes, and the term appears throughout SOA. Most of those federal references are based on the federal general fraud statute:

> *Whoever, in any manner within the jurisdiction of any department or agency of the United States, knowingly and willfully falsifies, conceals, or covers up by any trick, scheme, or device a material fact, or makes any false, fictitious, or fraudulent writing or document knowingly the same to contain any false, fictitious, or fraudulent statement or entry, shall be fined not more than . . . or imprisoned not more than . . . or both.*

Although stated in legalese, this is a strong statement. The auditor's word "material" is not included here, and anything false, fictitious, or fraudulent could be considered a violation in terms of the federal fraud statute. State statutes generally are modeled after the federal rules. An internal auditor should be aware of his or her state rules.

To help detect fraud, auditors also need to have an understanding of why people commit fraud. An organization can have the red flag environment described in Exhibit 8.1, but it will not necessarily be subject to fraudulent activities unless one or more employees decide to engage in fraud. Exhibit 8.2 lists some typical reasons for committing a fraud. These are all reasons where strong internal controls are in place and the fraud is typically committed by only one person. Fraud detection is harder when there is collusion between multiple persons. In the HealthSouth fraud, a very aggressive CEO assembled a top management team whom he called "the company" to prepare these fraudulent financial reports. Members of "the company" were highly compensated and received many incentives. The fraud did not become public until certain members of "the company" had personal concerns about the growing accounting fraud.

EXHIBIT 8.2   Reasons for Committing Fraud

- ***Employees have a desperate need for money.*** This probably is the major motivator and where fraud is most difficult to detect. Whether due to a nasty divorce or a drug problem, the need for money can cause employees to resort to criminal actions.
- ***Employees have job frustrations.*** Employees can feel their company "doesn't give a damn" about them and feel free to act inappropriately.
- ***Employees believe everybody does it.*** This type of situation is more common in smaller retail-type environments, where an employee thinks that everyone else is stealing as well. This attitude also can come up when senior managers seem to be living extravagantly while the company is incurring losses.
- ***Employees are challenged to beat the system.*** This is a particular problem with would-be hackers in an automated systems environment. However, in many other cases, employees, for example, try to set up fictitious transactions to see if they can bill the company and receive cash in return.
- ***Lax internal controls make fraud easy.*** Lax controls are a basic motivation to attempt almost any fraud.
- ***There is a low probability of detection.*** Similar to the weak internal controls point, if an employee knows that chances of getting caught are nil, the temptation to commit fraud is greater.
- ***There is a low probability of prosecution.*** When a company seemingly never takes action to bring criminal charges against violators, the word will get out.

Although major frauds involving senior management participation are difficult to detect, frauds that occur at much lower levels in the organization are easier to identify with a proper level of auditor investigation. For example, a payroll process can present a wide range of opportunities for fraud through the use of such mechanisms as inflating the actual hours an employee worked, generating checks for fictitious or terminated employees, or issuing duplicate checks for an employee. These are the classic types of issues that are part of many internal audit procedures. However, rather than just an internal control violation, an internal auditor should think of these items in terms of potential areas for employee fraud. Exhibit 8.3 is a checklist for

EXHIBIT 8.3   Fraud Detection Methods Checklist

- *Conduct unannounced cash counts.* Going all of the way from treasurer disbursement funds to petty cash, auditors should count the recorded cash and reconcile results to records.
- *Review the composition of deposits.* Company records will indicate the timing and amounts of bank deposits. Balances and timing should be reconciled.
- *Reconcile sequentially prenumbered documents.* Sequential numbering controls over paper and electronic documents should be reviewed. Gaps or missing documents should be investigated.
- *Review controls over the voiding of checks.* A check can be marked void in records but still released. Controls should be reviewed.
- *Review controls over authorization and issuance of checks.* Checks of any sort represent funds out and should contain adequate controls.
- *Determine that controls over electronic payments are adequate.* Automated payment systems sometimes do not have the same controls as traditional accounts payable processes. Controls should be reviewed.
- *Review bank reconciliations.* This is basic cash audit control. Obtain an independent confirmation of bank balances and reconcile to organization records.
- *Search for duplicate payments.* Computer-assisted techniques will allow searches for duplicates based on vendor number and amount.
- *Match vendor addresses with employee addresses.* Again, computer-assisted techniques will allow searches here for potentially fictitious vendors.
- *Confirm account balances with a sample of customers.* Independent confirmation letters, a traditional audit technique, are sent out with requests to return responses directly to the auditors.
- *Perform test counts of sample inventory items.* Sample sets of inventory should be test counted and reconciled to records.
- *Observe the existence of a sample of physical assets.* The existence and relative health of physical assets should be checked on a test basis.

some of these old, classic fraud detection methods. Auditors have performed these procedures for years but sometimes forget. In the HealthSouth fraud, it was discovered that the external auditors did not do a classic bank balance confirmation with HealthSouth's banks. In this time-tested procedure, the auditor asks the bank to independently confirm bank balance as of a certain date. In the promotion of audit efficiency over the years, auditors have dropped many of these traditional procedures. It may be time to revisit some.

PUBLIC ACCOUNTING'S NEW ROLE IN FRAUD DETECTION

The external auditor's responsibility for the detection of fraud in financial statements has been an ongoing but contentious issue over the years. The very first auditing standard, No. 1, of the AICPA's SASs provided: "The auditor has no responsibility to plan and perform the audit to obtain reasonable assurance that misstatements, whether caused by errors or fraud, that are not material to the financial statements are detected." In other words, the external auditor was responsible for determining if the debits equaled the credits but not for detecting fraudulent activity. The public accounting profession stood by this position for many years. Even during the numerous financial frauds that led to the 1987 Treadway Commission Report on Fraudulent Financial Reporting, AICPA auditing standards regarding the detection of fraud did not change.

Despite a fairly regular clamor for change, audit standards regarding auditor responsibility for fraud remained unaltered until 1997, when the auditor's responsibility for fraud was restated in SAS No. 82: "The auditor has a responsibility to plan and perform the audit to obtain reasonable assurance about whether the financial statements are free of material misstatement, whether caused by error or fraud." This revised but tighter standard was released, after much professional discussion, at about the peak of the dot-com bubble, when the public was concerned about how fast and how large their investments would surge forward; there was not that much concern with fraud then.

Moving to more recent times with Enron, WorldCom, and the host of others, concerns about fraudulent financial reporting certainly have changed. Given SOA and the new Public Corporation Accounting Oversight Board (PCAOB), it was perhaps too late, but the AICPA released SAS No. 99 in December 2002 on the auditor's responsibility for detecting fraudulent financial reporting. With this new standard, the external auditor now is responsible for providing reasonable assurance that the financial statements are free of material misstatement, *whether caused by error or fraud.*

We have italicized this phrase because this is a major change in external auditor responsibilities.

SAS No. 99 calls on financial auditors to increase their level of professional skepticism. Putting aside any prior beliefs as to management's honesty, the audit team members should exchange ideas or brainstorm on how frauds could occur in the organization they are about to audit. These discussions should identify fraud risks and always keep in mind the characteristics that are present when frauds occur: incentives, opportunities, and ability to rationalize. Throughout the audit, the engagement team should think about and explore the question, If someone wanted to perpetrate a fraud here, how would it be done? From these discussions, the engagement team should be in a better position to design audit tests responsive to fraud risks. External auditors always should go in to an audit anticipating there may be some level of fraudulent activity.

The external auditor engagement team is expected to inquire of management and others in the organization as to their perceptions of the risk of fraud and whether they are aware of any ongoing fraud investigations or open issues. The auditors should make a point of talking to employees in and outside management, giving people the opportunity to step forward or "blow the whistle" regarding any fraud. During an audit, the external audit engagement team should test areas, locations, and accounts that otherwise might not be tested and design tests that would be unpredictable and unexpected by the client.

SAS No. 99 recognizes that management is often in a position to override controls to commit financial statement fraud. The auditing standard calls for tests for the management override of controls on every audit. SAS No. 99 introduces a major external audit emphasis in detecting fraud. This is a significant change from the "let's take the afternoon off and talk about things over a game of golf" approach that was common in many past external audit engagements.

In addition to imposing a very tough fraud detection auditing standard on its members, the AICPA has taken strong steps to bring external auditors up to speed regarding situations that encourage fraud as well as providing them supporting educational materials. The AICPA's web pages are filed with case studies, publications, continuing professional education (CPE) courses, and other references on management fraud issues. AICPA membership is not required to access the site, but there are member and nonmember prices for purchasing items. As an example of the AICPA materials, Exhibit 8.4 shows a misappropriation of assets checklist for auditors. From an auditing and accounting professional organization that avoided getting involved in fraud prevention and detection over many years, SAS No. 99 raises the bar for all certified public accountants. Given SOA and other recent events, it is unfortunate that these audit standards were not released sooner.

EXHIBIT 8.4   Risk Factors Relating to Misappropriation
of Assets

Risk factors that relate to misstatements arising from misappropriation of assets also are classified according to the three conditions generally present when fraud exists: incentives/pressures, opportunities, and attitudes/rationalizations. Some of the risk factors related to misstatements arising from fraudulent financial reporting also may be present when misstatements arising from misappropriation of assets occur. For example, ineffective monitoring of management and weaknesses in internal control may be present when misstatements due to either fraudulent financial reporting or misappropriation of assets exist. Examples of risk factors related to misstatements arising from misappropriation of assets follow.

Incentives/Pressures

A. Personal financial obligations may create pressure on management or employees with access to cash or other assets susceptible to theft to misappropriate those assets.

B. Adverse relationships between the entity and employees with access to cash or other assets susceptible to theft may motivate those employees to misappropriate those assets. For example, adverse relationships may be created by:

- Known or anticipated future employee layoffs
- Recent or anticipated changes to employee compensation or benefit plans
- Promotions, compensation, or other rewards inconsistent with expectations

Opportunities

A. Certain characteristics or circumstances may increase the susceptibility of assets to misappropriation. For example, opportunities to misappropriate assets increase when there are:

- Large amounts of cash on hand or processed
- Inventory items that are small in size, of high value, or in high demand
- Easily convertible assets, such as bearer bonds, diamonds, or computer chips
- Fixed assets that are small in size, marketable, or lacking observable identification of ownership

B. Inadequate internal control over assets may increase the susceptibility of misappropriation of those assets. For example, misappropriation of assets may occur because there is:

- Inadequate segregation of duties or independent checks
- Inadequate management oversight of employees responsible for assets, for example, inadequate supervision or monitoring of remote locations
- Inadequate job applicant screening of employees with access to assets

EXHIBIT 8.4   Risk Factors Relating to Misappropriation
of Assets *(Continued)*

- Inadequate recordkeeping with respect to assets
- Inadequate system of authorization and approval of transactions, for example, in purchasing
- Inadequate physical safeguards over cash, investments, inventory, office equipment, or fixed assets
- Lack of complete and timely reconciliations of assets
- Lack of timely and appropriate documentation of transactions, for example, credits for merchandise returns
- Lack of mandatory vacations for employees performing key control functions
- Inadequate management understanding of information technology, which enables information technology employees to perpetrate a misappropriation
- Inadequate access controls over automated records, including controls over and review of computer systems event logs

---

Source: Reprinted with permission of the American Institute of Certified Public Accountants.

IIA STANDARDS FOR DETECTING AND INVESTIGATING FRAUD

Internal auditors are often in a better position than external auditors to detect fraud. Although many external auditors do not visit a client much more often than around the quarterly and annual financial statement dates, internal auditors are, by definition, internal to the organization and at the organization on a day-to-day basis. Through observation, internal auditors may be in a better position to see a red flag than an external auditor. The shipping supervisor who shows up at the annual holiday party in an expensive Italian suit and sporting a Rolex watch might raise a small blip on an internal auditor's radar screen that an external auditor might not see. There may be many very valid reasons to justify such a show of wealth, but it is something to remember going forward.

IIA general standards for Due Professional Care and Scope of Work cover fraud in a very general sense. The internal auditor is to be concerned about such matters as the possibility of wrongdoing and should consider evidence of any improper or illegal activities in an audit. However, the IIA Standards that provide specific guidance on fraud seem to follow the older external audit standards just discussed. Recognizing that it may be difficult to detect fraud, IIA Standard 1210.A2 provides the guidance: "The internal auditor should have sufficient knowledge to identify the indicators of fraud *but is not expected to have the expertise of a person whose primary responsibility is detecting and investigating fraud.*" Our italicized phrase recognizes that internal auditors are not expected to have the expertise to deal with fraud issues.

This same fraud standard is supported by an IIA Practice Advisory, 1210.A2-1, Identification of Fraud. Despite the words from the standard that internal auditors are *not expected to have the expertise,* the supporting Practice Advisory provides an internal auditor with some guidance on detecting and investigating fraud. We have included an adapted portion of this Practice Advisory:

> *Deterrence of fraud consists of those actions taken to discourage the perpetration of fraud and limit the exposure if fraud does occur. The principal mechanism for deterring fraud is control. Primary responsibility for establishing and maintaining control rests with management.*
>
> *Internal auditors are responsible for assisting in the deterrence of fraud by examining and evaluating the adequacy and the effectiveness of the system of internal control, commensurate with the extent of the potential exposure/risk in the various segments of the organization's operations. In carrying out this responsibility, internal auditors should, for example, determine whether:*
>
> - *The organizational environment fosters control consciousness, and realistic organizational goals and objectives are set.*
> - *Written policies (e.g., code of conduct) exist that describe prohibited activities and the action required whenever violations are discovered.*
> - *Appropriate authorization policies for transactions are established and maintained.*
> - *Policies, practices, procedures, reports, and other mechanisms are developed to monitor activities and safeguard assets, particularly in high-risk areas.*
> - *Communication channels provide management with adequate and reliable information.*
> - *Recommendations need to be made for the establishment or enhancement of cost-effective controls to help deter fraud.*
>
> *When an internal auditor suspects wrongdoing, appropriate authorities within the organization should be informed. The internal auditor may recommend whatever investigation is considered necessary in the circumstances. Thereafter, the auditor should follow up to see that the internal auditing activity's responsibilities have been met.*

This IIA Practice Advisory does not really educate internal auditors on red flag types of conditions that might suggest potential fraudulent activity. Rather, it suggests that if an organization does not have good policies and procedures, or lacks a code of conduct, such an environment could encourage fraud. This is often true, but the lack of a current code of conduct or poorly drafted policy statements should not be the major reason for an internal auditor to go on a hunt for potential fraudulent activities. The red flags of Exhibit 8.1 are better indicators.

The IIA has not, as yet, taken the strong position on detecting fraud as the AICPA has taken. A mid-2003 search to the IIA web site using the key word "fraud" does not give the wealth of material that is available on the AICPA site. There are references to articles on fraud in older issues of the IIA publication, *The Internal Auditor,* but not much more. Other fraud-related articles are listed but available only to IIA members. The previously referenced Practice Advisory is an example. The IIA also has special conferences on the topic. Fraud detection and prevention should be a concern for all internal auditors.

The IIA along with the AICPA, ISACA, the Association of Certified Fraud Examiners, Financial Executives International, the Institute of Management Accountants, and the Society for Human Resource Management have collaborated and sponsored fraud guidance materials published as a supplement to SAS No. 99. Other professional organizations that have participated in reviewing and developing fraud guidance include the American Accounting Association, the Defense Industry Initiative, and the National Association of Corporate Directors.

FRAUD INVESTIGATIONS FOR INTERNAL AUDITORS

In addition to establishing necessary controls to prevent and detect fraud, internal auditors sometimes become very involved in fraud investigations. Although appropriate legal authorities should be used for many fraud investigations, internal audit often is asked to play a key role in many fraud matters. Internal auditors should not play the role of a Sherlock Holmes but can help with smaller-scale discoveries or provide supporting materials for potentially more major fraud matters. Many times internal audit gets involved in a potential fraud issue here through an anonymous call or e-mail note.

When faced with potential fraud information, auditors' first step always should be to consult with the organization's corporate counsel. Because of the nature of the allegation as well as the extent of initial information, the matter may be turned over to legal authorities. In some cases, legal advice will suggest that other authorities get involved at once. In smaller, seemingly less major matters, internal audit often is asked to take responsibility for the investigation. In many instances, these investigations just involve a detailed review of documents where the evidence gathered from that review will become the basis for further actions.

Fraud-related investigations cause internal auditors to operate rather differently from normal financial or operational audits. In any fraud-related review, auditors should concentrate on three major objectives:

1. *Prove the loss.* Fraud-related reviews usually start out with the finding that someone stole something. The investigative review led by internal audit should assemble relevant material to determine overall size and scope of the loss.

2. *Establish responsibility and intent.* This is the "who did it?" step. As much as possible, the audit team should identify everyone responsible for the matter and determine if there was any special or different intent associated with the fraud action.

3. *Prove the audit investigative methods used.* The investigative team needs to be able to prove that its fraud-related conclusions were based on a detailed, step-by-step investigative process, not just a wild, uncoordinated witch hunt. The review should be documented using the best internal audit review processes. Of particular importance here, all documents used need to be secured.

Many other procedures are associated with a fraud-related examination. The objective of this book is not to describe the overall process of fraud examinations but to discuss the increased emphasis on fraud detection and prevention as outlined by new standards, particularly SAS No. 99. Internal auditors interested in learning more about fraud investigations should explore the publications of the Association of Certified Fraud Examiners (CFE) at *www.cfenet.com/home.asp*. This professional organization has a variety of educational and guidance materials that can supplement those provided by the AICPA.

INFORMATION SYSTEMS FRAUD PREVENTION PROCESSES

Information systems related fraud covers a wide range of issues. In today's business environment, information systems are virtually always the key component of any financial or accounting-related fraud. Because IT systems support so many areas and cross so many organization lines, IT fraud can be thought of in multiple dimensions, ranging from the "minor" to significant fraudulent activities:

- *Improper Personal Use of Computer Resources.* An organization may establish rules stating that there should be no personal files or programs on their work-supplied systems. Employees frequently ignore such rules.

- *Internet Access Issues.* Similar to personal use of the computer, organizations often establish guidelines and controls to restrict workplace

Internet use. Again, employees frequently ignore such rules, which sometimes are bypassed by software that allows employees to get around firewall barriers.

- *Illegal Software Use.* Employees sometimes attempt to steal/download
  copies of company software or install their own software on organization computer resources. They are violating organization rules and sometimes putting their employers in violation of software license agreements

- *Computer Security and Confidentiality Fraud Matters.* Employees can
  violate password protections and gain improper access to systems. Even
  if they are only trying to "see if it works," they are performing a fraudulent act.

- *Information Theft or Other Data Abuse Computer Fraud.* It is one thing
  to access a computer system improperly by violating password controls
  and another to view, modify, or copy data or files improperly. This is a
  significant area of computer crime.

- *Embezzlement or Unauthorized Electronic Fund Transfers.* Stealing
  money or other resources through improper or unauthorized transactions is the most significant cause of computer fraud. Whether initiating a transaction to send an accounts payable check to the home
  address or facilitating a major bank transfer, this is a major computer
  fraud area.

These examples run the course from what might be considered fairly
minor to significant information systems abuses. We mention the minor
items to point out the range of items that can be considered computer fraud.
If I am given a laptop computer for my work and told it is only for business use, but if I use it to run my child's homework, does this represent computer fraud? The answer here is really yes. The organization's rules were
set up for good reason, and employees should not violate them. However,
should internal audit launch a review to discover violations in this area?
Probably not; there are usually more important high-risk areas to spend
limited internal time and resources. A strong code of conduct and ethics
program, as discussed in Chapter 4, should be the predominant control procedure here.

This last example illustrates that there are many possibilities for computer fraud. In this very complex area, strong technical skills are needed.
This also is an area where the rules are changing. Individuals with a fraudulent intent are finding new ways to violate established automated controls,
and skilled professionals are finding ways to detect and protect this fraudulent activity. Consider the new concept of computer forensics. This is
the detailed examination of computers and their peripheral devices, using
computer investigation and analysis techniques, for finding or determining
potential legal evidence in a fraud situation. The evidence needed to be

found covers a wide range of subjects, such as theft of trade secrets, theft or destruction of intellectual property, fraud, and other civil cases involving wrongful dismissals, breaches of contracts, and discrimination issues. The idea here is that essentially anything written on a computer file can be recovered, even if it has been erased through an operating system command. Exhibit 8.5 provides examples of the deleted information recovery that a skilled computer forensics expert can accomplish.

Recovered computer data can often be a gold mine in a fraud investigation. Perpetrators often feel they have covered their tracks by deleting files, but computer forensics tools often allow full recovery. Forensic examinations involve the examination of computer media, such as floppy disks, hard disk drives, backup tapes, CD-ROMs, and any other media used to store data. The forensic specialist uses specialized software to discover data that resides in a computer system and can recover deleted/erased, encrypted, or damaged file information and passwords, so that documents can be read.

Computer forensics is a new audit investigation rule, or set of procedures, that will aid computer fraud investigations. This area requires specialized tools and training. The typical auditor probably will not have the skills to perform such an analysis but should obtain necessary help as required.

EXHIBIT 8.5   Computer Forensics File Recovery Approaches

Computer forensics specialists can recover data from erased or deleted files using some of these approaches:	
Deleted files	These are files that the user has deleted through a Windows delete command. In many cases specialists can use software tools to recover these files.
Password-protected files	Many times it is possible to remove the password from these files and gain access to their content.
Hidden files	These are files that are not usually visible using standard Windows programs. Specialized software can read these files.
Data in free space	Free space is the hard disk space that is not currently in use. Data in free space may contain deleted or overwritten files and can be recovered.
Data in slack space	Slack space is the space within the last cluster allocated to a file that may not be wholly occupied by the file. Computer forensics specialists can discover data here.

The web site *www.forensic.to/links/pages/* provides a large number of listings of consultants and other firms; this may be a good source for help.

Other than direct testimony by an eyewitness, documentary evidence is usually the most compelling form of evidence, and paper trails traditionally have been a gold mine for investigators where fraud is involved. In past years, documentary evidence was limited to paper. Where the best evidence rule applied, the original document was produced. However, documents today are produced through personal computer software such as Microsoft Word. Many are no longer printed but e-mailed to the recipient directly from the computer. Because of the change in the way information is distributed and/or the way people communicate, copies of computer files are now as good or legitimate as the original electronic document.

NOTES

1. *Fraud: The Unmanaged Risk* (New York: Ernst & Young, 8th Global Survey, 2003).
2. The organizations are the American Institute of Certified Public Accountants, the Association of Certified Fraud Examiners, Financial Executives International, the Information Systems Audit and Control Association, the Institute of Internal Auditors, the Institute of Management Accountants, and the Society for Human Resource Management. Other organizations that participated in reviewing and offering advice include the American Accounting Association, the Defense Industry Initiative, and the National Association of Corporate Directors.

CHAPTER 9

Enterprise Risk Management, Privacy, and Other Legislative Initiatives

The Sarbanes-Oxley Act (SOA) has caused major changes in accounting and auditing controls and in corporate governance, but it certainly is not the only new rule for internal auditors as we move into the twenty-first century. This chapter discusses several recent or newer initiatives including one that has just been released in draft as this book goes to press—the COSO ERM (the Committee of Sponsoring Organizations Enterprise Risk Management) framework—as well as other new U.S. federal regulations that will impact internal controls procedures and the internal auditors in many organizations. We introduce the Gramm–Leach–Bliley Act (GLBA) with its personal financial privacy controls as well as the Health Insurance Portability and Accountability Act (HIPAA). Depending on one's organization, some of these legislative initiatives may become almost more important than SOA. Rules are always changing, and the internal audit professional should be aware of the impacts of these initiatives and legislative directions.

ENTERPRISE RISK MANAGEMENT

All business activity as well as all personal/professional work involves some risks. An individual with savings to invest for a retirement nest egg can place those savings in a very stable and low-risk money market fund with some interest income but little opportunity for growth through market appreciation. At the other extreme, the individual can invest the money in hot but untested stock with the potential for a high return but a risk that the company will fail. Most of us do something more in the middle, such as investing in mutual funds that buy blue chip stocks with good but not exceptional returns and minimal risk. Organizations go through this same risk assessment process when deciding where to invest or direct resources.

The process of identifying, analyzing, and taking actions to manage risks is discussed frequently in business publications. However, internal audit professionals often do not have a good understanding of how to apply these principles to individual internal audits conducted within their organizations. This section discusses overall risk management as well as what will soon become a common new term or concept, Enterprise Risk Management (ERM). The Committee of Sponsoring Organizations of the Treadway Commission, the group that launched COSO, has initiated a study on ERM. As this book goes to press, the first draft of the COSO ERM report has just been released. Based on the transition of the original Treadway report to what became the COSO internal controls framework, we expect some time and redefinition will occur before the final ERM framework is released. Our comments on COSO ERM here are based on a variety of net-based published sources, ranging from the Institute of Internal Auditors (IIA) to various law firms.

Although ERM concerns the overall organization, internal auditors need to understand how to use risk management to evaluate and plan individual audit projects. The chapter briefly discusses risk management concepts with an emphasis on their applicability to individual internal audit projects. Risk analysis is an important project management tool that should be used by all internal auditors. This chapter also discusses business impact analysis (BIA), a current internal audit practice, and how BIA fits into the evolving concepts of ERM.

COSO Risk Management Initiative

To quote John Flaherty, the chairman of COSO in 2002, "Although a lot of people are talking about risk, there is no commonly accepted definition of *risk management* and no comprehensive framework outlining how the process should work, making risk communication among board members and management difficult and frustrating."[1] This was the same environment that faced the Treadway Commission some ten or more years earlier when it looked at internal control and its supporting definitions. Treadway found no common or consistent definition for "internal control." The result then was COSO, the almost universally accepted framework today for internal control. Soon ERM will probably become the accepted framework for risk management as well.

ERM represents a fundamental shift in the way an organization should approach broad areas of risk, including SOA-related corporate governance issues, currency fluctuations, human resources issues in foreign countries, evaporating distribution channels, and the prospect of technology failures. ERM is a process to uncover, identify, and evaluate these risks, both by the individual risk area and a larger context of the interrelationship of the differing risks impacting an organization. According to the new COSO ERM study, ERM is defined as a process, effected by an entity's board of directors, management, and other personnel, applied in a strategy-setting analysis across the enterprise. ERM's goal is to provide reasonable assurance regarding the achievement of organizational objectives by identifying events that may affect the entity. COSO ERM will emphasize the importance of managing risk within the entity's concept or level of risk appetite. "Risk appetite" means how much risk an organization is willing to accept. Our comments about the choice between investing in a money market fund or some hot technology start-up would be based on the investor's risk appetite.

The COSO ERM framework, according to information in the draft, breaks organizational risk management objectives into four broad categories:

1. *Strategic ERM Objectives.* These are high-level goals that support the organization's overall mission. A regional electrical utility company that wanted to stay and grow in its state or regional market would have a low appetite for risk as compared to some utilities that, in the late 1990s, made various electrical utility investments worldwide.

2. *Operational ERM Objectives.* These objectives focus on the effective and efficient use of the total organization resources. There are numerous ways that an organization can conduct its day-to-day operations in either a relatively conservative or a high-risk manner.

3. *ERM Reporting Objectives.* Objectives here primarily cover the reliability of reporting to internal and external parties. With SOA penalties for fraudulent reporting, one would think that today's organizations would be very careful in limiting their reporting objective risks. However, a sufficient number of reporting options still exist in which organizations can take higher- or lower- risk approaches,

4. *ERM Compliance Objectives.* These objectives cover compliance with applicable laws and regulations. Here too there are many areas in which an organization can take a higher- or lower-risk approach. An example would be operating in an area where environmental regulations are changing and seem to be murky. An organization can take a low-risk, tow-the-line approach or, at the other extreme, can assume it is in compliance with some difficult-to-interpret rule.

With an effective ERM that addresses the above objectives, organization management should have a reasonable assurance that it is taking steps to manage their overall risks. Senior management and the board should first identify the types and scope of risks that the organization is facing. Exhibit 9.1 shows some examples of the types of risks that an enterprise may face. The idea is for a management team to consider potential risks in each of multiple areas, such as financial or operational risks. The enterprise team assessing risks should not to try to quantify *every* potential risk but to consider

EXHIBIT 9.1   Examples of ERM Categories

Enterprises face a number of risks, which vary with the type of business and other factors. Organizations should examine their risks in each of these general category areas.

- *Financial Risks.* Every organization faces multiple financial risks, such as the risk of financial loss from investing in a new acquisition or currency losses from international operations exchange rate fluctuations.

- *Human Capital Risk.* Examples might include the risk of not having qualified staff due to a past deemphasis on college recruiting or the risk of losing key staff members due to a below-market compensation program.

- *Legal and Regulatory Risks.* Operating in a highly regulated industry, such as nuclear power, or merely operating "on the edge" can introduce risks.

- *Strategic Risks.* Growth through aggressive acquisitions can impose risks as can the risk of operating too conservatively and letting competitors pass the organization by.

- *Operational Risks.* A lack of documented processes can cause organizational risks as can the failure to act quickly due to strong, centralized administrative controls.

- *Technological Risks.* The failure to upgrade and modernize systems can cause risks. Systems privacy or security penetration violations also cause risks.

major risk areas that may impede organization progress or cause limitations. Management should take a hard look at these risks and then decide which are or are not acceptable risks. The result is that an organization will develop what the COSO ERM calls a picture of its *appetite* for risk. That is, some organizations and their managers are risk takers while others are not. Each has its potential rewards and punishments.

The draft COSO ERM framework then suggests that an organization should make its appetite for risk explicit and communicate that message throughout the organization. The idea is to align that level of risk acceptance to all managers, unit heads, and staff members as well as stakeholders. If corporate management is very conservative with little appetite for risky ventures, separate business units should recognize that philosophy and also limit their risk-taking activities in order to protect the overall organization. A conservatively managed organization does not need some separate "lone ranger" unit or executive taking risks that could impact the entire organization.

As part of this identification and review of potential risks, the organization should attempt to quantify the magnitude and potential impact of each risk. This type of analysis can be performed through a series of hypothetical scenarios. Often internal audit can be of help here, as many times it goes through this type of analysis as part of internal audit reports. In some cases, risks that appeared to be enormous are seen as actually being manageable.

A next step is to create what can be called risk portfolios to identify the interrelationships among the organization's various risks. Because many of these risks are not correlated, viewing risk as part of a portfolio can reduce volatility significantly, making individually hedged risk more efficient. That is, a human resource risk from Exhibit 9.1 may have nothing to do with a technological risk in the same business area, but if both appear in the same risk portfolio, their combined potential will be greater. Based on an analysis of these potential risks, the organization should develop a strategy to provide it with some protection.

The COSO ERM framework, in its current draft form, outlines an approach to understanding enterprise-wide risks and developing a strategy for handling them. By "handling," we mean that an organization can develop controls to avoid the risk, can modify operations to all but eliminate the risk, or can acquire insurance or other controls to accept the risk. Similar to the COSO framework discussed in Chapter 5, the proposed COSO ERM currently proposes a framework of eight separate ERM components:

1. ***Internal ERM Environment.*** This component reflects the organization's appetite for risk and should help to influence the risk and control consciousness of all members of the organization. Management is responsible for establishing this foundation of attitudes toward risk for all members of the organization as a set of guidelines. There are some similarities here to the COSO control environment.

2. ***Strategic and Risk Objectives Setting.*** The organization should set objectives in the broad terms of strategies and the risks it is willing to accept. The strategic objectives will reflect management's choice as to how the organization will seek to enhance value, usually shareholder value. Following the general strategic objectives discussed previously, an organization should establish some overall risk-related objectives. For example, senior management may decide that it does not want its international operations to include ventures in the Middle East, or a retailer may determine that it does not want to have restaurant services in its store operations. These strategic and risk-based objectives will drive other business decisions.

3. ***Events Identification.*** Following the COSO internal controls concepts, management should have processes in place to implement its ERM successfully and to identify events that may have positive or negative impact on those risk-related strategies. Based on its overall risk tolerances, management should consider both internal and external events that may introduce new risks or reduce existing risk areas. These events might include changes in the competitive environment, economic or social trends, or automation developments among others.

4. ***Risk Assessments.*** As a risk event occurs, management needs to consider how the event might impact the effect of its ERM objectives in terms

of both the likelihood of an event and its impact. Chapter 7 discusses the importance of an emergency response plan in the event of a business continuity event or disaster. Although probably not documented in the formal sense, as would be done for computer systems disaster recovery, the organization should have plans in place to respond to the various risk challenges it faces.

5. ***Responses to Risks.*** Management should identify various risk response options and consider their effect on event likelihood and impact, in relation to the organization's tolerance for risk. Risk responses will include avoidance, reduction, sharing, and acceptance of the risk. The assessment of risk responses and the assurance that some risk response has been selected and implemented is a key component of the organization's ERM framework. However, an effective ERM does not mean that the *best* response to the risk was selected, only that the response selected should bring the risk likelihood and impact within the organization's established risk appetite.

6. ***Control Activities.*** Policies and procedures should be in place to ensure that appropriate risk responses are executed. These control activities should occur throughout all levels and functions within the organization, including approvals, authorizations, performance reviews, safety and security issues, and appropriate segregation of duties. There are many similarities here between COSO internal controls and the new COSO ERM framework.

7. ***Information and Communication.*** Risk-related information from internal and external sources must be identified, captured, and communicated in a form that allows appropriate members of the organization to carry out their responsibilities here. Effective communication should flow throughout the organization at all levels as well as to such external parties as customers, vendors, regulators, and shareholders.

8. ***Risk Monitoring.*** Ongoing procedures should be in place to monitor the ERM program and the quality of its performance over time.

An ERM can be judged as effective when all of these eight components are present and operating. This is true regardless of the size of the organization, although some smaller entities may implement their ERM framework somewhat differently. From a broader perspective, the draft ERM framework is a useful tool that boards and other stakeholders can use to measure how well their management teams are handling the risks they face. It is designed to answer the question: Do we have a risk management program in place in our organization?

Exhibit 9.2 shows the ERM framework as proposed in COSO's initial draft report. This framework was released at the time of our publication and may change with the final release of ERM. This three-dimensional framework covers the issues discussed in this chapter and is similar to the COSO internal control framework discussed in Chapter 5 but with some subtle differences. For example, the COSO internal control framework shown in Exhibit 5.9 places the Control Environment at the base or as the foundation for internal control while internal control monitoring is at the highest level. The reverse is true for the ERM framework, and there are now additional levels to consider. While COSO internal control had separate categories for each business unit, ERM considers risks from an entity level to a subsidiary unit level. As stated, COSO ERM is still in draft form as of mid 2003 with some modifications almost certainly to come. It does provide a comprehensive way for managers at all levels to consider risks throughout the enterprise, and it should be a useful model for senior managers coping with SOA.

At this time, COSO ERM is not even a "new rule"; its initial draft study has been released for comment with the possibility of changes to come. However, internal auditors should be aware that this new standard in process probably will impact the way an organization identifies, understands, and responds to the many risks it faces. ERM almost certainly will align with an organization's COSO internal controls framework as we move forward. The important component here of recognizing one's appetite for risk is useful for many internal audit activities.

EXHIBIT 9.2   COSO Enterprise Risk Management Framework—Exposure Draft, 2003

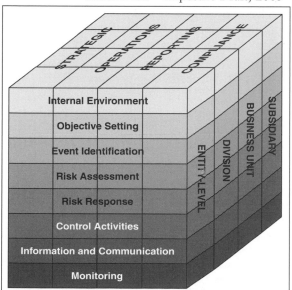

Source: Used with permission. PricewaterhouseCoopers.

Risk Assessment for Internal Auditors

While the COSO ERM framework describes a general model for understanding and assessing risks for the overall enterprise or organization, internal auditors have a need to understand and control the risks surrounding their individual audit plans and activities. Project managers have used risk management approaches for some years, and this is not a new rule or tool for internal auditors. However, internal auditors often do not use a formal risk management approach in planning and completing audit projects. Other professionals do use risk management techniques for such projects as information systems implementations or new business launches. These other professionals often use the tools and techniques promoted by the Project Management Institute (PMI),[2] which sponsors the Project Management Professional (PMP) examination and provides a wealth of published literature on project management. PMI maintains a document called the Project Management Book of Knowledge (PMBOK) that is a compilation of many good project management practices that should be helpful for internal auditors. The PMBOK focuses on broad project management concepts, and it is updated from time to time.

Internal auditors might benefit from using these PMI risk management concepts as part of normal audit activities. Every internal audit faces a range of uncertainties ranging from having no information about some subject area to total certainty and complete information, and internal audits should be planned and managed with these concepts in mind. Exhibit 9.3 shows this uncertainty spectrum, ranging from none to complete information. Assume the organization has decided to purchase some new subsidiary unit and internal audit is sent out to help on a due diligence review. The internal auditor

EXHIBIT 9.3 Project Risk Uncertainty Spectrum

No Information	Partial Information	Complete Information
(Unknown Unknowns)	(Known Unknowns)	(Knowns)

←————————————————————————————————→

Total Uncertainty	General Uncertainty	Specific Uncertainty	Total Certainty

Scope of Project Risk Management*

*Note: In this range, the information to be sought is known.

will have to approach this environment with almost total uncertainty and, thus, with a relatively high risk of encountering problems. On the other side of the spectrum, a regular compliance audit, such as an annual physical inventory observation, represents almost total certainty with little risk. To better manage higher-risk audit projects, internal auditors should focus on those more uncertain projects with an objective of gathering as much information as possible and moving to environments of greater certainty.

PMI's literature suggests that project risk should be managed following four phases of risk management. Although designed for considering risk in a wide variety of projects, these concepts are useful for better understanding risks in internal audit projects.

Risk Management Phase One: Identification

The internal auditor should attempt to identify all the possible risks that could impact the success of an upcoming internal audit project, ranging from high impact/high probability all the way to low impact/low probability. The whole idea is that internal audit should identify all of the risks it may in fact encounter when planning a new internal audit. The developer planning a multimillion-dollar project will go through an elaborate risk assessment process here; yet this step should be a useful quick exercise for all planned internal audit projects.

Risk Management Phase Two: Assessment

Having identified a range of risks, a next step is to rank them in terms of the type of risk, their potential impact, and probability. Although there are complex procedures available for such a risk ranking, most internal audit projects can be risk assessment ranked through simple subjective evaluations. The idea is to go through the possible risks that may impact an audit project and to both rank and document those risk assessment decisions. Later, internal audit may be in a position to say "Yes, we considered the risk, but did not feel there was a high probability of its occurrence."

Risk Management Phase Three: Response

After identifying all risks that may impact an internal audit project and estimating their potential impact, the internal audit risk manager should develop appropriate response strategies. These strategies may range from the simple decision to accept the risk if it occurs to comprehensive plans for deployment of resources to control a risk event. In our example of an internal audit–led due diligence review, the response plan might include tentative plans to add more resources to the effort if serious problems are encountered.

Risk Management Phase Four: Documentation

Other project managers often miss this step, but internal auditors should be well aware of the need for documentation. However, this overall risk management process always should be documented in some detail.

Our purpose in this chapter is to not go through the total formal risk management process as would a PMP project manager when launching a major development effort. Rather, we are suggesting that internal auditors should use these PMI-type risk management processes for assessing risk in individual audit projects. Internal auditors typically go through a formal risk assessment process when selecting individual audit projects from their audit universe of a wide population of potential audit candidates. This type of process should result in individual audits that are better planned with consideration given to the many things that can go wrong on an internal audit project.

Business Impact Analysis

Professionals live in a world where terminology frequently changes or is redefined. Chapter 7 discussed how the phrase "disaster recovery planning" has been largely replaced by the term business continuity planning (BCP). The concept of disaster recovery has not gone away, but BCP means a bit more. Business impact analysis is another of those terms. It frequently pops up as part of the mainstream disaster recovery/BCP literature; and others speak of BIA as a separate and different risk management process. From our perspective, BIA is an evaluation of the strengths and weaknesses of an organization's disaster preparedness and the impact an interruption would have on business operations.

The objective of a BIA process is to understand the organizational impact if the operations of some business unit or a separate department become disrupted and unable to continue with their core activities. BIA thinks of disruptions in a very broad sense, such as the risk of losing a brand name through litigation or the loss of prestige associated with that brand name through, for example, a well-publicized product recall. The BIA process is initiated through interviews and evaluations of each area of the business. The process is accomplished by interviewing on-site managers who are both senior enough to have a mature and pragmatic outlook and close enough to business activities really to understand the effects of a potential disruption. The ideal BIA candidate is often a middle-level manager with a good operational knowledge of his or her area of the business. A critical difference between BIA and the BCP process discussed in Chapter 7 is that BIA focuses on *recovery throughout the organization*. It looks at business impacts, but more than just the impact of an information systems failure.

A BIA analysis should break down the critical functions or activities for each business department. Based on interviews and other analyses, it then measures the impact of various classes of business disruptions for predefined periods of time, such as one day, two days, five days, and one month. The analysis can take many forms and include such analyses as the impacts of revenue or margin losses, the direct financial costs of replacing uninsured items, reduction in demand, possible financial penalties from regulatory bodies, expected compensation payments, the loss of market reputation, loss of key staff, and the costs associated with a loss of productivity. As much as possible, these factors would be explored during the BIA interview phase and then evaluated and quantified.

Although a prime BIA objective should be to measure impacts in financial terms, this may not always be possible. Interviewees may say that the financial impact of a disruption may be "disastrous" but provide only qualitative, no quantitative, estimates. This can be expected; many organizations have never measured such things as the cost of a missed customer call, although they recognize that there will be massive bad consequences were a customer order line to go down. A BIA should attempt to estimate risks and costs from qualitative and quantitative perspectives, comparing and rating each department under evaluation against each other. An alternative BIA approach is to analyze the potential effects of each loss on the organization's overall revenue stream and to attempt to break this effect down into its operating components. In many large and complex organizations, however, this BIA estimation process can be extremely difficult, leading to the possibility of distorted and misleading data.

If BIA is properly executed—with department-by-department interviews results with mid-level managers carried out, documented, and classified—it can help an organization achieve a number of objectives often missed in classic BCP processes. These might include the complete identification of all significant financial and nonfinancial costs, establishing more accurate time window estimates in which recovery has to take place, and raising the awareness of both BIA and BCP in the organization. For many organizations, a proposed BIA project may be a difficult sell for internal audit or the corporate security function. Historically, BIA projects were launched by some of the major public accounting firms during the 1990s. SOA and most of the major public accounting firms ending their consulting practices have changed things.

A major value of BIA can be a focus on such significant items as the effect of a catastrophe on shareholder values. We have discussed BIA in a very general manner, but the lines between BIA, BCP, and disaster recovery planning are blurred. A web browser search based on any one of these three terms will point to some of the same web sites. BIA emphasizes gaining an understanding of the costs facing an organization in the event of an information systems disaster event, while BCP emphasizes the steps necessary to recover business operations through restoration of key information systems resources. BIA requires a bit more risk analysis than does BCP and asks the analyst to focus on a wider range of issues, as outlined in Exhibit 9.4.

EXHIBIT 9.4 Business Impact Analysis Loss Consideration Areas

The following potential costs or items might be considered as part of an organization business impact analysis (BIA) exercise. An organization should focus in on key cost areas and develop recovery strategies based on areas of higher risk and higher potential loss. The BIA process should include all costs here including those that can be covered through insurance.

1. Loss of capital stock value due to shareholder desertions
2. Brand image recovery
3. Delays in customer accounting, accounts receivable, and billing/invoicing
4. Loss of control over debtors
5. Loss of credit control and increased bad debt
6. Delayed achievement of benefits of profits from new projects or products
7. Loss of revenue for service contracts from failure to provide service or meet service levels
8. Lost ability to respond to contract opportunities
9. Penalties from failure to produce periodic accounting or mandated reports or to make timely tax payments
10. Where company share value underpins loan facilities, share prices could drop and loans be called in or be rerated at higher interest levels
11. Cost of replacement of buildings and plant
12. Cost of replacing equipment
13. Cost of replacing software
14. Salaries paid to staff unable to undertake billable work
15. Salaries paid to staff to recover work backlog and maintain deadlines
16. Cost of re-creation and recovery of lost data
17. Loss of cash flow
18. Interest value on deferred billings
19. Penalty clauses invoked for late delivery and failure to meet service levels
20. Loss of customers (lifetime value of each) and market share
21. Loss of profits
22. Additional cost of credit through reduced credit rating
23. Recruitment costs for new staff on staff turnover
24. Training/retraining costs for staff
25. Fines and penalties for noncompliance
26. Liability claims
27. Additional cost of advertising, public relations, and marketing to reassure customers and prospects to retain market share
28. Additional cost of working; administrative costs; travel and subsistence; and so on

Although the BIA process is different from BCP and from disaster recovery, the basic steps for all three are very similar. The objectives of BIA, BCP, and disaster recovery are to recognize key loss areas and to determine the resources necessary to get the organization back in operation. BIA is one of the new approaches used by auditors; internal auditors, however, should not split hairs but instead should help members of the organization get the business back in operation in the event of a disaster contingency event. Doing so can best be accomplished through an effective BCP process as discussed in Chapter 7.

CONCURRENT WITH SOA: OTHER LEGISLATION IMPACTING INTERNAL AUDITORS

As emphasized throughout this book, SOA is the most significant U.S. accounting and securities legislation since the early 1930s, and it certainly has launched a series of new rules. Other recent legislation also has introduced other new rules as well. This section briefly discusses two other new items of federal legislation that have a privacy protection focus and should impact the modern organization and its internal auditors as we go forward.

Federal legislation often is named after its main legislative sponsors. Senator Sarbanes and Representative Oxley brought us the Sarbanes-Oxley Act that we have referenced throughout this book as SOA. Another newer legislative item is the Gramm–Leach–Bliley Act of 1999 (GLBA). The GLBA requires financial institutions to further protect and audit their data and to take special care when sharing this data with others. Although the GLBA is directed at financial institutions, it will impact many organizations. Here, we discuss its main components that impact internal auditors.

The Health Insurance Portability and Accountability Act (HIPAA), which does not carry the names of its legislative sponsors, has introduced a new set of privacy and security rules covering personal healthcare records. Although its focus is on healthcare providers, HIPAA covers the kinds of personal privacy records that impact all of us, and it has caused changes in such areas as human resource functions. Internal auditors should have a general understanding of the still-evolving HIPAA rules.

It is sometimes difficult to predict whether new legislation will have a continuing and lasting impact or whether it will be just a law on the books with little ongoing compliance activity. Chapter 2 of *Brink's Modern Internal Auditing*, for example, talked about the Foreign Corrupt Practices Act (FCPA) of the late 1970s.[2] That legislation's strong documentation requirements had many internal auditors thinking they would be very busy in perpetuity keeping in compliance with FCPA provisions. Although the legislation still remains on the books, there has been limited enforcement action since its enactment, and today the FCPA's requirements have been all but forgotten. We do not think that the GLBA, HIPAA, and certainly not SOA will go the same way as the FCPA, but such actions and interests rise and fall. Internal auditors need to be aware of such legislation and plan their review and internal control activities accordingly.

The Gramm–Leach–Bliley Act

The Financial Modernization Act of 1999, also known as the Gramm–Leach–Bliley Act, is a privacy-related set of requirements that aim to protect consumers' personal financial information held by financial institutions. This legislation has three principal parts, the Financial Privacy Rule, the Safeguards Rule, and the "pretexting provisions," which are discussed in the following sections. The act gives authority to eight federal agencies and the states to administer and enforce its rules. The "financial institutions" to which these rules apply include not only banks, securities firms, and insurance companies, but also companies providing many other types of financial products and services to consumers. Among these services are lending, brokering, or servicing any type of consumer loan; transferring or safeguarding money; preparing individual tax returns; providing financial advice or credit counseling; providing residential real estate settlement services; collecting consumer debts; and an array of other activities. With GLBA, these nontraditional "financial institutions" are now regulated by the Federal Trade Commission (FTC).

An internal auditor working for a bank or insurance company today probably has been involved already with GLBA and its privacy-related provisions; however, the act is a new rule that may impact many organizations due to its expanded definition of what is a financial institution. GLBA rules also are being applied to some state-regulated financial institutions. As an example, insurance companies in the United States are regulated on a state-by-state basis with the National Association of Insurance Commissioner (NAIC) acting as a central coordinating and standards-setting group. The NAIC is in the process of imposing GLBA rules on its individual state-regulated insurance companies. This is another example of how the new rules regulations evolve in some instances from a U.S. authority like the SEC for SOA matters to the similar international rules discussed in Chapter 10. We often forget that in the United States, some corporate regulation is on a state-by-state basis. Through the authority of the NAIC, GLBA rules are being adopted by most states in the United States.

Financial Privacy Rule

Consumers frequently encounter the GLBA Financial Privacy Rule today when they receive a note from a credit card provider talking about privacy rules.

The rule requires that customers receive these privacy notices explaining the financial institution's information collection and sharing practices. The privacy notice must be a clear, conspicuous, and accurate statement of the company's privacy practices; it should include what information the company collects about its consumers and customers, with whom it shares this information, and how it protects or safeguards the information. The notice applies to the "nonpublic personal information" the company gathers and discloses about its consumers and customers; in practice, that may be most—or all—of the information a company has about them. For example, nonpublic personal information could be information that a consumer or customer puts on an application; information about the individual from another source, such as a credit bureau; or information about transactions between the individual and the company, such as an account balance. Indeed, even the fact that an individual is a consumer or customer of a particular financial institution is nonpublic person information. Information that the company has reason to believe is lawfully public—such as mortgage loan information in a jurisdiction where that information is publicly recorded—is not restricted by the GLBA rules.

Many consumers today pay little attention to these notices, even though they may state that the company may share consumer names with others. GLBA gives the customer the right to opt out of or say no to having information shared with certain third parties. The privacy notice must explain how, and offer a reasonable way, for customers to do that. For example, providing a toll-free telephone number or a detachable form with a preprinted address is a reasonable way for consumers or customers to opt out; requiring someone to write a letter as the only way to opt out is not. The privacy notice also must explain that consumers have a right to say no to the sharing of certain credit report or application information with the financial institution's separate divisions or affiliates.

GLBA puts some limits on how anyone who receives nonpublic personal information from a financial institution can use or redisclose the information. If a lender discloses customer information to a service provider responsible for mailing account statements, where the consumer has no right to opt out, that service provider may use the information only for limited purposes—such as for mailing account statements—and may not sell the information or use it for marketing.

This GLBA Federal Privacy Rule gets more complex as we get into its details. Our intention here is not to give a detailed explanation of this portion of GLBA but to explain these privacy rules in general. An internal auditor should recognize that all personal financial information is very private and cannot just be arbitrarily sold or otherwise distributed. Consumers have rights to opt out and say no, and the organization must keep appropriate records of these actions and respect consumer privacy rights. Internal auditors working with any financial institutions or applications should be aware of how GLBA privacy rules apply to their organization. A risk to an organization is that it may take the privacy rules as an almost trivial matter, perhaps fail to honor an opt-out request or improperly sell a mailing list, and then find itself facing some type of class action litigation for damages.

GLBA Safeguards Rule

The act's Safeguards Rule requires financial institutions to have a security plan in place to protect the confidentiality and integrity of personal consumer information. When consumers open an account or purchase some product, they often disclose some personal information—such as address, telephone number, or credit card number—as part of that transaction process. An organization must have a security plan in place to protect the confidentiality and integrity of that personal data. It should cover more than just the business continuity risks discussed in Chapter 7 and include controls to prevent hackers from accessing data files, disgruntled employees from accessing customer information, or just simple carelessness. The GLBA Safeguards Rule requires that every financial institution, regardless of size, must create and implement a written information security plan for the protection of customer data. The scope and complexity of the security plan may be scaled to the size of the institution and the sensitivity of the information it maintains. The plan should be based on a risk analysis that identifies all foreseeable threats to the security, confidentiality, and integrity of customer information. Based on that risk analysis, financial institutions must document and implement security measures that include administrative measures such as employee training; technical protections including passwords, encryption controls, firewalls; and physical safeguards such as locks on doors and computers. Financial institutions must designate one or more employees to coordinate the safeguards and must conduct periodic reviews to determine whether their security programs require updating in light of changed circumstances.

An organization can take five steps to start becoming compliant with the GLBA Safeguards Rule:

1. ***Environmental Risk Analysis.*** The organization should formally identify the internal and external risks to the security, confidentiality, and integrity of customer personal information. Risk analysis was discussed earlier in this chapter. This process should cover all sources of personal information, whether on automated systems or manual records.

2. ***Designing and Implementing Safeguards.*** These safeguards are the internal controls discussed in Chapter 5 and elsewhere throughout this book.

3. ***Monitoring and Auditing.*** Continuous monitoring processes, such as are discussed in Chapter 11, should be in place. Internal audit can play an important role here by regularly scheduling reviews of the adequacy of the security plan, coupled with appropriate compliance tests.

4. ***Constant Improvements Program.*** The organization should have a program in place to constantly improve its security plan, based on results of audits and other tests.. That program should be well documented to describe the plan's progress.

5. ***Overseeing Security Providers and Partners.*** Many partners and other organizations may have access to this same personal information or may have access to systems network connections where that personal privacy can be violated. Policies, controls, and audit procedures need to be in place here as well.

The Safeguards Rule applies to a wide range of providers of financial products and services, including mortgage brokers, nonbank lenders, appraisers, credit reporting agencies, professional tax preparers, and retailers that issue their own credit cards. Banks are not subject to the Safeguards Rule, but must comply with similar counterpart regulations that have been issued by federal banking agencies. The Safeguards Rule was not applicable to nonbank financial institutions before May 23, 2003. Failure to comply with the Safeguards Rule may result in fines or other enforcement action by the Federal Trade Commission.

GLBA Pretexting Provisions

GLBA prohibits "pretexting"—the use of false pretenses, including fraudulent statements and impersonation—to obtain consumers' personal financial information, such as bank balances. Pretexters use a variety of tactics to get personal information. For example, a pretexter may call, claim she's from a survey firm, ask a few questions to get the name of one's bank, and then use the information gathered to call the target person's financial institution, pretending to be that person or with authorized access to the account. She might claim that she's forgotten her checkbook and needs information about the account. In this way, the pretexter may be able to obtain personal information about people, including Social Security numbers, bank and credit card account numbers, information in credit reports, and the existence and size of savings and investment portfolios.

Under GLBA's Pretexting Provisions, it is illegal for anyone to:

- Use false, fictitious, or fraudulent statements or documents to get customer information from a financial institution or directly from a customer of a financial institution.

- Use forged, counterfeit, lost, or stolen documents to get customer information from a financial institution or directly from a customer of a financial institution.

- Ask another person to get someone else's customer information using false, fictitious or fraudulent statements or using false, fictitious, or fraudulent documents or forged, counterfeit, lost, or stolen documents.

  Pretexting leads to a new security and privacy risk or exposure, identity theft. Identity theft occurs when someone hijacks personal identifying information to open new charge accounts, order merchandise, or borrow money. Consumers targeted by identity thieves usually do not know they have been victimized until the hijackers fail to pay the bills or repay the loans, and collection agencies begin dunning the consumers for payment of accounts they did not even know they had.

A separate federal law related to GLBA, the Identity Theft and Assumption Deterrence Act, makes it a federal crime when someone "knowingly transfers or uses, without lawful authority, a means of identification of another person with the intent to commit, or to aid or abet, any unlawful activity that constitutes a violation of federal law, or that constitutes a felony under any applicable state or local law." Here, a name or Social Security number is considered a "means of identification," as is a credit card number, cellular telephone electronic serial number, or any other piece of information that may be used alone or in conjunction with other information to identify a specific individual.

GLBA is one of the new rules that will impact many internal auditors, particularly those in any type of financial institution. Many aspects of GLBA are designed to protect consumer financial information, the definition of which has become so broad that GLBA impacts many internal auditors in the United States.

HIPAA and Internal Auditors

An internal auditor for a manufacturing company or a financial services organization might ask, "Why should I care about HIPAA?" Legislation that affects healthcare privacy records has an impact on all of us. Enacted in 1999 with final rules still being released as this book went to press, the Health Insurance Portability and Accountability Act (HIPAA) will have a major impact on the privacy and security of personal medical records and other personal records. As individuals, we see HIPAA's impact when we visit our doctor's office for an annual physical and are asked to sign what looks like an innocuous disclosure statement before getting started. Human resource (HR) functions in organizations are seeing the impact of HIPAA requirements today in their administration of employee healthcare plans and medical treatment records. Of course, HIPAA has caused a large and ever-growing impact on the entire healthcare industry and all affiliated delivery providers. In addition, it will improve standards for business processes based on electronic commerce.

The original HIPAA legislation had four primary objectives:

1. *Ensure health portability by eliminating preexisting condition job locks.* This was the original motivation for the passage of HIPAA. People were diagnosed with some condition and then unable to change jobs or acquire new health coverage because information about that condition often was shared cavalierly with others.

2. *Reduce healthcare fraud and abuse.* Our words here are from the congressional hearings leading to the legislation when some examples of alleged fraud and abuse were cited.

3. *Enforce standards for health information.* The HIPAA privacy and security rules outlined below cover this area.

4. *Guarantee security and privacy of health information.*

This section provides a brief overview of HIPAA objectives and the resultant rules covering privacy and security. Our intent is not to provide an exhaustive introduction to all aspects of HIPAA but to introduce it as another of the legislatively driven new rules that will impact many internal auditors. The progress of the HIPAA legislation illustrates how the government-sponsored rule-making process often works and, perhaps, shows that we can expect the new Public Corporation Accounting Oversight Board (PCAOB) auditing standards rules will take some time to develop and get issued. HIPAA rules initially were issued in draft form following an early published schedule. The drafts resulted in lots of comments; revised rules drafts were issued with still more comments; and the final rules were issued much later than originally planned. The PCAOB auditing standards rules to come, discussed in Chapter 2, probably will proceed in a similar manner.

HIPAA Patient Record Privacy Rules

Patient privacy is the reason why we have HIPAA. We visit our medical care providers, discuss some concern that we have, and then expect treatment in a manner that is confidential or private. We do not want the results of that physician visit to be communicated back to our employer's HR department, to some other insurance company that has no need to know, or to be left on a desk in the medical care provider's office for anyone to pick up. Even worse, we do not want what we think are confidential matters to be shared in a manner that may limit our job transfer options. However, many parties need to have some information about our healthcare condition to provide adequate coverage or reimbursement, and virtually all healthcare operations require detailed and complex supporting systems. HIPAA privacy rules cover five general areas, which are outlined briefly in the next paragraphs. These comments do not provide exhaustive coverage of and do not intend this material to be a reference source for HIPAA rules; we only aim to provide the internal auditor nonmedical professional with an overview of these HIPAA new rules.

1. *Medical Records Uses and Disclosures.* An organization that is subject to HIPAA rules must take steps to limit the use and disclosure of personal medical information to "the minimum necessary to accomplish the intended purpose of the use, disclosure, or request" for non–treatment-related matters. HIPAA contains many guidelines that will be subject to organization-by-organization specific rules with practices tested through other rulings or litigation over time.

   HIPAA specifies that individual health information loses its HIPAA protection if the individual covered is "de-identified" in a manner that this health information will not contain any of 18 specific identifiers of the individual and his or her relatives, employers, or household members. This requirement says a lot about HIPAA. The legislation identifies these 18 specific factors that a specialist in data mining, as briefly discussed in Chapter 11, might use to identify the individual.

2. *Authorization Requirements.* Many users of healthcare services encounter this section of HIPAA first. Healthcare providers must obtain written approval to disclose healthcare information on everything with the exception of emergency situations. An individual has the right to refuse such a disclosure, and healthcare providers must have a strong record retention requirement to keep track of all of these disclosures.

3. *Privacy Practice Communications.* Healthcare providers must have published Privacy Practices that they should provide to healthcare users. Individuals then have the right to formally request restrictions in this policy, and providers must accommodate reasonable requests.

4. *Medical Record Access and Amendment Rights.* Individuals have the right to inspect and copy all or a portion of their personal health information. In addition, individuals have the right to request amendments to those healthcare records. Finally, the healthcare provider must keep a record of all other parties that requested access to these personal healthcare records in the six-month period prior to any request.

5. *HIPAA Privacy Administration.* Going beyond the records access and disclosure rules, HIPAA has an extensive set of administrative requirements. These rules apply to what are called "covered entities"— medical offices, laboratories, hospitals, and all others involved with personal healthcare. These privacy administration rules include:

   a. The provider must designate a "privacy official" who is responsible for the development and implementation of these policies and procedures.

b. The provider must train members of its workforce on these HIPAA-related policies and procedures and must maintain documentation that the training has been provided.

c. A healthcare provider must have in place administrative, technical, and physical safeguards to protect the privacy of personal health information.

d. The healthcare provider must apply "appropriate sanctions" against employees who fail to comply with these privacy polices and procedures.

e. The provider must develop and implement policies and procedures that are designed to comply with the elements of the HIPAA regulations, and this documentation must be maintained in written or electronic form for six years.

Besides covering access to personal healthcare information, these HIPAA rules outline other areas that really define good operating practices that should be implemented elsewhere in the organization. An example would be the requirement that healthcare providers maintain documentation covering their training programs. These types of rules that have existed for Food and Drug Administration medical or drug programs, are now part of HIPAA, and are a good idea for most corporate training programs. Organizations sometimes spend resources in training their employees but do not bother to document that activity very well.

Cryptography, PKI, and HIPAA Security Requirements

In addition to its medical records authorization and release privacy rules, HIPAA contains some very specific and perhaps difficult-to-implement information systems security requirements. It pushes to the edges of today's common computer security practices and requires such things as secure electronic signatures even though, at the time of this publication, there are no technically mature techniques to provide such security on open networks such as the Internet. We are still at a point where a skilled computer hacker can intercept a cellphone call, and such a call covering healthcare-related matters could be in violation of HIPAA security requirements. Technology will change, control procedures will improve, the hackers will get ever smarter, and violations will be settled in the courts.

The basic concept behind these security rules is that the pre-HIPAA security of healthcare administrative systems is often inadequate. Organizations can improve their security not by purchasing and installing new software but by improving human-driven policies first. The HIPAA Security Standards rules were not finalized and put into effect until April 2003. Full compliance will not be required until April 21, 2005, a date that still seems far in the future but will be a challenge for many organizations to implement.

Security is a key element of keeping personal health information private, and many first steps are mainly a matter of improving the design and function of organizational security-related systems. The following paragraphs summarize some of these HIPAA security rules. They cover good security practices for much more than just medical records, such as requirements for strong disaster recovery standards.

HIPAA Security Administrative Procedures

HIPAA requires administrative procedures to be in place to guard data integrity, confidentiality, and availability. These procedures must be carefully documented per HIPAA rules. Exhibit 9.5 lists these required administrative procedures. We have listed the implementation rules here in a very general manner; published HIPAA rules tend to be very detailed. Many of these requirements, such as a documented and tested contingency plan or formal policies for information access controls, are similar to the control procedures internal auditors have been recommending over the years. Now, as an administrative rule, a HIPAA-impacted healthcare provider will face a penalty if its established rules and procedures are found inadequate.

EXHIBIT 9.5   Administrative Procedures Required for HIPAA
Computer Security

Security Requirement	Implementation Requirements
Certification	The organization is required to certify that it has performed internal quality assurance testing both internally and with an external certification entity.
Chain of Trust Agreements	Formal agreements should be in place between all medical partner providers.
Contingency Plans	Contingency processes must be in place including: ■ Application and data criticality analysis ■ Data backup plans ■ Formal disaster recovery plans ■ Emergency operations plans ■ Contingency testing and revision processes
Formal Mechanisms for Processing Records	Strong applications controls that emphasize security and integrity need to be in place.

EXHIBIT 9.5   Administrative Procedures Required for HIPAA
Computer Security *(Continued)*

Security Requirement	Implementation Requirements
Information Access Controls	Controls here should cover access authorization, establishment, and modification.
Internal Audit Requirements	Security procedures should be audited on a regular basis to assess quality, currency, and documentation controls.
Personnel Security	Strong procedures here should include: ■ Adequate supervision of maintenance personnel ■ Personnel access and clearance procedures ■ Security-related training for all personnel
Security Configuration Management	Strong configuration management processes need to be in place that reflect the ITIL configuration management processes mentioned in Chapter 10.
Security Incident Procedures	There should be effective procedures for reporting incidents with consistent response mechanisms.
Security Management Processes	Documented procedures should be in place for risk analysis, risk management, and the overall security policy.
Termination Procedures	Strong procedures should be in place to manage and monitor employee terminations including removal from all user accounts and access files, turning in user access key, and changing combination locks, if used.
Training	Training programs must include: ■ Awareness training for all personnel including management ■ Periodic reminders to all on security policies ■ User education concerning log-in processes, reporting discrepancies, password protection, and information systems virus protection

HIPAA security requirements also include some physical safeguard rules. These rules are similar to physical access controls that have existed over data centers going back to the days of mainframe computers. Here, however, HIPAA calls for strong guidelines and documentation over workstation use and location. While we typically do not think much of the physical controls surrounding the many networked terminals in a business environment, a medical workstation, such as a nurse's, requires strong controls in a medical environment.

Technical Security Services and Mechanisms

Processes should be put in place to guard data integrity, confidentiality, and availability and to prevent unauthorized access to data that is transmitted over communications networks. The rules here, which will not be effective until 2005, will require some very strong information systems security controls, controls that are stronger than those found in many large corporations today. These HIPAA technical security requirements include:

- *Access Control.* Strong control mechanisms based on the context of the data or the role/position of authorized users must be established. In addition, control processes always must be in place to allow emergency access if required.
- *Audit Controls.* Here and throughout all of the HIPAA rules are requirements for strong audit controls, including such things as documentation of revisions and traditional audit trails.
- *Data Authentication.* Strong systems controls are required here.
- *Entity Authentication.* Controls must be in place such that when one workstation attempts to access another, it is authenticated. This process may include passwords, telephone call backs, or even biometric controls.
- *Communications and Network Controls.* A wide range of controls are suggested here, including alarms, encryption, event reporting, message authentication, and others. The HIPAA-impacted organization must implement a very secure network.

Electronic Signatures

HIPAA requires that electronic controls be established that will provide the same legal weight to electronic data signatures as is associated with an ordinal signature on a paper document. HIPAA rules require message integrity, nonrepudiation, and user authentication. However, it is well recognized that no technically mature techniques currently exist here in an open network environment. Digital signature processes are in place today, but they are often somewhat cumbersome. Nevertheless, these digital signatures will be required until other techniques are developed.

Going Forward: HIPAA and e-Commerce

Although designed to protect and authenticate medical information, HIPAA rules outline some strong guidelines for all electronic commerce processes. A major requirement here will be improved standards and processes for electronic signatures. There is still much to be accomplished before processes become common and commercially available, and the National Institute of Standards and Technology (NIST) is taking a leadership role in the development of a Federal Public Key Infrastructure that supports digital signatures and other public key-enabled security services. NIST is coordinating with industry and technical groups developing technology to foster interoperability of public key incryption (PKI) products and projects.

The HIPAA 2005 due date will almost certainly push progress in this area. There had been many predictions for improved e-commence control procedures prior to the dot-com bust of the early 2000s. These HIPAA rules should serve as a strong incentive to move things along. They will become additional new rules for internal auditors. Of course, in worst case, if we approach 2005 with nothing acceptable, the rules will have to change.

NOTES

1. Cited on the COSO home page, *www.coso.org.*
2. Project Management Institute, Newtown Square, PA, *www.pmi.org.*

CHAPTER 10

Rules and Procedures for Internal Auditors Worldwide

The Sarbanes-Oxley Act (SOA) is a U.S. law that was enacted in response to financial frauds in U.S. corporations such as Enron and WorldCom. When these frauds were first discovered, the only non-U.S. corporation with an Enron-like accounting scandal was Tyco, with headquarters in Bermuda. Tyco, whose chief executive officer (CEO) was involved in flagrant financial excesses, was really a U.S. corporation that had transferred its corporate registration to Bermuda for tax purposes. At that time, journalists and politicians elsewhere in the world and particularly in European Union (EU) countries tut-tutted that this financial fraud was just a U.S. problem. Later, they particularly resented the plans of the Security and Exchange Commission (SEC), as discussed in Chapter 2, to impose SOA rules on all international corporations whose securities are registered on U.S. exchanges.

It did not take long to realize that the United States was not the only country with financial fraud issues. In February 2003, the major Dutch food distributor Royal Ahold admitted an "accounting irregularity" of some $500 million. Ahold had operations throughout the world and was found to have misstated its accounting and financial records to show better results. While the investigations of Ahold were continuing at the time of this publication, that same period saw a corruption trial in France for some 37 people from the major oil company Elf who were accused of siphoning off over $400 million of corporate funds through the 1990s. The Elf CEO was the main miscreant there. When asked at the trial to justify the use of Elf corporate funds for the purchase of a $9.3 million Paris mansion as well as a country chateau and $4.5 million to help with a personal divorce settlement after 18 months of marriage, the ex-CEO stated, "I allowed myself to get carried away."

This chapter looks at SOA from an international perspective. Although some rules are yet to be released, we look at the act from the focus of a non-U.S. corporation. The emphasis will be on internal auditor responsibilities. The chapter also provides an overview of International Auditing Standards

(IAS), a set of guidelines with U.S. roots that are now evolving into their own set of guidance standards.

Many professionals have seen the words "ISO Registered" included in customer brochures and other advertising materials. Although the United States often pushes its standards on the rest of the world, ISO (the International Standards Organization) is an international set of guidelines that many U.S. organizations have adopted. ISO is important for today's global economy, and internal audit can help to ensure effective ISO compliance. ISO quality standards, the ISO registration process, and ISO quality audits are introduced in this chapter. This chapter also introduces the Information Technology Infrastructure Library (ITIL) of service delivery and support processes, an important set of guidance material that originated in the United Kingdom, is common in Europe, has become established in Canada, and is just being introduced in the United States. Although not a new rule, ITIL represents some best practices procedures that should become better recognized by internal auditors worldwide.

SOA INTERNATIONAL REQUIREMENTS

When SOA was enacted in 2002, the legislation covered all companies with SEC registration, whether U.S. based or internationally based. Many foreign-registered companies initially assumed they would be exempted from all or at least some of these requirements as these final SEC rules were issued. As of the beginning of 2003, for example, the New York Stock Exchange listed 474 non-U.S. companies from 51 countries with a combined global market capitalization of approximately $4.3 trillion. Among other differences, these soon-to-come-under-SOA organizations do not always follow U.S. generally accepted accounting principles (GAAP), their audit committee rules are different, and they sometimes only report financial results annually. To appease these foreign companies, the SEC offered a number of limited exemptions or special accommodations, including attorney conduct rules and clarifications on the use of non-GAAP financial measures, among others. However, SOA essentially applies to all foreign companies that have any securities registered on U.S. exchanges.

Like their U.S. counterparts, foreign companies are required to provide certification of their financial statements by their chief executive officers (CEOs) and chief financial officers (CFOs). Thus, foreign CFOs and CEOs are subjecting themselves to possible U.S. legal liabilities. For violators, the prosecution process may be challenging, but a foreign national who is even indicted under a U.S. law will have trouble visiting the United States until the matter is resolved. Foreign-registered organizations must either begin to comply with SOA rules or seek delisting of their securities that are registered on U.S. exchanges. At the time of this publication, only a few foreign companies have openly opted out of the U.S. markets because of this new SOA regulatory environment.

SOA has raised the bar for foreign corporations listed on U.S. exchanges, but the United Kingdom and the European Union (EU) currently are studying some similar SOA-like requirements. In years to come there will be a move toward tighter governance standards in all major foreign countries, making those SOA and related regulations more palatable. This chapter discusses the increasingly important International Accounting and Auditing (IAA) standards, the Committee of Sponsoring Organizations (COSO) internal control standards worldwide, such as Canada's Criteria of Control (CoCo), and the ISO registration process.

INTERNATIONAL ACCOUNTING AND AUDITING STANDARDS

Internal and external auditors based in the United States had thought of the American Institute of Certified Public Accountants (AICPA) and its Auditing Standards Board (ASB) as the authority that had established auditing standards for U.S. organizations up until SOA and its Public Accounting Oversight Board (PCAOB). Of course, the whole purpose of any audit is to review compliance against some recognized standard or principle. One of the major tenets of internal control, under COSO and any other internal audit standard for that matter, is compliance with laws and regulations. That legal compliance becomes a standard for audits of internal controls, and financial audits also assess the fairness of accounting procedures based on established accounting standards. In the United States, those standards are based on GAAP as well as very specific accounting rules prescribed by the Financial Accounting Standards Board (FASB). These auditing and accounting standards are not necessarily the same throughout the world.

Although standards such as double-entry bookkeeping are used and recognized throughout the world, other practices may be different in various countries or regions. The practice of driving on the right- or left-hand side of the road is an example of a country or regional practice. No matter which standard is followed, drivers still can get from point A to point B as long as all drivers follow the same rule. The same is true for effective auditing and accounting standards and practices. The situation becomes a bit more complex because we are an increasingly global economy and accounting and auditing practices in Belgium, for example, need to be comparable with nearby neighbors France and Germany. In addition, there is a need for some consistency between Belgium and a broad range of other countries, including the United States. As individual organizations become increasingly global, internal auditors should at least have a general understanding of the differences and consistencies across international borders.

Accounting and auditing standards were established on a country-by-country basis by national professional or governmental boards with some guidance from international standards-setting bodies. Individual countries may fully or only generally accept these international standards. The United States is an example of the latter. With strong established practices in many areas, often the United States takes the lead or goes its own way regarding auditing and accounting standards. U.S. auditors working in an international environment must gain a general understanding of these worldwide "rules" and how they might apply to auditors' organizations, and also of what body sets the appropriate auditing and accounting standards. The latter can be confusing.

As we move into the world of international organizations, we run into a gaggle of initials to describe the international rules-setting organizations. Consider the United Nations (UN) with its UNESCO, FAO, UNICEF, UNCTAD, and many more organizations. International auditing and accounting standards are tied to the same confusing sets of initials. There are ISAs (International Standards of Auditing), as well as IASs (International Accounting Standards). The ISA auditing standards are established by the International Federation of Accountants (IFAC) through its International Auditing and Assurance Standards Board (IAASB), which issues these ISAs as well as International Auditing Practice Statements (IAPSs). To complicate the picture, there is also the International Organization of Supreme Audit Institutions (INTOSAI), whose Auditing Standards Committee contributes to the work of IAASB.

The ISA auditing standards are somewhat consistent with the U.S. pre-SOA Statements of Auditing Standards (SAS documents) and probably will be consistent with the auditing standards to be issued under PCAOB as well. Exhibit 10.1 lists the current ISA auditing standards. Similar to the earlier SAS process in the United States, ISAs are released after publication of an exposure draft but are published in over 20 languages, including French, German, Russian, and Spanish. More than 70 countries have indicated that they either have adopted IASs or feel there are no significant differences between their standards and the ISA international standards. The United States is one of the countries with no significant differences here. In many cases, an ISA has followed the issuance of a U.S. SAS, a process that almost certainly will continue with the PCAOB's auditing standards. For example, the recently revised ISA 240 closely follows SAS No. 99 on auditing for fraud, as discussed in Chapter 8. To provide a flavor of these standards, Exhibit 10.2 shows ISA 610 on considering the work of internal auditors. The typical U.S. auditor, and particularly an internal auditor, does not need to have a detailed understanding of these international standards of auditing at present. However, as we work in a more global environment, these standards will become increasingly important.

EXHIBIT 10.1 International Standards on Auditing

Introductory Matters

ISA 100   Framework of International Standards on Auditing

ISA 120   Assurance Engagements

Responsibilities

ISA 200   Objectives and General Principles Governing an Audit of
              Financial Statements

ISA 210   Terms of Audit Engagements

ISA 220   Quality Controls for Audit Work

ISA 230   Documentation

ISA 240   The Auditor's Responsibility to Consider Fraud and Error
              in an Audit of Financial Statements

ISA 250   Consideration of Laws and Regulations in an Audit of a
              Financial Statement

ISA 260   Communication of Audit Matters with those Charged with
              Governance

Planning

ISA 300   Planning

ISA 310   Knowledge of Business

ISA 320   Audit Materiality

Internal Control

ISA 400   Risk Assessments and Internal Control

ISA 410   Auditing in a Computer Information Systems Environment

ISA 420   Audit Considerations Relating to Entities using Service
              Organizations

Audit Evidence

ISA 500   Audit Evidence

ISA 510   Initial Engagements—Opening Balances

ISA 520   Analytical Procedures

ISA 530   Audit Sampling and Selective Testing Procedures

ISA 540   Audit of Accounting Estimates

ISA 550   Related Parties

ISA 560   Subsequent Events

ISA 570   Going Concern

ISA 580   Management Representations

(continues)

EXHIBIT 10.1 International Standards on Auditing *(Continued)*

Using Work of Others

ISA 600 Using the Work of Another Auditor

ISA 610 Considering the Work of Internal Auditing

ISA 620 Using the Work of an Expert

Audit Conclusions and Reporting

ISA 700 The Auditor's Report on Financial Statements

ISA 710 Comparatives

ISA 720 Other Information in Documents Containing Audited Financial Statements

Specialized Areas

ISA 800 The Auditor's Report on Special Purpose Audit Engagements

ISA 810 The Examination of Prospective Financial Information

Related Services

ISA 910 Engagements to Review Financial Statements

ISA 920 Engagements to Perform Agreed-Upon Procedures Regarding Financial Statements

ISA 930 Engagements to Compile Financial Information

The International Accounting Standards Board (IASB) publishes accounting standards in a series of pronouncements called International Financial Reporting Standards (IFRSs). Those pronouncements, designated International Accounting Standards, provide a basis for all countries worldwide and, in particular, provide accounting standards for developing countries that do not have established auditing standards. Most developed countries have established auditing standards that generally follow U.S., British, German, Swiss, or French standards. The IAS standards historically were not inconsistent with those country-by-country standards. An auditor doing work in a developing country, with weak accounting and auditing standards, should look to the IAS materials to form a basis for appropriate standards. Going forward, all countries that are members of the European Union (EU) will be required to adopt the IASB international auditing standards by 2005. This will eliminate country-by-country standards differences within EU countries.

In a step toward eliminating the existing differences between U.S. GAAP and international standards, FASB and IASB are examining and selecting the better of these standards in each of 15 areas, including how companies make restatements when accounting standards change as well as a consistent

EXHIBIT 10.2   ISA 610—Considering the Work
of Internal Auditing

Introduction

1. The purpose of this International Standard on Auditing (ISA) is to establish standards and provide guidance to external auditors in considering the work of internal auditing. This ISA does not deal with instances when personnel from internal auditing assist the external auditor in carrying out external audit procedures. The procedures noted in this ISA need only be applied to internal auditing activities which are relevant to the audit of the financial statements.

2. The external auditor should consider the activities of internal auditing and their effect, if any, on external audit procedures.

3. "Internal auditing" means an appraisal activity established within an entity as a service to the entity. Its functions include, amongst other things, examining, evaluating and monitoring the adequacy and effectiveness of the accounting and internal control systems.

4. While the external auditor has sole responsibility for the audit opinion expressed and for determining the nature, timing and extent of external audit procedures, certain parts of internal auditing work may be useful to the external auditor.

Scope and Objectives of Internal Auditing

5. The scope and objectives of internal auditing vary widely and depend on the size and structure of the entity and the requirements of its management. Ordinarily, internal auditing activities include one or more of the following:

- Review of the accounting and internal control systems. The establishment of adequate accounting and internal control systems is a responsibility of management which demands proper attention on a continuous basis. Internal auditing is ordinarily assigned specific responsibility by management for reviewing these systems, monitoring their operation and recommending improvements thereto.

- Examination of financial and operating information. This may include review of the means used to identify, measure, classify and report such information and specific inquiry into individual items including detailed testing of transactions, balances and procedures.

- Review of the economy, efficiency and effectiveness of operations including non-financial controls of an entity.

- Review of compliance with laws, regulations and other external requirements and with management policies and directives and other internal requirements.

(continues)

EXHIBIT 10.2   ISA 610—Considering the Work
of Internal Auditing *(Continued)*

Relationship between Internal Auditing and the External Auditor

6. The role of internal auditing is determined by management, and its objectives differ from those of the external auditor who is appointed to report independently on the financial statements. The internal audit function's objectives vary according to management's requirements. The external auditor's primary concern is whether the financial statements are free of material misstatements.

7. Nevertheless some of the means of achieving their respective objectives are often similar and thus certain aspects of internal auditing may be useful in determining the nature, timing and extent of external audit procedures.

8. Internal auditing is part of the entity. Irrespective of the degree of autonomy and objectivity of internal auditing it cannot achieve the same degree of independence as required of the external auditor when expressing an opinion on the financial statements. The external auditor has sole responsibility for the audit opinion expressed, and that responsibility is not reduced by any use made of internal auditing. All judgments relating to the audit of the financial statements are those of the external auditor.

Understanding and Preliminary Assessment of Internal Auditing

9. The external auditor should obtain a sufficient understanding of internal audit activities to assist in planning the audit and developing an effective audit approach.

10. Effective internal auditing will often allow a modification in the nature and timing, and a reduction in the extent of procedures performed by the external auditor but cannot eliminate them entirely. In some cases however, having considered the activities of internal auditing, the external auditor may decide that internal auditing will have no effect on external audit procedures.

11. During the course of planning the audit the external auditor should perform a preliminary assessment of the internal audit function when it appears that internal auditing is relevant to the external audit of the financial statements in specific audit areas.

12. The external auditor's preliminary assessment of the internal audit function will influence the external auditor's judgment about the use which may be made of internal auditing in modifying the nature, timing and extent of external audit procedures.

13. When obtaining an understanding and performing a preliminary assessment of the internal audit function, the important criteria are:

    a. *Organizational Status:* Specific status of internal auditing in the entity and the effect this has on its ability to be objective. In the ideal situation, internal auditing will report to the highest level of management

EXHIBIT 10.2   ISA 610—Considering the Work
of Internal Auditing *(Continued)*

and be free of any other operating responsibility. Any constraints or restrictions placed on internal auditing by management would need to be carefully considered. In particular, the internal auditors will need to be free to communicate fully with the external auditor.

b. *Scope of Function:* The nature and extent of internal auditing assignments performed. The external auditor would also need to consider whether management acts on internal audit recommendations and how this is evidenced.

c. *Technical Competence:* Whether internal auditing is performed by persons having adequate technical training and proficiency as internal auditors. The external auditor may, for example, review the policies for hiring and training the internal auditing staff and their experience and professional qualifications.

d. *Due Professional Care:* Whether internal auditing is properly planned, supervised, reviewed and documented. The existence of adequate audit manuals work programs and working papers would be considered.

Timing of Liaison and Coordination

14. When planning to use the work of internal auditing, the external auditor will need to consider internal auditing's tentative plan for the period and discuss it at as early a stage as possible. Where the work of internal auditing is to be a factor in determining the nature, timing and extent of the external auditor's procedures, it is desirable to agree in advance the timing of such work, the extent of audit coverage, test levels and proposed methods of sample selection, documentation of the work performed and review and reporting procedures.

15. Liaison with internal auditing is more effective when meetings are held at appropriate intervals during the period. The external auditor would need to be advised of and have access to relevant internal auditing reports and be kept informed of any significant matter that comes to the internal auditor's attention which may affect the work of the external auditor. Similarly, the external auditor would ordinarily inform the internal auditor of any significant matters which may affect internal auditing.

Evaluating and Testing the Work of Internal Auditing

16. When the external auditor intends to use specific work of internal auditing, the external auditor should evaluate and test that work to confirm its adequacy for the external auditor's purposes.

17. The evaluation of specific work of internal auditing involves consideration of the adequacy of the scope of work and related programs and whether

(continues)

EXHIBIT 10.2   ISA 610—Considering the Work
of Internal Auditing *(Continued)*

the preliminary assessment of the internal auditing remain appropriate. This evaluation may include consideration of whether:

a. the work is performed by persons having adequate technical training and proficiency as internal auditors and the work of assistants is properly supervised, reviewed and documented;

b. sufficient appropriate audit evidence is obtained to afford a reasonable basis for the conclusions reached;

c. conclusions reached are appropriate in the circumstances and any reports prepared are consistent with the results of the work performed; and

d. any exceptions or unusual matters disclosed by internal auditing are properly resolved.

18. The nature, timing and extent of the testing of the specific work of internal auditing will depend on the external auditor's judgment as to the risk and materiality of the area concerned, the preliminary assessment of the internal auditing and the evaluation of the specific work by internal auditing. Such tests may include examination of items already examined by internal auditing, examination of other similar items and observation of internal auditing procedures.

19. The external auditor would record conclusions regarding the specific internal auditing work that has been evaluated and tested.

Note: This document is one of the ISA International Auditing Standards as used in the European Union and other countries outside of the United States.

classification of short- and long-term liabilities. This effort toward harmonization comes as all publicly listed European companies prepare to meet international IASB accounting standards by 2005. Companies that are also publicly listed in the United States will have to meet the U.S. standards under SOA as well. The goal is to reach a consensus on standards by at least 2005. This push for a convergence of standards is really a result of the U.S. corporate scandals that led to enactment of SOA. The more recent Dutch accounting scandal at Ahold will have the same effect. Soon we should see the two sets of standards—international and U.S. GAAP—gradually converge.

For internal auditors, the IIA Standards, as discussed in Chapter 6, are international standards that apply to internal audits no matter what the country. Internal auditors may encounter different accounting standards or even different local financial statement auditing standards, but they always should follow the overall IIA professional standards. It is almost certain that the ISA and IAS standards will take the place of country-by-country standards, with the exception of the United States with its international leadership role. The Information Systems Audit and Control Association (ISACA) control objectives for information and related technology (CobiT) framework also is a worldwide standard.

COSO WORLDWIDE: INTERNATIONAL INTERNAL CONTROL FRAMEWORKS

Chapter 5 discussed the COSO internal control standard that has been part of U.S. auditing standards and almost certainly will be a component of SOA internal control requirements under the PCAOB. COSO was launched in the United States; other countries have implemented their own internal control frameworks. This section introduces two of them, the CoCo framework from Canada and the United Kingdom's Turnbull report guidance. These frameworks were released after COSO, and each has some very attractive features.

As internal auditors increasingly work on a worldwide, global basis, there is much value in at least having an understanding of these slightly different internal control standards. Just as we are seeing some convergence in auditing standards, we should see the same with international internal control frameworks. CoCo and Turnbull are different, but each has similar overall internal control objectives.

CoCo: Canada's Variation of COSO

The Canadian Institute of Chartered Accountants (CICA) is the professional financial auditing and accounting organization in Canada. Similar to the AICPA's certified public accounting (CPA) certificate, the CICA awards chartered accountant (CA) certifications. After the release of the COSO framework and the AICPA's incorporation of it in U.S. audit standards, the CICA established a study group in 1995 to issue guidance on designing, assessing, and reporting on the control systems for organizations in Canada. The result was the Criteria of Control framework.

According to CoCo, control comprises those elements of an organization—including its resources, systems, processes, culture, structure, and tasks—that, taken together, support its people in the achievement of the organization's objectives. There are some slightly different words here when compared to the U.S.-oriented COSO. CoCo emphasizes that the essence of control is purpose, commitment, capability, monitoring, and learning within the internal control framework, as represented in Exhibit 10.3. Each term represents a set of the internal control criteria. The criterion for commitment, for example, consists of these areas:

- Shared ethical values, including integrity, should be established, communicated, and practiced throughout the organization.

- Human resource policies and practices should be consistent with an organization's ethical values and with the achievement of its objectives.

EXHIBIT 10.3 CoCo Framework

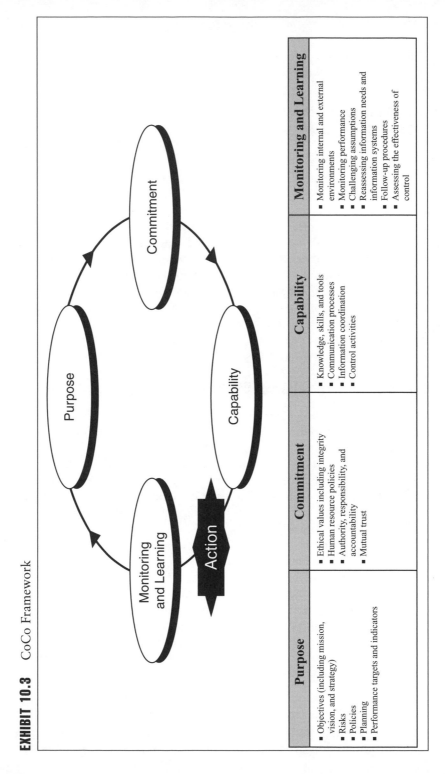

Purpose	Commitment	Capability	Monitoring and Learning
▪ Objectives (including mission, vision, and strategy) ▪ Risks ▪ Policies ▪ Planning ▪ Performance targets and indicators	▪ Ethical values including integrity ▪ Human resource policies ▪ Authority, responsibility, and accountability ▪ Mutual trust	▪ Knowledge, skills, and tools ▪ Communication processes ▪ Information coordination ▪ Control activities	▪ Monitoring internal and external environments ▪ Monitoring performance ▪ Challenging assumptions ▪ Reassessing information needs and information systems ▪ Follow-up procedures ▪ Assessing the effectiveness of control

- Authority, responsibility, and accountability should be clearly defined and consistent with an organization's objectives so that decisions and actions are taken by the appropriate people.

- An atmosphere of mutual trust should be fostered to support the flow of information between people and their effective performance toward achieving the organization's objectives.

The CoCo model has similar detailed criteria for its other three major elements. Based on these elements, the model helps to shape internal control concepts while developing a new terminology that might become codified in future standards. The CICA CoCo guidance goes on to state that management's overriding objective is to ensure, as far as practical, the orderly and efficient conduct of the entity's business. Management discharges its internal control responsibilities through actions directed to:

- ***Optimizing the Use of Resources.*** Internal control assists management in optimizing the use of resources by ensuring as far as practical that reliable information is provided to management for the determination of business policies and by monitoring the implementation of those policies and the degree of compliance with them.

- ***Prevention or Detection of Error and Fraud.*** A management internal controls objective is the prevention and detection of unintentional mistakes or errors and fraud—the intentional misrepresentation of financial information or misappropriation of assets. The guidance goes on to state that any controls here should be *cost-effective*. The cost of a possible control should be weighed against the relative likelihood of error and fraud occurring and the consequences if any were to occur, including their effect on the financial statements.

- ***Safeguarding of Assets.*** An organization's assets should be safeguarded, partly through internal controls and partly through business policies. Internal control protects against loss arising from *unintentional* exposure to risk in processing transactions or handling related assets. The degree of *intentional* exposure to risk is determined by business policies.

- ***Maintaining Reliable Control Systems.*** These are the policies and procedures established and maintained by management to collect, record, and process data and report the resulting information or to enhance the reliability of such data and information. Management requires reliable control systems to provide information necessary to operate the entity and produce such accounting and other records necessary for the preparation of financial statements.

The preceding paragraphs have briefly outlined the CoCo framework. While it is consistent with the U.S. framework, CoCo represents a tighter, easier-to-grasp model of internal control than the somewhat complex

COSO framework. The CoCo control framework represents a different way of thinking about internal control and provides a good way for managers to consider how their organizations are performing. All auditors, whether in Canada, the United States, or elsewhere, should take a more detailed look at the CoCo model. A good starting point is *www.cica.ca.*

Internal Control Standards in the United Kingdom

Auditing and accounting professional organizations seem a bit more complex as we move over to the United Kingdom. Similar to Canada, the professional designation is Chartered Accountant, a certificate that candidates obtain through their auditing experience and passing a comprehensive examination. The professional organization here is the Institute of Chartered Accountants in England and Wales, with separate organizations in Ireland and in Scotland. There also are separate chartered accountant designations and organizations for management accounting and public finance. Affiliated with the Charted Accountant institutes, the Auditing Practices Board (APB) establishes and publishes statements of auditing principles and guidelines similar to the U.S. SAS documents. These are called, for example, APB Guideline No. X with a title.

The United Kingdom had some of the same concerns as the United States regarding improper financial reporting during the 1990s. Although its focus was more on inappropriate statements made by directors, it also included failures of internal control. The result of a 1999 study similar to the U.S. Treadway Commission report, became known as the Turnbull Report on Internal Control. The Turnbull Report, oriented toward directors of public companies, places a strong emphasis on objective setting, risk identification, and risk assessment when evaluating internal controls. The report calls on directors to regularly consider:

- The nature and extent of the risks facing the company
- The extent and categories of risk that it regards as acceptable for the company to bear
- The likelihood of those risks materializing
- The company's ability to reduce the incidence and impact on the business risks that do materialize
- The costs of operating particular controls relative to the benefit thereby obtained in managing the related risks

This set of considerations is very similar to the risk assessment approaches discussed in Chapter 9. What is significant about the Turnbull approach is the emphasis on understanding business objectives and then analyzing risks as first steps in designing effective internal controls. The Turnbull Report then suggests a framework for evaluating the effectiveness of internal controls based on understanding the risks, designing controls based on those risks, and performing tests to evaluate the controls.

Although there are some differences in the text, the report provides the same three basic objectives of internal controls as do COSO and CoCo: effectiveness and efficiency of operations, reliability of internal and external financial reporting, and compliance with applicable laws and regulations. The really important concept of the Turnbull approach is the emphasis on risk assessment. It states that emphasis should be placed on developing controls for high-impact and higher-likelihood risks. COSO provides the same general guidance, but the Turnbull approach does a better job in establishing a risk-based internal control environment. The new COSO ERM, discussed in Chapter 9, perhaps catches up here. There is nothing in conflict with COSO, and a U.S. internal auditor involved in international assignments might find value in reviewing the Turnbull Report in greater detail.

Internal Control Frameworks Worldwide

With the wide range of independent national accounting authorities and some differences in business practices, there are some variations in internal control frameworks or models worldwide. Most follow the COSO framework with its CoCo or Turnbull variations. For example, Australia has the Australian Conditions for Control (ACC). It is not the objective of this book to summarize internal control practices on a country-by-country basis.

Although not discussed specifically in the COSO framework, internal audit often has a more prominent role in other models. Perhaps because internal auditors in the past in the United Kingdom sometimes were regarded as little more than corporate "police officers," the Turnbull materials stress the importance of internal audit in improving an organization's internal control framework. The Turnbull Report states that an internal audit function should be able to:

- Provide objective assurance to the board and management as to the adequacy and effectiveness of the company's risk management and internal control framework

- Assist management to improve the processes by which risks are identified and managed

- Assist the board with its responsibilities to strengthen and improve the risk management and internal control framework

Developed before SOA, this is excellent guidance for internal audit to understand risks and to help improve the internal control structure in any organization, no matter where in the world it is based.

ISO AND THE STANDARDS REGISTRATION PROCESS

Standards—documented agreements containing technical specifications or other precise criteria to be used consistently as guidelines, or definitions, to ensure that products, processes, and services are fit for their purpose—at all levels—are essential in our global economy. For example, the format of a credit card is based on a standard that defines such features as an optimal thickness so that the cards can be inserted in reader devices worldwide. Standards contribute to making life simpler and to increasing the reliability and effectiveness of the goods and services we use.

Most international standards are based on guidelines from the International Standards Organization located in Geneva, Switzerland. Founded in 1946, the ISO has some 200 technical committees covering a wide range of areas. Virtually all countries in the world are ISO members. ISO Standards follow recognized numbering schemes. The ISO 90000 series covers quality standards and describes the documentation requirements to support such quality assertions. For an organization to claim that it follows a certain level of quality under the ISO 90000 series, it first must document its processes in exacting and precise detail and then must describe such things as the practices in place to train staff on the use of these standards. The organization then must invite an outside auditor or registrar to review this documentation and concur that the documentation is appropriate, in a process similar to a financial external audit. This quality audit process was discussed as part of Chapter 6. The organization then can claim that it is ISO compliant with the standard of interest.

In some respects, ISO Standards and registrations do not really fit in with the "new rules" theme of this book. ISO Standards have been in place for some years, and the quality auditors introduced in Chapter 6 have been responsible for auditing according to the ISO standards. With the ever-increasing globalization of businesses, however, all internal auditors should have an understanding of these ISO 90000 quality standards as well as the process for achieving ISO certification.

ISO 90000 Quality Standards: Overview

Earlier, we mentioned the gaggle of letters and acronyms associated with international auditing and internal control standards. The same is true—and perhaps more so—for the ISO series of standards and guidelines. We will not attempt to cover all of them here; much more information is available at *www.iso.ch*. The ISO quality standards important to internal auditors are:

- *ISO 9000:2000, Quality Management Systems—Fundamentals and Vocabulary.* This standard is a starting point and defines the fundamental terms and definitions used in the ISO 9000 family.

- **ISO 9001:2000, Quality Management Systems—Requirements.** The requirements standard is used to assess the ability to meet customer and applicable regulatory requirements and to address customer satisfaction. This is the only standard in the ISO 9000 family against which a third-party certification can be implemented (discussed later).

- **ISO 9004:2000, Quality Management Systems—Guidelines for Performance Improvements.** This standard provides guidance for continual improvement of quality management systems to benefit all parties through sustained customer satisfaction.

These are the three prime ISO quality standards; the *2000* means this set was updated in the year 2000. In addition, there are numerous supporting guidelines with numbers such as ISO 10005:1995, ISO 10006:1997, and ISO 10012–2:1997 covering such standards as for preparing the quality assurance (QA) plan, project planning standards, and statistical process controls. There are general standards or guidelines for virtually all areas of the quality process. For example, there is a guideline for training the staff in quality processes, ISO 10012:1999. If an organization or one of its functions is asked whether it has trained the staff adequately in certain quality processes, the response might be to point to this guideline and the detailed documentation developed to support compliance.

Exhibit 10.4 describes this ISO-based Quality Management implementation process. We have taken this exhibit from the public access ISO web site, *www.iso.ch,* but have eliminated some decision steps. The whole process here is similar to a normal internal audit in that the organization establishes goals, applies the appropriate standards, implements those standards, and then reviews them. The actual ISO standards referenced here are very detailed. For example, ISO 19011 for auditing covers over 30 printed pages and describes the entire quality audit process. Other ISO standards are just as detailed.

The overall ISO process is one of establishing effective documentation over existing procedures and processes. If an organization claims that it has "world-class" production standards under ISO, it needs to develop detailed documentation to support that contention. This documentation may include the results of detailed testing or a statistical process analysis. A strong system of documentation is key to establishing a level of ISO quality standards compliance.

Quality Audits and Registration

Although neither IIA internal nor AICPA financial attest auditors give much attention to ASQ quality auditors in their professional literature, there are some strong analogies among the three groups of auditors. In a financial statement attest audit, the internal and external auditors perform periodic reviews of internal accounting controls installed by management prior to the

EXHIBIT 10.4   Implementing an ISO 9001:2000 Quality Management System

1. *Identify the goals you want to achieve.*

   Typical goals may be:
   - Be more efficient and profitable.
   - Produce products and services that consistently meet customer requirements.
   - Achieve customer satisfaction
   - Increase market share.
   - Maintain market share.
   - Improve communications and morale in the organization.
   - Reduce costs and liabilities.
   - Increase confidence in the production system.

2. *Identify what others expect of you.*

   These are the expectations of interested parties (stakeholders), such as:
   - Customers and end users.
   - Employees.
   - Suppliers.
   - Shareholders.
   - Society.

3. *Obtain information about the ISO 9000 family.*
   - For general information, look at *www.iso.ch.*
   - For more detailed information, see ISO 9000:2000, ISO 9001:2000, and ISO 9004:2000.
   - For implementation case studies and news of ISO 9000 developments worldwide, read the ISO publication *ISO Management Systems.*[1]

4. *Apply ISO 9000 standards in your management system.*
   - Use ISO 9001:2000 as the basis for certification.

5. *Obtain guidance on specific topics within the quality management system—see:*
   - ISO 10006 for project management.
   - ISO 10007 for configuration management.
   - ISO 10012 for measurement systems.
   - ISO 10013 for quality documentation.
   - ISO/TR 10014 for managing the economics of quality.
   - ISO 10015 for training.
   - ISO/TS 16949 for automotive suppliers.
   - ISO 19011 for auditing.

EXHIBIT 10.4   Implementing an ISO 9001:2000 Quality
Management System *(Continued)*

6. *Establish current status, and determine the gaps between your quality management system and the requirements of ISO 9001:2000.*

   You may use one or more of the following:

   - Self-assessment.
   - Assessment by an external organization.

7. *Determine the processes that are needed to supply products to your customers.*

   Review the requirements of the ISO 9001:2000 section on Product Realization to determine how they apply or do not apply to your quality management system including:

   - Customer-related processes.
   - Design and/or development.
   - Purchasing.
   - Production and service operations.
   - Control of measuring and monitoring devices.

8. *Develop a plan to close the gaps in step 6 and to develop the processes in step 7.*

   Identify actions needed to close the gaps, allocate resources to perform these actions, assign responsibilities, and establish a schedule to complete the needed actions. ISO 9001:2000 Paragraphs 4.1 and 7.1 provide the information you will need to consider when developing the plan.

9. *Carry out your plan.*

   Proceed to implement the identified actions and track progress to your schedule.

10. *Undergo periodic internal assessment.*

    Use ISO 19011 for guidance in auditing, auditor qualification, and managing audit programs.

11. *Do you need to demonstrate conformance?*

    If yes, go to step 12.

    If no, go to step 13.

    You may need or wish to show conformance (certification/registration) for various purposes, for example:

    - Contractual requirements.
    - Market reasons or customer preference.
    - Regulatory requirements.
    - Risk management.
    - To set a clear goal for your internal quality development (motivation).

(continues)

EXHIBIT 10.4   Implementing an ISO 9001:2000 Quality
Management System *(Continued)*

12. *Undergo independent audit.*

Engage an ISO accredited registration/certification body to perform an audit and certify that your quality management system complies with the requirements of ISO 9001:2000.

13. *Continue to improve your business.*

Review the effectiveness and suitability of your quality management system. ISO 9004:2000 provides a methodology for improvement.

[1] A subscription publication available through the ISO website, *www.iso.org.ch.*

Source: International Organization for Standardization, Geneva, Switzerland.

period end date. Their work is based on auditing standards, and management procedures will have been based on strong, supporting internal control processes. As a final step, the CPA external auditor reviews the financial reports for the period as well as other supporting materials and attests to the fairness of these financial reports by signing the report. The audited financial statements are filed with the Securities and Exchange Commission (SEC) and become part of the annual report to shareholders.

Quality audits are based on the ISO standards just discussed. Management should have established quality processes as part of normal operations and will be reviewing compliance to those standards through internal self-checks or reviews by the organization's quality audit function. In order to state that the organization is ISO compliant, its quality systems are reviewed and registered through an external quality auditor function, called a quality audit registrar. Although not tied to the same SEC reporting cycle, the results of quality audits allow organizations to tell outsiders that they are ISO compliant. Just as investors sometimes require a set of audited financial reports, customers often will require that same ISO certification, particularly in international transactions.

A major difference between an audited financial statement following SAS or PCAOB financial auditing standards and ISO quality standards is that when an organization adopts ISO quality standards, it must have processes in place for the continual improvement of its quality management system along with ongoing customer satisfaction. Continual improvement is a process of increasing the effectiveness of the organization to fulfill its quality objectives, and ISO 9001 requires that an organization plan and manage the processes necessary for the continual improvement of its quality management system. Data should be obtained from various sources, both internal and external, to assess the appropriateness of these quality system goals and to improve the performance of processes. These processes must be strengthened through effective ASQ internal auditing as well as management reviews of overall systems and process performance. Like all systems, quality processes either improve over time or atrophy and become less effective. Nothing remains static for long.

ISO Standards provide guidance to establish and maintain an ongoing set of quality audits for an organization. They are based on what was called a Plan-Do-Check-Act cycle, developed by the father of the quality movement, Edward Deming, in the late 1940s. Under this, the key actions to define an audit program are:

- Establish the objectives and extent of the audit program.

- Establish responsibilities, resources, and procedures.

- Ensure the implementation of the audit program.

- Monitor and review the audit program to improve its efficiency and effectiveness.

- Ensure that appropriate program records are maintained.

Documentation is a key element in any quality system. Exhibit 10.5 illustrates the tiered level of ISO quality documentation. At Tier 1, or the very top, there is a need for a very high level ISO quality document for the organization. There is a hierarchy of more detailed documentation as we step down tiers to the detailed forms, files, and records at the Tier 4 foundation. This is the same level of documentation requirement that internal auditors have been commenting on for years. The difference with ISO quality audits is that an organization *must have* an adequate set of documentation as well as an ongoing process to improve it. Otherwise, it fails the audit—similar to the almost improbable event of a CPA refusing to sign or certify a financial statement.

In our discussion of new rules for internal auditors, we have introduced the ISO continuous improvement and quality audit process only very briefly. As discussed in Chapter 8 and again here, the typical IIA-trained and oriented operational or financial internal auditor is somewhat isolated today from quality auditors, even within the same organization. This situation should change. Quality auditors are moving out of the production floor and are more frequently calling themselves internal auditors. However, the name and title is not as important as the overall function. ASQ quality auditors often are much more concerned about the importance of continuous improvement processes and the necessary supporting documentation than typical internal auditors today. This should be an important aspect of the work of all internal auditors.

All internal auditors should gain at least a general understanding of the ISO 9000 quality management standards and processes. Acceptance of ISO 9000 standards allows essentially any organization to improve its standards of quality and service to customers and to internal members of the

EXHIBIT 10.5   ISO Quality System Documentation Tiers

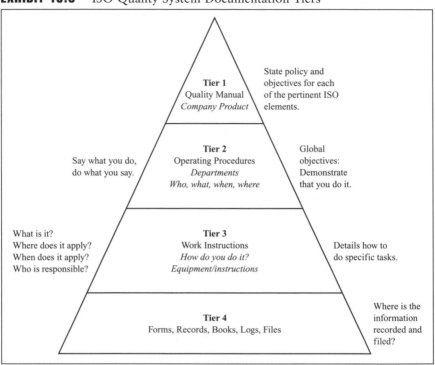

organization. Exhibit 10.6 summarizes the major principles behind ISO 9000. If an internal auditor's organization is already involved in an ISO registration effort, internal audit should get involved with the process, helping where it can and otherwise embracing ISO's concepts. If the organization has done nothing with ISO, the chief audit executive (CAE) should better understand the costs and benefits of ISO registration and potentially consider recommending it to members of the senior management team.

EXHIBIT 10.6   ISO Quality Management Principles

Principle 1. Customer Focus

Organizations depend on their customers and therefore should understand current and future customer needs, should meet customer requirements and strive to exceed customer expectations.

Principle 2. Leadership

Leaders establish unity of purpose and direction of the organization. They should create and maintain the internal environment in which people can become fully involved in achieving the organization's objectives.

EXHIBIT 10.6   ISO Quality Management Principles *(Continued)*

Principle 3. Involvement of People

People at all levels are the essence of an organization, and their full involvement enables their abilities to be used for the organization's benefit.

Principle 4. Process Approach

A desired result is achieved more efficiently when activities and related resources are managed as a process.

Principle 5. System Approach to Management

Identifying, understanding, and managing interrelated processes as a system contributes to the organization's effectiveness and efficiency in achieving its objectives.

Principle 6. Continual Improvement

Continual improvement of the organization's overall performance should be a permanent objective of the organization.

Principle 7. Factual Approach to Decision Making

Effective decisions are based on the analysis of data and information

Principle 8. Mutually Beneficial Supplier Relationships

An organization and its suppliers are interdependent, and a mutually beneficial relationship enhances the ability of both to create value.

ITIL SERVICE SUPPORT AND SERVICE DELIVERY BEST PRACTICES

As we become a more global economy, the audit professional is constantly confronted with new standards and processes. Some of these tend to be oriented to one industrial group while others really do not cross national borders. An example of the former might be the Basle II Accords, an important set of risk management standards with some internal audit responsibilities. The Accords primarily are applicable to major international banks and auditors involved in the banking industry; because of that limitation, we have not discussed Basle II. Other topics not covered in this book are standards or issues that are primarily specific to one non-U.S. country or group countries, such as EU standards.

Other standards do originate in one country and then gravitate to others over time. COSO is certainly an example here. It started as primarily a U.S. matter and has become a fairly consistent standard worldwide. In other instances, standards have originated in other international spheres and then gravitated to the United States. Because of its size and economic power, the United States sometimes has to be brought to a given international practice "kicking and screaming"; in other instances, it readily adopts these standards. Metric units of measure are one example here. Although this standard is used extensively in U.S. manufacturing companies and elsewhere in order to compete worldwide, the U.S. consumer seemingly refuses to adopt it. Initially, the United States did not readily embrace the ISO quality standards. Only in recent years, as the United States has seen these standards being established in other international markets, has the country begun to embrace ISO seriously.

The Information Technology Infrastructure Library (ITIL) set of process best practices is an example of standards that have not yet been fully embraced by the United States. Developed in the late 1980s by the United Kingdom's Central Computer and Telecommunications Agency (CCTA), ITIL is now considered the de facto standard for information technology (IT) service management and service delivery and has been embraced by organizations worldwide. By service management, we mean virtually all of the IT processes beyond actual application development. The concept here is that organizations often are highly dependent on their IT services and expect them not only to support the organization, but also to present new options to achieve the objectives of the organization.

Originally published as a series of separate manuals or guides, ITIL is organized into a series of sets, which themselves are divided into two main areas: service support and service delivery:

- Service support is the practice of those disciplines that enable IT services to be provided effectively. These include processes for release, change, configuration, problem, and incident management.

- Service delivery covers the management of the IT services themselves. It involves a number of management practices to ensure that IT services actually are provided as agreed between the service provider and the customer. The processes here are service level, financial, capacity, availability, and continuity management.

Each of these processes, whether in the service support or service delivery areas, supports the overall IT infrastructure in an organization. ITIL concepts got started in the United Kingdom and then in the EU to support ISO; today its usage is fairly widespread in Canada. It is just beginning to penetrate into larger U.S. organizations.

While not a specific set of standards, ITIL should be seen as a series of processes to reduce costs while maintaining and improving the quality of service. Auditors should find ITIL useful as an approach to understanding best practices and controls over overall IT operations. In the paragraphs following, we briefly discuss each of these ITIL service management areas. There is no defined order to our listing of practices, and each practice somewhat relates to another. Each describes processes that are needed to allow an organization to manage the given ITIL process area successfully.

ITIL Service Support Release Management

Release management is the process to manage all software and hardware in the facility, from purchase to development and until testing and eventual migration to production. The overall process starts with a secure and well-documented new release of an IT component until its migration to production. Processes that need to be implemented for an IT function to have effective release management are:

- A release policy that describes the frequency of regular releases as well as the handling of emergency releases. The policy should specify standards for testing as well as subsequent releases to production. As much as possible, the release policy should describe the scope of what items will be included under this policy and what will not. A structured approach should be used for all releases, including:

  □ The contents of a given release package, including a definition of all release components as well as its schedule

  □ Overall software and hardware release requirements as well as roles and responsibilities

  □ A backup plan for the release

  □ A quality and acceptance plan

- A formal process for the design, building, and configuration of releases. This is the technical portion of release management. Of particular importance here is the design of a back-out plan that will become part of the change management process to be described.

- Procedures for the testing and sign-off of new releases. The lack of testing is the most common cause of failure for new releases. Business unit representatives—users—should participate to ensure all software roll-outs are fully tested before being released into the production environment.

The benefits to an organization for having an effective release management process include the controlled release of components to production. Properly executed, the software to be released can be held in a secure location before release, which can greatly reduce the possibility of illegal copies. Exhibit 10.7 shows the relationship of release management to other ITIL processes. Requests for changes (RFCs) from other processes will initiate change management with the results flowing to the release management process.

Release management can cause problems for some organizations if established procedures are ignored. Both IT and operations staff may resist following a formal release process that includes necessary testing. There is sometimes a tendency to ignore the established test plan and roll out the

EXHIBIT 10.7   Relationship of Change Management
with other ITIL Processes

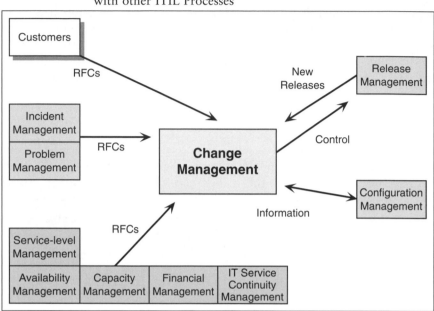

release with inadequate testing. The risk of subsequent problems can be high. An internal auditor should understand the release management process in place and, if appropriate, make suggestions for its improvement.

ITIL Service Support Change Management

An effective and efficient IT service delivery organization needs the capability to implement changes efficiently and correctly. Although an IT organization usually must make changes because of problems, many changes are initiated proactively by seeking such business benefits as reducing costs or improving services. The goal of an IT service change management process is to ensure that standardized methods and procedures are used for efficient and prompt handling of all changes, in order to minimize the impact of any change-related incidents on service quality, and consequently to improve the day-to-day IT and overall organization operations. The goal of this process should be to ensure that standardized methods and procedures are in place for the prompt and efficient implementation of changes to minimize any disruption to the quality of IT service delivery. An old line from quality management literature describes this important process: "Not every change is an improvement, but every improvement requires a change!"[1]

An organization normally formalizes its change management processes through the use of an RFC control document and by launching a change review board (CRB) to review, approve, and monitor the progress of RFCs. These requests should be evaluated in terms of their potential risks, resource requirements, and any impacts on business continuity. Exhibit 10.8 shows this change management process with the CRB monitoring all steps. It is important that change management processes have high visibility and open channels of communication to promote smooth transitions when changes take place. Change management depends on the accuracy of the configuration data (discussed next) to ensure the full impact of making changes is known. There should be a very close relationship among the configuration management, release management, and change management processes.

ITIL Service Support Configuration Management

Configuration management is the process that focuses on the identification, recording, and reporting of all IT hardware and software components and their relationships. An organization requires quality IT services, and configuration management provides a logical model for the infrastructure by identifying, controlling, maintaining, and verifying the versions of all of the installed components in place, often called configuration items (CIs). The goals of configuration management are to:

- Account for all the IT assets and configurations within the organization.

- Provide accurate information on configurations and their documentation to support all the other processes, including incident, problem, change, and release management.

- Verify the configuration records, from a configuration management database (CMDB), against the infrastructure and correct any exceptions.

The configuration management system identifies relationships between an item that is to be changed and any other components of the infrastructure, allowing owners of these components to be involved in an impact assessment process. A key component to this process is building a CMDB for the selection, identification, and labeling of the hardware, software, or documentation CIs, including their respective "owners" and the relationships between them. Examples of CIs include vendor-provided services, servers, network components, desktops, mobile units, applications, telecommunication services, and other facilities. Building such a CMDB initially requires a detailed inventory of all CIs, including individual versions of each and references to supporting documentation. Other records and data associated with a CI include documentation covering incidents, known errors and problems, and other supporting data regarding suppliers or procedures. Identifying all CI's and structuring them in a hierarchy can be a difficult

EXHIBIT 10.8   Change Management Processes

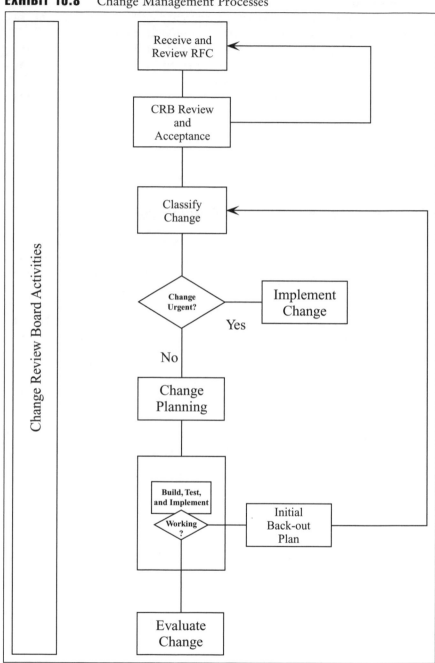

process initially but should yield savings in the effective management of this service delivery process.

A configuration management process and its supporting CMDB can provide for the better management of all IT resources, including the effective and efficient processing of changes as well as more efficient problem resolution. Such a process can very much enhance overall IT internal controls by supporting software license legal requirements, security issues, and budgeting and component spending matters.

ITIL Service Support Problem Management

The goal of the problem management process is to minimize the adverse impact of IT infrastructure incidents and problems and to prevent any recurrence of these errors. To achieve this goal, problem management seeks to get to the root cause of incidents and then to initiate actions to improve or correct matters. The problem management process has both reactive and proactive aspects. The reactive aspect is concerned with solving problems in response to one or more incidents, and the proactive element is concerned with identifying and solving problems and known errors before any incidents occur.

Most IT operations today have some type of "help desk" where users and others report IT troubles. Few incidents received at the help desk are new or mysterious to the support staff; nevertheless, relevant and easily applied advice should be available to resolve nonfamiliar incidents effectively. Although there may exist a second line or third line of support to resolve more difficult problems, the best use of resources is to document them in such a way that front-line staff can handle them.

An effective problem management process should reduce both the number and severity of IT incidents and problems on the business. ITIL problem management has four primary activities:

1. *Problem Control.* The main activities here are the identification and recording of reported problems processes outside of problem management, such as capacity management issues. Problems then should be organized in terms of their impact, urgency, and priority. The IT team should attempt to understand what is causing the problem. This step is vastly different from incident management investigation, where the focus should be on "rapid restoration" of service.

2. *Error Control.* Known errors should be resolved and corrected, and new or unknown errors should be researched and documented. Once a solution has been determined, an RFC should be released if needed to fix the problem.

3. *Proactive Problem Management.* The organization should redirect efforts away from just reacting and fixing problems, to proactively preventing incidents from occurring in the first place. This activity includes problem trend analysis to highlight potentially weak areas and taking steps to initiate corrective preventive actions.

4. *Problem Review Follow-up.* At the end of any major problem resolution as well as periodically, there should be a review to learn what things were done right, what could have been done differently, and what were the lessons learned.

A formal IT problem management process improves the IT service quality by resolving the root cause of problem incidents. This leads to better quality for overall IT service management and a higher resolution rate for incidents at the help desk the first time around. As with all ten of the ITIL process areas, this is an area internal auditors should include in their reviews of IT processes and internal controls.

ITIL Service Support Incident Management

Closely related to problem management, incident management includes activities aimed at restoring IT services following a disruption. The help desk is usually the owner for this process; however, all IT support groups may become involved. The disruption of an IT service, questions about the functionality of an application, or requests for advice are all regarded as incidents included in this process. The primary goal of incident management is to restore normal service operation as quickly as possible, to minimize adverse impacts on business operations, and to ensure the best possible levels of service quality and availability. Normal service operations are defined as part of the service level management process.

In ITIL terminology, an incident is defined as:

> *any event which is not part of the standard operation of a service and which causes, or may cause, an interruption to, or a reduction in, the quality of that service.*[2]

There should be a close interface between the incident management process and the problem management and change management processes. If not properly controlled, changes may introduce new incidents.

Although the above process includes most IT incidents, there can be major incidents where the degree of impact on the user community is extreme. Incidents for which the time scale of disruption—to even a relatively small percentage of users—becomes excessive also should be regarded as major. These incidents may require a series of formal meetings with key in-house support staff, vendor support, and IT services management, with the purpose of reviewing progress and determining the best course of action.

Unlike some other ITIL processes where benefits may be hard for end users to identify, a well-implemented incident management process will have easily visible benefits.

ITIL Service Delivery Service-Level Management

The major component of the service-level management (SLM) process is the written agreement between the users and IT department called the service-level agreements (SLAs). In these formal agreements, IT promises to deliver services according to an agreed-on set of schedules and understands there will be penalties if service standards are not met. The goal of SLM is to maintain and improve service quality through a constant cycle of agreeing, monitoring, reporting, and improving the current levels of IT service. It is strategically focused on the business and on maintaining the alignment between the business and IT.

Exhibit 10.9 shows this SLM process. Customers or IT users initially define the service requirements that they are seeking, such as average response times no more than X hours or the financial systems close processing completed by X o'clock or a variety of other factors. These requirements will be prepared according to specifications prepared by the SLM process function, and, after some negotiation, formal SLAs will be established. Performance against these SLAs will be monitored on an ongoing basis with performance reported regularly. Failure to meet these standards may result in additional negotiations and SLA adjustments.

Service-level management provides the following benefits for the business and the IT organization:

- Because IT will be working to meet these standards, IT services should be of a higher quality, causing fewer interruptions. The productivity of the IT customers will improve as well.

- IT staff resources will tend to be used more efficiently as the IT organization provides services that better meet the expectations of the customers.

- With SLAs, the service provided can be measured and the perception of IT operations generally will improve.

- Services provided by the third parties are more manageable with the underpinning contracts in place, and any possibility of negative influence on the IT service provided is reduced.

- Monitoring overall IT services under SLAs makes it possible to identify weak spots that can be improved.

The SLA process should be an important component of all IT operations. If an organization does not use formal SLAs, internal auditors reviewing IT operations should consider recommending the implementation of formal SLA processes.

EXHIBIT 10.9   Service-level Management Activities

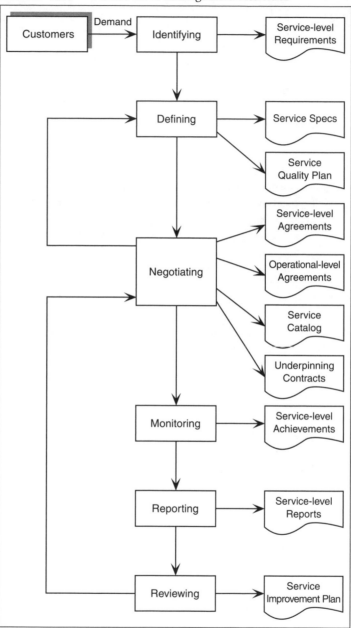

ITIL Service Delivery Financial Management

The function and overall processes in any organization should operate as a business, and financial management is an important and key ITIL process. The objective of the IT service financial management process is for IT to provide cost-effective stewardship of the assets and resources used in providing IT services. IT should be able to account fully for its spending on IT services and allocate these costs to the services delivered to IT users or customers. Three separate subprocesses are associated with ITIL financial management: budgeting, accounting and charging processes.

Financial management for IT services provides important information to service-level management about the introduced costing, pricing, and charging strategies. Although generally not operated as a profit center, the financial management process suggests that both IT and its customers should think of IT service operations in business terms. The financial management process may allow IT and overall management to decide what, if any, functions should be retained in-house or outsourced to an external provider.

The financial management process allows accurate cost–benefit analyses of the IT services provided and allows the IT organization to set and meet financial targets. It also should provide timely reporting to the service-level management process such that customers can understand the charging and pricing methods used. Auditors should use their financial skills to review and assess financial management process internal controls with process improvement suggestions as appropriate.

ITIL Service Delivery Capacity Management

The capacity management process is designed to ensure that the capacity of the IT infrastructure is aligned to business needs and that it maintains the required level of service delivery at an acceptable cost through appropriate levels of capacity. Through gathering business and technical capacity data, this process creates a capacity plan to deliver the cost-justified capacity requirements for the business. In addition to a main objective to understand the business's IT capacity requirements and deliver against them both in the present and the future, capacity management also is responsible for understanding the potential advantages new technology could have and assessing its suitability for the organization.

The capacity management process should be considered in terms of three subprocesses covering business, service, and resource capacity management. Business capacity management is a long-term process to ensure that the future business requirements are taken into consideration and then planned and implemented as necessary. Service capacity management is responsible for ensuring that the performance of all current IT services falls within the parameters defined in the existing SLAs. Finally, resource capacity management has more of a technical focus and is responsible for the management of the individual components within the infrastructure. There are multiple inputs to these three capacity management subprocesses including:

- SLAs and SLA breaches
- Business plans and strategies
- Operational schedules as well as schedule changes
- Application development issues
- Technology constraints and acquisitions
- Incidents and problems
- Budgets and financial plans

As a result of these multiple inputs, the capacity management processes —often under a single designated capacity manager—should manage IT processes, develop and maintain a formal capacity plan, and make certain capacity records are up to date. In addition, the capacity manager must be involved in evaluating all changes to establish the effect on capacity and performance. This capacity evaluation should happen both when changes are proposed and after they are implemented. Capacity management must pay particular attention to the cumulative effect of changes over a period of time that may cause degraded response times, file storage problems, and excess demand for processing capacity. Other roles within capacity management are the roles of the network, application, and system manager. They are responsible for translating the business requirements into required capacity to meet these requirements and to optimize performance.

The implementation of an effective capacity management process offers IT the benefits of an actual overview of capacity in place and the ability to plan capacity in advance. Effective capacity management should be able to estimate the impact of new applications or modifications as well as provide cost savings that are in tune with the requirements of the business. Proper capacity planning can reduce significantly the overall cost of ownership of IT resources. Although formal capacity planning takes time, internal and external staff resources, and software and hardware tools, the potential losses incurred without capacity planning can be significant. Lost productivity of end users in critical business functions, overpaying for network equipment or services, and the costs of upgrading systems already in production can more than justify the cost of capacity planning. This is an important ITIL process.

ITIL Service Delivery Availability Management

Organizations increasingly depend on IT services being available 7 days per week 24 hours a day, often called 24/7. When IT services are unavailable, often the business stops as well. It is vital that an IT organization manage and control the availability of its IT services. This can be accomplished by defining the requirements from the business regarding the availability of the IT services and then matching them with the possibilities of the IT organization.

Availability management depends on multiple inputs to function well. These inputs include requirements regarding the availability of the business; information regarding reliability, maintainability, recoverability, and serviceability of the configuration items; and information from the other processes, incidents, problems, SLAs, and achieved service levels.

The activities within the availability management process are planning, improving, and measuring. Planning involves determining the availability requirements to find out if and how the IT organization can meet them. The service-level management process maintains contact with the business and will be able to provide the availability expectations to availability management. The business may have unrealistic expectations with respect to availability without understanding what this means in real terms. For example, it may want 99.9 percent availability yet not realize that this will cost five times more than providing 98 percent availability. It is the responsibility of service-level management and the availability management process to manage expectations and outline these options.

When the business can tolerate some downtime of services or a cost justification cannot be made for building in additional resources into the infrastructure, designing for recovery is the appropriate approach. Here the infrastructure will be designed such that in the event of a service failure, recovery will be "as fast as possible." Designing for recovery is a more reactive management approach for availability. In any event, processes such as incident management need to be in place to recover as soon as possible in case of a service interruption.

The main benefit of availability management is a structured process to deliver IT services according to the agreed requirements of the customers. This process should result in a higher availability of the IT services and increased customer satisfaction.

ITIL Service Delivery Continuity Management

As businesses are becoming more dependent on IT, the impact of the unavailability of IT services has increased drastically. Every time the availability or performance of a service is reduced, systems users cannot continue with their normal work. This dependence on IT services will continue and increasingly influences users, managers, and decision makers. That is why it is important that the impact of a total or partial loss of the IT services is estimated and continuity plans be established to ensure that the business always will be able to continue.

ITIL calls for an appropriate strategy to be developed that contains an optimal balance of risk reduction and recovery options. Some of these business continuity and disaster recovery strategies were discussed in Chapter 7. Using the approaches outlined there, an IT organization can implement an effective set of service continuity processes.

NOTES

1. A frequent phrase in the quality management literature. See W. Edwards Deming's *Out of the Crisis* (Cambridge, MA: MIT Press, 2000).
2. *ILIL Service Delivery Handbook* (London: Office of Government Commerce, 2003). This work is updated periodically.

CHAPTER 11

Continuous Assurance Auditing Future Directions

Continuous assurance auditing (CAA) is the process of installing control-based monitors in automated systems such that these monitors would send signals to auditors—usually internal auditors—when the automated process deviates from one or another audit-defined limit or parameter. The concept has been around for some years. In the earlier days of information systems auditing, the literature referred to similar concepts called Integrated Test Facilities (ITFs) or System Continuous Audit Review File (SCARF) facilities.[1] These terms sounded good, but they were seldom if ever implemented. Those real-time audit monitors could not be implemented in that earlier era of batch processing and magnetic tape storage. The concept subsequently began to be described as continuous assurance monitoring and was a frequent topic at internal audit future technology conferences throughout the 1990s, but there were few actual implementations. Finally, technology and, to some extent the Sarbanes-Oxley Act (SOA), are making CAA a very practicable alternative for auditing automated systems.

The testimony of the chair of the American Institute of Certified Public Accountants (AICPA), James Castellano, to the Congress during its hearings on the fall of Enron emphasizes the importance of this approach. In his February 2002 comments, he said:

> The transition to new reporting and auditing models is going to demand not only new audit approaches but personnel of the highest caliber. With this in mind, the profession has been working actively in the following areas: continuous auditing or continuous assurance that involves reporting on short time frames and can pertain to either reporting on the effectiveness of a system producing data or more frequent reporting on the data itself.

This chapter introduces continuous assurance auditing (CAA) as a "new rule" for reviewing today's automated systems. Technology today makes continuous auditing approaches much easier to implement, and SOA's requirements for "almost real-time" financial reporting makes CAA very attractive. Some larger organizations already have implemented continuous auditing processes, and the chapter considers some example implementations. Continuous assurance auditing represents a dramatic change in the audit model and may change auditor skill requirements as it becomes more widely accepted.

A large database or data warehouse environment is an almost necessary component for implementing CAA, as are the data warehouse tools of data mining and online analytical processing (OLAP). We briefly discuss these concepts and their applicability to internal audit processes. Internet concepts and the use of an extensible mark-up language (XML) is another key CAA component. We also introduce use of the AICPA-initiated XBRL (extensible business reporting language). Technology is creating some new rules for internal auditors worldwide.

IMPLEMENTING CONTINUOUS ASSURANCE AUDITING

Auditing has gone through a stream of conceptual changes over the years. In its earliest days, auditing was a process of vouching and testing. Using dictionary definitions of these terms, to "vouch" means to attest, guarantee, or certify something as being true or reliable, and an auditor performed tests to support that vouching process. This vouching process had been used as a prime audit approach for years. As systems later became highly automated, auditors began to rely primarily on reviews of internal controls to support their audit conclusions. If the controls were adequate and found to be working through tests, there was less need to perform the detailed vouching or transaction testing. Over time, through the early 1990s, auditors placed a major emphasis on reviews of internal controls as the major component of their attest work.

With too many systems and diverse controls to consider coupled with an ongoing emphasis on increased audit efficiency, auditors—particularly external auditors—began to perform a formal risk analysis over these control environments, placing audit emphasis on higher-risk internal control areas. The audit risk analysis process was discussed in Chapter 9 as part of our introduction to the COSO Enterprise Risk Model (ERM) and could be considered a third phase of auditing, following first, vouch and test, and second, internal control reviews. Many analyses of what happened after Enron and a host of other failures questioned the audit procedures used. How could these failures have happened? Why did the external auditors not see these internal control weaknesses, strange-looking financial ratios, and other problems? One often-cited concern was the unreliability of audited financial reports delivered well after the official business closing dates and containing many pro forma numbers. SOA now requires that financial reports be issued on a much tighter schedule, closer to period ending dates, along with generally accepted accounting principles (GAAP) numbers and reconciliation to any pro bona numbers. That rapid close requirement points to the need for continuous assurance and what may become the next generation of audit techniques.

What Is a Continuous Assurance Audit System?

CAA is an audit technique that produces audit results simultaneously with, or a very short period of time after, the occurrence of actual events. As a first step, auditor-supervised controls are installed in major, enterprise-wide resource systems. Such controls include alarm monitors and continuous analytical analysis routines to either test results or highlight items for immediate audit analysis. CAA is generally independent of the underlying business application with processes that test transactional data against defined control parameters or rules. CAA processes today run on a daily or weekly basis and generate exception reports or alerts for auditor follow-up.

In its most basic design, CAA is an independent application that monitors another critical application. Exhibit 11.1 shows a CAA monitoring application for an automated payments system. Here CAA software monitors activity through periodic reviews of activity through a payments transaction file. Activity summaries are reported periodically, and any unusual items are highlighted in an exception report, probably through an e-mail notice. This type of system is very similar to the kinds of password security monitors in place today in many organizations. The exception activity is reported on a regular basis, and "red flag" violations are highlighted.

CAA applications can be more than just monitors running against application transaction files to highlight exceptions. Applications are much more complex in, for example, an enterprise resource planning (ERP) system. These are the all-inclusive application packages, by vendors such as SAP, PeopleSoft, Oracle, or Lawson, that provide a total systems solution from accounting and the general ledger, to human resources, and through purchasing—covering virtually all processes and applications in the enterprise. In these complex systems, an average ERP implementation may cost some $12 million and take 20 months to implement. They also are built around a single or a closely linked set of databases. CAA monitors here must be quite complex, as multiple transactions may be updating or depending on linked multiple tables. CAA is very useful in ERP applications as it allows monitoring to be installed over a complex set of interrelated processes.

Exhibit 11.2 shows how CAA might be implemented in such an environment. At the base of the exhibit is a stream of measurable, operational processes such as might occur in a complex ERP. The audit team would establish metrics it wishes to monitor as well as supporting standards for those metrics. As a simple example, the United States has established some money-laundering banking rules stating that all transactions over $10,000

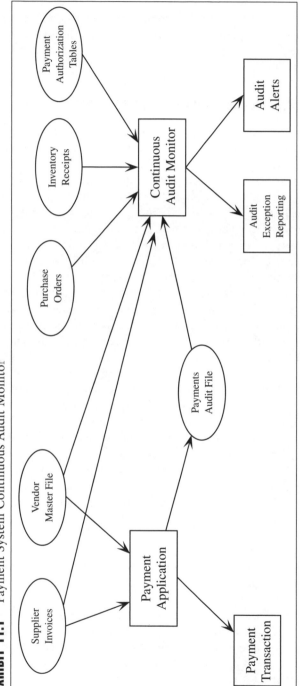

EXHIBIT 11.1 Payment System Continuous Audit Monitor

EXHIBIT 11.2 Continuous Audit Assurance Process

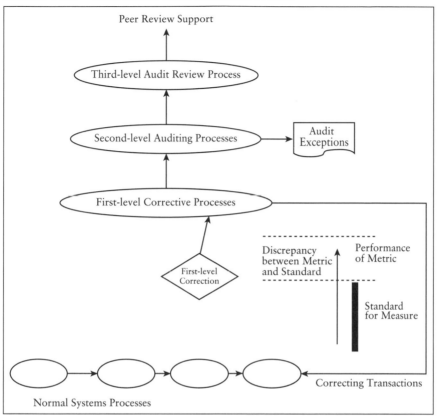

Peer Review Support

Third-level Audit Review Process

Second-level Auditing Processes — Audit Exceptions

First-level Corrective Processes

First-level Correction

Discrepancy between Metric and Standard — Performance of Metric

Standard for Measure

Normal Systems Processes — Correcting Transactions

are to be reported to regulators. Metrics tools could be built into the ERP processes to monitor all accounts payable and other cash transfer transactions with a standard that any over $10,000 should be flagged. The process could have multiple levels of metrics and standards with exceptions fed up to a first-level assurance process that would monitor the difference and, in some instances, send back a correcting feedback transaction to the ongoing process. The warning notes sent to systems users that their mailboxes are over 90 percent full are another such example.

Other discrepancies would flow up to what the exhibit shows as a second level monitoring or auditing process. This level would produce the reports to management or emergency exception notices, as shown on Exhibit 11.1. Beyond reports, this level could produce more significant audit or assurance actions. In the mailbox-full example, this is where CAA would initiate a transaction to prevent further accesses to the offending user. There is also a third CAA level to monitor the auditing process. Control procedures would be built to monitor ongoing CAA activity. The organization could use this level to report CAA activities to external auditors or regulators.

The monitoring processes just described can be performed on multiple levels. The first CAA level might be to flag and extract all transactions that pass resources between the organization and some entity of interest, extracting all transactions that match the criteria for further analysis, vouching, or reporting. An example might be monitors for all financial transactions with some group of countries or companies of interest. A second level would be a bit more sophisticated, as it would include some limits or logical templates in the evaluation process, such as maximums and minimums. On a third and more analytical level, CAA could examine the formal rules relative to the process monitored. An example here might be the use of system-generated values, such as interest rates or asset returns, and a comparison of auditor-initiated reasonable tests of those assumptions with historical values.

At its most basic level, CAA introduces a heightened level of monitoring to application systems. Classic auditor points of control will "disappear" into the processing system, changing recording and measurement tools. The cycle time for making audit-based decisions or actions should decrease as they are based on systems measures. CAA creates an environment for 24/7 continuous auditing.

CAA processes already have been implemented in some larger organizations. The long-distance telecommunications provider AT&T was an early adopter, and CAA has become common in the insurance and medical claims processing industries. Built around an organization's ERP system, CAA is particularly useful for monitoring purchase and payment cycle applications with an emphasis on controls over potential vendor-related fraud. CAA is a valuable tool for any application area where cash is going out the door, including employee travel accounting, insurance claims, and money-laundering controls.

Resources for Implementing CAA

Although the basic concept of implementing an audit monitor in an ERP or other business application seems relatively straightforward, the actual execution of CAA in an organization presents challenges. In order to be independent of other IT applications, the CAA process must be installed with some level of independence from other outside parties. That is, if CAA has an objective to monitor all transactions over X dollars as well as certain other conditions, those monitoring controls must be installed independently such that the controls cannot be bypassed easily. However, installing CAA in an ERP or any other business applications requires some complex technical skills, often beyond the capabilities of many internal auditors. Conversely, even if internal audit has the technical skills to install CAA in an organization's applications, information technology (IT) management will look at any such proposal with a high degree of skepticism. IT management typically will not trust auditors to install their own CAA monitoring software in an operating production system. If IT does agree to take the CAA software module and test and modify it for production installation, the CAA's independence could be compromised.

As an option, there are several vendor-supplied software solutions to install CAA. The products or approaches discussed are not the *only* solutions to installing CAA, but represent some good starting points for the organization considering CAA. Although CAA implementations have been described for some time by "voices in the wilderness" at academic conferences, they are beginning to be more widely recognized. A good source for more information is the Rutgers University Accounting web site, *http:// raw.rutgers.edu/*. The site includes papers from an annual international conference on continuous assurance auditing and reporting. The discussion here is based on several selected CAA implementation examples.

KPMG CAA Approach

The external audit firm KPMG in the United Kingdom has developed a CAA approach called KOLA, KPMG On Line Auditing.[2] KPMG installs its own desktop computer at the audit client site for CAA reviews, with read-only access to relevant databases running behind the organization's firewall. No software is loaded on the company's system, to avoid security issues data do not routinely leave the client, and the organization's e-mail system is used to carry program instructions and report audit test outcomes. Databases are monitored using automated routines to notify the auditor about various levels of audit events, including preprogrammed responses for automatic escalation or prompts calling for manual responses for certain events conducted either remotely or in person. KOLA also allows data to be sent as file attachments for further analysis. Exhibit 11.3 shows this KOLA process as presented at the previously mentioned Rutgers University continuous auditing conference.

KPMG has reported that its KOLA system is still in a test mode. It appears to be an excellent approach to implementing CAA, as it is described as platform independent, working with any database but with no software loaded onto the client organization's system. The KOLA computer, shown on the lower right side of the exhibit, provides the capability to audit controls online for early, proactive audit problem identification.

ACL Continuous Assurance Systems

Many auditors have used software products developed by ACL Services, a popular software producer for computer-assisted audit analysis and retrievals.

EXHIBIT 11.3 KPMG KOLA Continuous Audit Assurance Process

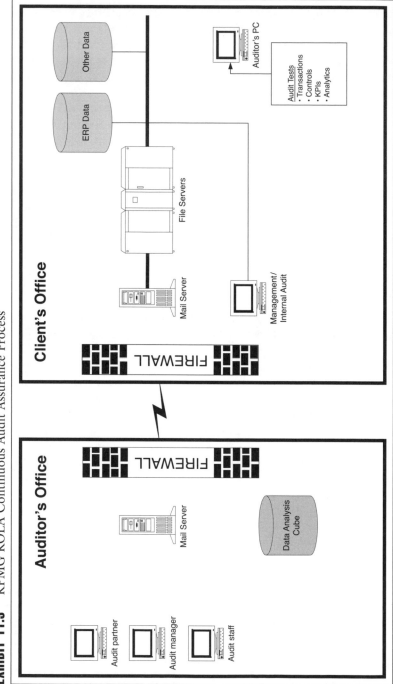

ACL also provides an effective tool for CAA. The ACL approach might be described as first-generation CAA, as was shown in Exhibit 11.1. ACL takes the approach that few organizations today have fully embedded and automated continuous auditing or monitoring applications and that most audit-related testing applications are simply a series of data analysis tests that are manually initiated and run on a regular basis. The ACL approach goes a step further such that the auditor does not need to formally start and run the monitoring program. The ACL software is linked to organization files and applications so that it can run in the background. The software is useful for such areas as detecting unusual transactions, detecting indicators of fraud, or identifying duplicate or overpayments. Although the software is not truly continuous, ACL suggests that auditors install and run this software based on completion of process steps and at periodic time intervals. The software then takes a slice of the data, capturing all transactions since the last test process. ACL continuous assurance software is used today by all of the Final 4 major public accounting firms as well as a large number of major corporations in the United States. An organization interested in implementing some beginning level of CAA might well consider starting with ACL's assurance product.

Dashboard Approach to Monitoring: Business Objects and Others

The driver of an automobile faces a dashboard that monitors performance by showing speed, progress by showing miles traveled, status by showing the fuel remaining, and problems by warnings for such items as low fuel. This dashboard approach allows the driver to monitor overall progress while the vehicle is in operation and to take action as required. That same dashboard approach can be used with complex business information systems with active monitors to review performance and highlight potential problems.

Many online applications today have a continuous display. In a sales order application, designated users can access the progress of sales recorded, perhaps by product line or region, through an online terminal. However, that monitoring typically covers just that one sales application; another screen must be called up to review related activities handled by other applications, such as ongoing cash collections or returns. Today's ERP applications provide a better environment for such cross-application monitoring under a common database structure. In addition, several good current software products are structured as dashboard monitors to review the overall status of business transactions and other activities. Two of the better of these software tools are the offerings of BusinessObjects and Cognos. Each allows an organization to tie a wide variety of diverse applications to a dashboard monitor that allows users to watch overall activity. This can be a very effective approach to implementing CAA.

INTERNET-BASED EXTENSIBLE MARK-UP LANGUAGES: XBRL

We are all operating in an environment of Internet-supported systems and processes. The paper-based information reports and the batch systems that once supported them have largely gone away. Although the Internet is a very flexible approach, management and auditors often have reasons to question document integrity over Internet-produced reports. When reports were being produced in the classic closed-shop data center, whether on paper or in an online system, there were few questions about the reported data. As long as there were appropriate general and application controls in place, auditors were comfortable with data integrity and performed just traditional audit tests to acquire a level of assurance. The "free and open" nature of the Internet can raise questions about the integrity of transmitted data. A common question here is: How does the user know that the file is actually what it is represented to be?

XBRL, a proposed industry standard for the publishing, exchange, and analysis of financial and business reports and data, offers a solution. XBRL (eXtensible *Business Reporting Language*) is an open standard developed by a consortium of over 200 companies and agencies, delivering benefits to investors, accountants, regulators, executives, business and financial analysts, and information providers. XBRL provides for the publication, exchange, and analysis of complex financial information in corporate business reports in the dynamic and interactive realm of the Internet. It provides a common format for critical business reporting processes, simplifying the flow of financial statements, performance reports, accounting records, and other financial information between software programs. XBRL defines a consistent format for business reporting to streamline the preparation and dissemination of financial data and allow analysts, regulators, and investors to review and interpret it. As a result, XBRL should save time and money when information consumers within and outside an organization analyze complex data. In the post-Enron era of SOA, XBRL is an important tool for providing consistent business and financial reporting.

XBRL Defined

XBRL is a new Internet standard similar to HTML for Internet browsing, MP3 for digital music, or XML for electronic commerce. XBRL uses standard Internet XML data tags to describe financial information. A professional organization, XBRL International, produces standard specifications that can be licensed royalty-free for use in applications. Just as established formats exist for Internet e-mail addresses (e.g.: name@ispname.xxx) or web access links, XBRL provides both a standard description and classification system for accounting reports. Data can be taken from an accounting information system and XBRL coded to produce an electronic annual report including all financial statements, the auditors' report, and 10-K disclosures. The document then can be read directly by computer programs or end users or, more likely, coupled with a style sheet to produce a printed annual report, user-friendly web pages or Adobe Acrobat files. Similarly, internal business reports and regulatory filings can be output in a variety of forms.

According to the September 2000 issue of *Accounting Today,* "XBRL is . . . perhaps the most revolutionary change in financial reporting since the first general ledger." XBRL provides a method for organizations to report their financial information in a format that can be easily read and understood by others. It allows for efficient data collection and publishing as well as serving as a tool for improved data validation and analysis. Exhibit 11.4 illustrates how XBRL can improve the transfer of data and information across systems and entities. As the exhibit shows, financial data from an ERP, general ledger, and other financial systems can be all coded in XBRL. That coded information then can be used, either at the present time or in the future, for reporting to banks, their annual reports, Securities and Exchange Commission (SEC) EDGAR[3] filings, and others. XBRL is a consistent approach for reporting to investors, credit agencies, and governmental units.

Implementing XBRL

XBRL is an evolving standard. Visionaries have praised the concept, tools and standards have been established, but only a few organizations have been early adopters. Microsoft Corporation filed its SEC 10-K report in XBRL format for the year 2002, and General Electric is using it for its internal company reporting. Governmental regulators have seen the value of financial reports issued in a consistent and traceable format, and the U.S. Federal Deposit Insurance Corporation (FDIC) now requires that federal bank status call reports be submitted in XBRL format. The standard can save on costs and provide reporting flexibility by eliminating proprietary accounting system dump formats and doing away with manual copy-and-paste consolidation and reporting. In the coming years, the SEC probably will require the use of XBRL.

Under XBRL, Internet financial data is tagged in a manner to be recognized and properly interpreted by other using applications based on a standardized XBRL vocabulary of terms, called a *taxonomy,* to map results into agreed-on categories. An example of this XBRL taxonomy is the markups or coding for well-defined concepts within the U.S. GAAP including "Accounts Receivable Trade" or "Allowance for Doubtful Accounts." No matter where it is located in the report format, a value can be recognized as the "Allowance for Doubtful Accounts," whether within one organization's reports or across multiple organizations. However, GAAP may vary

EXHIBIT 11.4 XBRL Interoperability Uses

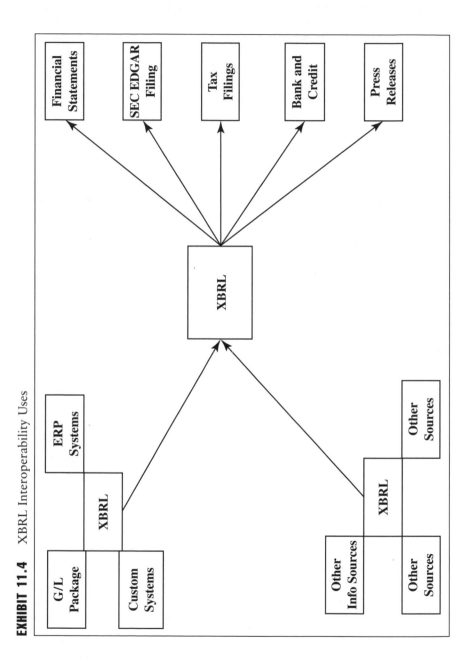

somewhat depending on whether the organization is a retailer, a minerals extraction mining company, or any of some other variations. XBRL qualifiers establish unique categories. A major saving with XBRL is the reduction of the data manipulation required when an organization needs to reposition the output from its financial systems to meet the needs of diverse users. A quarterly Internal Revenue tax form is very different in format and content from a quarterly SEC filing, although the information needed to file both typically comes from the same financial database. With XBRL, information will be entered *once;* that same information can be "rendered" as a printed financial statement, an HTML document for a web site, an EDGAR SEC file, a raw XML file, or a specialized reporting format such as periodic banking and other regulatory reports.

Prior to XBRL, it was necessary to extract financial information for reports from databases such as a general ledger, and that extracted information then would need to be processed multiple times depending on user needs. For example, a typical balance sheet would need to be processed individually for SEC filings, for placement in the annual report, for examination by external auditors, and for analysis by management. Each process could require an extra handling and transfer of the information to create the desired report. With XBRL, the information is coded once and ready for extraction electronically into reports for all information users. With the proper tools in place, the desired output for all uses of balance sheet information can be transmitted electronically, without the need for paper-based reports, and only one authorized version of that balance sheet with its data appears anywhere.

Because it is a new, evolving technology, there are some risks of error here. The organization needs to select an appropriate taxonomy and to tag data appropriately. Going back to our earlier example, there will be one taxonomy for a manufacturing and distribution organization and quite another for a petroleum refinery. Starting with the wrong taxonomy will cause multiple control problems. Once a taxonomy is selected, procedures need to be in place to ensure that the tagging of data is complete and accurate. This is the same type of control concern that Internet browser users occasionally encounter when clicking on a link and getting pointed to the wrong or a nonexistent site. The problem is frustrating when surfing the web, but critical when retrieving or reporting financial data. Internal audit should review procedures to ensure that controls are in place for XBRL data tagging in the organization. Even though these kinds of endeavors often start as a pet project by some member of the IT organization, tagging should be documented in a controlled environment.

XBRL is rapidly becoming a "new rule" standard for web-based financial reporting and supporting systems in the United States, the European Union, and throughout the world. Some have predicted it will become a standard to SEC reporting by as early as 2006. As John Connors, chief financial officer of Microsoft, stated in 2002 on releasing his company's financial reports in XBRL, "We see XBRL as not only the future standard for publishing, delivery and use of financial information over the web, but also as a logical business choice." The interested internal auditor can gain some XBRL knowledge through the official web site, *www.xbrl.org*, which has links to a wide variety of papers, presentation sets, and descriptions of XBRL use.

DATA WAREHOUSES, DATA MINING, AND OLAP

For many years, data storage was considered a rather mundane component of the IT infrastructure. Data needed for immediate short-term access were stored on mass storage disk drives; other, less-essential data were copied to magnetic tape drives. However, those old rules just did not work as application system tools grew more complex and users became more interested in analyzing and understanding that protected data. Data storage has now become a major component of the IT organization with many new tools and technologies.

Although space limitations in this book as well as the breadth of the topic restrict our discussion of storage management, internal auditors should develop an understanding of this increasingly important component of information systems. Storage management control procedures are an important part of information systems general controls that are too often ignored.

Importance of Storage Tools

Manufacturers had been experimenting with and introducing new storage devices over the years, besides the already mentioned tape drives and disk devices. In the mainframe, legacy systems world, the emphasis was on trying to pack more data storage capacity on a reliable device. During the 1970s, storage techniques ranged from large rotating magnetic drum devices, milled from steel sewer pipes on old Univac mainframes, to experiments with holographic light-based storage devices. Rotating disk and magnetic tape prevailed, and computer operations centers in the 1980s had large amounts of floor space devoted to these storage management devices. During that same period, an increasing amount of storage resided on desktop microcomputers, each with its own very reliable and increasingly high-capacity C drive hard disk. Systems and databases were getting larger, and reliable tools were needed to handle these ever-larger storage needs. Although there were other new product attempts, the storage world really changed when EMC Corporation launched a product called a Symmetrix, a refrigerator-size array of several hundred very-high-speed hard disk devices controlled through a series of controllers attached to each other and connected to computer servers through extremely fast and reliable fiber channels. Soon other competitors launched similar storage management devices, capabilities increased, and storage costs dropped dramatically. Storage management as a separate technical profession was launched.

Many organizations experimented with these new storage device offerings, trying one or another unit due to user demands for more and more storage capacity. This led to storage management configurations in data centers called JBOD (just bunches of disks) with these storage devices all connected as best as possible to servers or central computer systems. A concept called NAS (network attached storage) soon evolved where storage devices were connected to a network to provide file-level access to the stored data. Specialized NAS servers were added to allow applications to determine the locations of stored data such that anyone on the NAS could access data, and additional capacity could be added easily. From NAS, we have moved to SAN (storage area networks), where all storage devices are installed in a configuration similar to the local area network of office desktop computer systems. With SANs, stored data can be spread across multiple devices with easy switching from one to another.

Technology moves forward, and today we have CAS (content addressed storage), which moves storage management from being just an archive to an environment that can more easily respond to direct user and application requests in formats ranging from classic database to digital photos. Our point here is merely to highlight the fact that storage management is an increasingly important component of an organization's IT environment. Internal auditors can provide a major service to management through reviews of storage management capabilities including device utilization, performance, and traffic patterns. Storage management problems can limit systems availability and present difficulties in meeting service-level agreements.

Data Warehouses and Data Mining

Recently the concept of data warehousing has evolved into a unique and separate business application class. But internal auditors still may ask: What is a data warehouse? Simply put, a data warehouse is managed data situated after and outside of the operational information systems. In this section, we provide a brief definition of a data warehouse system and discuss some of its key attributes. Our objective is to allow auditors and other members of management to understand the concept at a high level. The primary concept of data warehousing is that the data stored for business analysis can be accessed most effectively by separating it from the operational systems. The reasons for this separation have evolved over the years. In the past, legacy systems archived inactive data onto tapes; and analysis reports ran from these tapes to minimize the performance impact on the operational systems. Advances in technology and changes in the nature of business have made many of these analysis processes much more complex.

Data warehousing systems are most successful when data can be combined, in the true concept of a physical central warehouse, from multiple operational systems to a place independent of the source applications. The data warehouse also can combine data from multiple applications such as sales, marketing, and production systems. Many large data warehouse architectures allow for the source applications to be integrated into the data warehouse incrementally. This allows for cross-referencing and time dimension data filtering, allowing an analyst to generate queries for a given week, month, quarter, or a year or to analyze data from the old and the new applications.

Building a data warehouse can be a complex task. Data must be gathered from multiple sources, scrubbed to clean up problems, and then converted or transformed to the data warehouse database. Exhibit 11.5 shows this general concept. Assume an organization has separate systems for order processing, product management, and marketing. The key information elements here will be transformed to a consistent data warehouse format, existing backups will be converted, and these systems will feed the data warehouse on a regular basis. The idea is not necessarily to move all application operations to the data warehouse repository, but to convert from separate applications for future analysis. Our purpose here is to provide internal

EXHIBIT 11.5   Data Warehouse Transformation Example

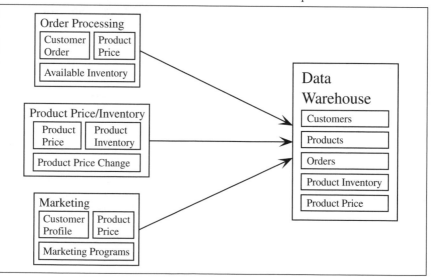

auditors, who will not be involved in building a data warehouse, with the knowledge to understand general concepts and ask appropriate questions.

An objective of a data warehouse is to make information retrieval and analysis as flexible and as open as possible. Low-end tools such as simple query capabilities may be adequate for users who only need to reference the data warehouse quickly, but other users may require powerful multidimensional analysis tools. Data warehouse administrators should be established to identify and assign access to these query tools. Often there is a progression path to the higher-level tools for data warehouse users. After becoming familiar with a low-level data warehouse tool, users may be able to justify the cost and effort involved with using a more complex tool. Internal auditors should be aware of the processes in place and the controls to limit access to authorized users. Because of the massive amount of historical data contained in a data warehouse, a high level of security and privacy tools are needed.

Reports often can be generated from a data warehouse facility, with many just "canned" reporting tools against warehouse summary data. In other instances, users may perform specific queries against the data warehouse accumulated summary data. The real strength of the data warehouse is its ability to allow analysts to perform what is called data mining. In this evolving science, the user starts with summary data and drills down into the detail data looking for arguments to prove or disprove a hypothesis. The tools for data mining are evolving rapidly. Even though data mining may account for a small percentage of the data warehouse activity, this is the key strength of the data warehouse for most organizations. The reports and queries of the data warehouse summary tables may be adequate to answer many "what" questions; the mining-like drill down into the detail data provides answers to "why" and "how" questions.

A data warehouse can be a better single and consistent source for many kinds of data beyond operational systems. However, because most information will not be carried over to the data warehouse, it cannot be the source of all system interfaces. Data warehousing is certainly a part of the new rules for internal auditors discussed throughout this book. We are introducing the concept in a very general manner, and the internal auditor seeking more information should do a web search for some of the many sites discussing the topic.

Online Analytical Processing

OLAP (online analytical processing) is a set of processes and tools that support a range of essential business applications, including sales and marketing analysis, planning, budgeting, statutory consolidation, profitability analysis, balanced scorecard, performance measurement, and data warehouse reporting. Although OLAP is neither a new nor an obscure concept, it is not widely understood by management, internal auditors, and even many IT professionals. OLAP is a category of software that enables analysts, managers, and others to gain insight into data through fast, consistent interactive access to a wide variety of possible views of information that has been transformed from raw data to reflect the real dimensionality of the enterprise as understood by its users. The problem for many organizations is the mass of data and the need to better understand any related trends. Consider an organization selling multiple product lines from various facilities. Which product lines are the most profitable? In which area or markets are sales increasing or declining? Do customer return patterns represent any overall trends? Answers to these and more are the functions of OLAP.

OLAP is the dynamic, multidimensional analysis of consolidated enterprise data supporting the end user analytical and navigational data. One way of thinking about OLAP concepts is to consider the model of a very complex, very large spreadsheet. We normally think of spreadsheets as two-dimensional arrays of rows and columns where we can do searches, calculations, and various types of analysis across these rows and columns and over multiple two-dimensional pages. However, sometimes data are too complex or there is just too much of data to place everything in an Excel-type spreadsheet. Some of the major attributes of an OLAP application are:

- *Multidimensional Conceptual Views.* Calculations and modeling are applied across multiple dimensions, through hierarchies, and/or across members. Software tools are available to allow analysis across eight to ten dimensions.

- *Trend Analysis over Sequential Time Periods.* Beyond the multidimensional approach of looking at data, OLAP tools can consider any data item in terms of sequential time period trends.

- *Drill-down Capabilities to Deeper Levels of Consolidation.* Using OLAP, the user can highlight a data element and then easily "drill down" to examine the basic data that created that item of interest.

- *Intuitive Data Manipulation.* OLAP tools have the ability to allow "If A, does this imply B?" levels of data manipulation.

- *Rotation to New Dimensional Comparisons in the Viewing Area.* OLAP allows a user to flip a complex database on its side and examine all of the data from that different perspective.

Organizations typically implement OLAP in a multiuser client/server mode with the aim of offering users rapid responses to queries, regardless of database size and complexity. OLAP helps users synthesize enterprise information through comparative, personalized viewing, as well as through analysis of historical and projected data in various "what-if" data model scenarios.

Various software products perform OLAP functions. All of them comply with a basic set of features that were first defined by the computer scientist E.F. Codd. Codd was the inventor of the relational database model now used in many if not most information systems databases today. Two examples of his relational database design are the Oracle and IBM's DB2 products, both built around his specifications. The general characteristics of an OLAP application are part of Codd's general model and should be part of any installed OLAP application.

OLAP is not necessary for every organization. In some instances, an organization does not have enough diverse data to make OLAP implementation cost beneficial. Many other organizations know that they need OLAP-based solutions, but those tasked to select and implement these solutions may be new to the area or may have lost track of its rapid developments. The selection of the right OLAP product can be challenging, but is very important if projects are not to fail. If an organization is considering the purchase of an OLAP product, internal audit should review the control procedures for the new software. For the organization using OLAP software, internal audit should attempt to become familiar with the software product used. Although we have talked about OLAP as a useful analytical tool for general business purposes, it also may be very useful for extensive audit queries over data.

NEWER TECHNOLOGIES, THE CONTINUOUS CLOSE, AND SOA

In this chapter, we have introduced some important newer and evolving technologies important for internal auditors. Storage management represents a new field of growing importance to the organization and its information systems resources. Organizations have always had data storage concerns, going back to the days of punched cards, but needs for accurate and efficient storage processes are increasing. Internal auditors whose reviews of information systems have been limited to computer hardware and network general control issues should begin to devote more attention to storage management.

Continuous assurance auditing soon may impact all internal auditors. SOA, as discussed in Chapter 2, requires organizations to close their books for periodic financial reporting on tighter and tighter schedules. The external auditors performing those reviews as well as management will be requesting timely internal control assessments of those supporting systems. This really points to the growing importance of the continuous assurance auditing as well as the XBRL techniques discussed in this chapter. As these time requirements get tighter, management may ask to reduce the time needed to close the books. The result will be the continuous close, where the summarized results at the end of a business day represent the overall results for the organization up to that period. Some organizations are already experimenting with these approaches. The increasing SOA regulatory requirements as well as capabilities offered by technology today point to that direction. The continuous close will introduce a whole new set of new rules for internal auditors.

NOTES

1. The first edition of Robert Moeller's *Computer Audit, Control, and Security* (New York: John Wiley & Sons, 1989) discussed how internal auditors could build ITF and SCARF facilities.
2. Kevin Handscombe, "KOLA, KPMG On Line Auditing,," paper presented at the Fourth World Continuous Auditing and Reporting Symposium, April 2002, Salford University, England.
3. A long acronym whose meaning really does not matter today, EDGAR is the SEC's forms and filing database; it can be found at *www.sec.gov.edgar.*

CHAPTER 12

Summary: Internal Auditing Going Forward

The prime objective of this book has been to describe the major elements of the Sarbanes-Oxley Act (SOA) and its impact on corporate governance, financial reporting, and internal auditing. SOA has had a major impact on the public accounting industry and its professional organization, the American Institute of Certified Public Accountants (AICPA). Auditing standards will no longer be set by the AICPA's Auditing Standards Board, the somewhat congenial process of external auditor peer reviews and self-governance has changed to a rules-based environment, and chief financial officers (CFOs) are faced with the danger of personal criminal liability for issuing fraudulently incorrect financial statements. As some wags have said, a CFO risks going from pinstripes to prison stripes through the release of a fraudulent financial report. In some respects, we may see auditing rules moving in the direction of other government-mandated rules, such as the Food and Drug Administration rules for the pharmaceutical industry and the Department of Defense for defense contracting. If things move in that direction, supporting documentation will become increasingly important.

Societal concerns over privacy and security will increase in importance. In an Internet-dominated world of ever-increasing wireless devices, multiple connections and linkages are easy. But in this world where anyone can find out information about almost anything, we need to respect personal privacy. Chapter 9's discussions of HIPAA and GLBA are two examples of legislative initiatives to protect this personal privacy, but effective internal controls implemented by organizations also will help to provide this protection.

FUTURE PROSPECTS FOR INTERNAL AUDITORS

Some might argue that SOA might be better named the Internal Auditors' Full Employment Act. It certainly has increased the importance of internal audit as a key component of corporate governance. The outsourcing of internal audit functions, which began in the 1980s, grew in the 1990s when more and more internal audit functions often were outsourced to "independent" groups managed by an organization's external auditors. Investigations following the fall of Enron and others suggested that those outsourced internal audit functions were not always as independent as a true internal audit function in the spirit of the Professional Standards of the Institute of Internal Auditors (IIA). As discussed in Chapter 2, SOA has changed all of this. The remaining public accounting firms (the Final 4) are no longer allowed to assume the responsibilities for their audit clients' internal audit functions through an outsourcing arrangement. An audit committee still can arrange for an external provider to perform internal audit services, and several large U.S.-based internal audit consulting firms can provide such services. However, all in all, the ball is back in internal audit's court.

The future looks brighter than ever for internal audit professionals. Shortly after the enactment of SOA and going forward—but we do not have any strong statistics here —the job market for internal audit professionals in the United States has increased. Newly empowered audit committees are realizing that their organization's internal audit functions are an important component of overall corporate governance. Internal auditors and their professional organization, the IIA, are accepting this challenge, and the Information Systems Audit and Control Association (ISACA) also has promoted this governance concept.

Internal audit functions need to accept this new challenge. The designated accounting and financial expert on the audit committee needs the help of internal audit to explain internal control issues within the organization, to better assess audit risks, and to plan and perform effective internal audits. Internal audit now typically has a level of responsibility for SOA Section 404 reviews of internal controls in the organization; the external auditors merely attest to the adequacy of that review. This is a very major change that will alter the relationships between internal and external auditors. Prior to the implementation of SOA, external auditors often assessed internal control risks, did some of the audit work themselves, and then asked internal audit to perform other review work under their general supervision. Although there will be no doubt much planning and coordination, internal audit through the audit committee—per SOA—is often responsible for reviewing and testing the results of internal controls and presenting those documented results to external audit. Some coordination will be necessary, but internal audit really is responsible here. There will certainly be some rough spots until internal audit assumes full responsibility for internal control reviews following the evolving PCAOB internal control auditing standards as well as the requirements of the external audit firms, but internal audit is assuming a role of increasing importance in the organization today.

Internal audit functions also need to get more involved in other SOA-related issues. One area of particular importance is the ethics and whistle-blower function in an organization. As discussed in Chapters 2 and 3, the audit committee is responsible for establishing a financial reporting–related whistle-blower function in the organization. Rather than limiting the scope of any such function, an organization should consider expanding any such program to all functions in an organization and including all employees and other stakeholders. Although such functions can be managed by a human resources function or some specialized ethics function, internal audit and its chief audit executive (CAE) should get their hands on such functions to assess that they are in compliance with SOA and meet the expectations of the audit committee.

SOA has introduced a wide set of new rules for corporate governance, financial reporting, and auditing. This book has introduced the Sarbanes-Oxley Act to internal auditors and other interested parties, including audit committee members and corporate financial and general management. We also have introduced some other new rules and technology trends that will impact internal controls and corporate governance going forward.

New rules are never sealed in cement but tend to change as society, legislation, and business practices change. The corporate accounting scandals of recent years, the demise of the major public accounting firm Arthur Andersen, and the introduction of SOA have all been drivers for these changes. In upcoming years, as the PCAOB becomes established or as we experience more international auditing and accounting standards convergence, these rules will continue to evolve as future new "new rules."

glossary

All specialized professions and disciplines are filled with acronyms—initials that become words unto themselves—and specialized terms and references. Many of the special terms used in this book are defined when they appear in the text. Some other terms used throughout the chapters of this book are defined in greater detail here.

AICPA   American Institute of Certified Public Accountants. The professional organization for Certified Public Accountants in the United States. Responsible for the CPA examination and, up until the Sarbanes-Oxley Act, for establishing public accounting auditing standards through its ASB and CPA self-discipline programs.

ASB   Auditing Standards Board. The AICPA body that set standards for CPA external auditors before SOA and the PCAOB.

ASE   American Stock Exchange.

ASQ   American Society for Quality. A major U.S. organization responsible for a series of quality-related publications, certifications, and educational offerings (*www.asq.org*).

Attributes Sampling   A form of audit sampling where a mathematical procedure is used to extract a sample from a population of data items to assess whether some internal control or other attribute is working. Based on the results from this sample, a conclusion can be drawn as to whether the attribute tested—often an internal control objective—is working as intended or not.

BASLE II Accord   An international banking capital regulation designed to encourage better and more systematic risk management practices, especially in the area of bank credit risk

CAE   Chief Audit Executive. The individual responsible for the internal audit function in an organization and reporting to the audit committee of the board. Previously, this person often was called the Audit Director.

Certified Fraud Examiner   An experience- and examination-based professional examination that results in this professional CFE designation.

CoCo   Criteria of Control. The Canadian equivalent of the COSO internal controls framework or standards. Developed by the Canadian Institute of Chartered Accounts (CICA), an organization similar to the AICPA.

CobiT   Control Objectives for Information Technology. A comprehensive internal control framework developed by ISACA and discussed in Chapter 5.

Due Diligence Review   The type of audit or review often associated with potential acquisitions. Company A plans to acquire company B in a friendly manner. B then gives A the right for an auditor to examine its books and records in what is called a due diligence review, where A should make every effort to observe the correct records and ask the right questions, but B is not obligated to reveal anything unless asked.

EDGAR   An SEC database. All companies, foreign and domestic, are required to file registration statements, periodic reports, and other forms electronically through EDGAR. Anyone can access and download this information for free (*www.edgar.gov*).

Ethics Officer Association   A U.S. professional organization that sponsors ethics-related conferences and educational programs (*www.eoa.org*).

FASB   Financial Accounting Standards Board. The independent, nongovernmental agency that establishes U.S. accounting standards and rules. The board is the keeper of U.S. GAAP and has issued many specialized numbered FASB statements.

FDA   Food and Drug Administration. The U.S. regulator for food and healthcare matters.

FDIC   Federal Deposit Insurance Corporation. The U.S. banking regulator that insures bank depositors and regulates banks. Individual deposits in U.S. federally chartered banks are insured within a statutory limit in the event of bank failure.

GAAP   Generally Accepted Accounting Principles. The recognized procedure for handling all financial accounting transactions. Many have been in place as basic accounting procedures over the years—such as how to record an asset and the periodic depreciation charged against that asset. Other more technical or special transaction practices have been defined through standards set by the FASB.

GLBA   Gramm–Leach–Bliley Financial Privacy Act. This is discussed in Chapter 9.

IIA   Institute of Internal Auditors. The professional organization for internal auditors worldwide. Administers the Standards for the Professional Practice of Internal Auditing as well as the CIA (Certified Internal Auditor) examination and certificate (*www.theiia.org*).

Internal Audit Charter   A formal document, authorized by the Audit Committee of the Board of Directors, that describes the responsibility and role of an organization's internal audit function. See the fifth edition of *Brink's Modern Internal Auditing* for more details.

ISACA Information Systems Audit and Control Organization. The major information systems audit professional organization, it is responsible for the CobiT control objectives framework, the CISA (Certified Information Systems Auditor) examination and certificate, as well as the CISM security examination.

ISO International Standards Organization. A Geneva, Switzerland-based standard-setting body that issues worldwide standards in many areas. ISO standards are discussed in Chapter 10.

NAIC National Association of (State) Insurance Commissioners. Many insurance companies are organized in what are called mutual companies and are owned by their policyholders. They have not issued stock and not registered through the SEC. These mutual insurance companies are regulated by the insurance departments of their parent or home states. The NAIC tries to establish consistent accounting and auditing rules across all state-by-state insurance commissions.

Nasdaq The initials stand for the National Association of Securities Dealers, but today the term normally refers to a large group of electronically traded securities, with many in technology sectors.

PCAOB Public Corporations Accounting Overview Board. The independent authority responsible to the SEC that regulates the public accounting profession and sets financial auditing standards.

PMBOK Project Manager's Book of Knowledge. A collection of project management best practices published by PMI and a basis for its PMP examination.

PMI Project Management Institute. A professional organization for project managers and publishers of the PMBOK guides and the PMP professional examination.

PMP Project Management Professional. A designation awarded after completion of experience requirements and an examination. Ongoing continuing education is a necessary requirement to keep the PMP designation.

Pro Forma Financial Reports Financial reports that present an "as if" picture of a firm's financial status by leaving out nonrecurring earnings expenses such as restructuring charges or merger-related costs.

SAS Statement on Auditing Standards. A series of numbered statements— SAS No. 98, SAS No. 99—that defines auditing standards in a specific area of interest. These had been issued by the AICPA's ASB until the launch of the PCAOB. CPAs who are members of the AICPA agree to follow these SAS's as part of their membership requirement to follow AICPA standards.

SDLC Systems Development Life Cycle. The classic process to develop, implement, monitor, or modify, and eventually replace information systems. Originally developed by IBM many years ago to design and build new applications, the basic process and its concepts continue today.

SEC Securities and Exchange Commission. The regulator for securities and financial reporting in the United States. The SEC has overall responsibility for SOA and its PCAOB auditing rule-setting authority.

SEC Form 10-K The SEC-mandated annual financial report.

SOA Sarbanes-Oxley Act. The July 2002 congressional act that regulates public accounting, establishes new rules for corporate governance, and introduces other changes to the audits of SEC-registered corporations.

SOX Another shortcut abbreviation for the Sarbanes-Oxley Act. Some publications use this abbreviation, but this author feels SOA is a better acronym.

SSAE Statements on Standards for Attestation Engagements. Attestation engagements cover situations where a CPA reviews or even just carefully observes some area but does not perform formal audit tests. The CPA then attests to what was found in the area or circumstance.

SSAR Statements on Standards for Accounting and Review. A series of AICPA standards covering areas that are not part of a formal audit. A CPA, for example, might compile a financial statement for a small retail business to give to its banker. SSARs cover standards for such matters as preparation and documentation.

Terabyte A computer file or storage management capacity term. A terabyte is a measure of computer storage capacity and is 2 to the 40th power, or approximately a thousand billion bytes (i.e., a thousand gigabytes).

Treadway Report A report issued in 1987 by the National Commission on Fraudulent Financial Reporting and Internal Control. A recommendation of this report led to the COSO study, named after the Treadway Report's sponsoring organizations.

Variables Sampling A form of audit sampling where a mathematical procedure is used to extract a sample from a population of individually valued items resulting in some total value. Based on the audited results from that variables sample, the auditor can reach a conclusion for an audited estimated total value with a plus-or-minus error range.

Work Breakdown Structure A project management step for breaking down a proposed project into each of its task components along with interrelationships between each.

index